NEWS OF CRIME

COURTS AND PRESS IN CONFLICT

J. EDWARD GERALD

CONTRIBUTIONS TO THE STUDY OF MASS MEDIA
AND COMMUNICATIONS, NUMBER 1

GREENWOOD PRESS
WESTPORT, CONNECTICUT ● LONDON, ENGLAND

Library of Congress Cataloging in Publication Data

Gerald, J. Edward.
  News of crime.

  (Contributions to the study of mass media and
communications, ISSN 0732-4456 ; no. 1)
  Bibliography: p.
  Includes index.
  1. Free press and fair trial—United States. 2. News-
paper court reporting—United States. I. Title.
II. Series.
KF9223.5.G44   1983   345.73'056   83-10732
ISBN 0-313-23876-6 (lib. bdg.) 347.30556

Library of Congress Catalog Card Number: 83-10732
ISBN: 0-313-23876-6
ISSN: 0732-4456

First published in 1983

Greenwood Press
A division of Congressional Information Service, Inc.
88 Post Road West
Westport, Connecticut 06881

Printed in the United States of America

10 9 8 7 6 5 4 3 2 1

Contents

Preface

This study focuses on mass media reporting of crime. It reports long-term interaction between the media and the judicial establishment characterized, in some instances, by exasperation and bitterness, and in others by a certain reasonable nobility.

The language of interaction is found, on the one hand, in the opinion of courts and, on the other, in popular journalism. The translation and reporting of such communication seems to involve certain obligations: (1) to describe fundamental aspects of both institutions in sufficient detail to reveal their common humanity, (2) to maintain a visible balance in reporting conflicts in point of view and factual claims, and (3) to reach an evaluation derived from critical observation of the values and acts of both institutions.

Much of what the media and the judges communicate about themselves is refracted through the lens of self-interest. The court decisions, while conforming to law, are sometimes tilted because some judges believe that publicity ordinarily enhances chances for fairness while others regard it as an impediment. Some judges favor less governmental control than others.

The public must decide whether justice has been done. The press is the medium by which the public becomes informed. The public is equally entitled to truthful information about the press in order to decide whether and to what extent the messenger has been fair and equitable in reporting the facts.

The general reader cannot translate the language of the courts without taking the time to become a specialist, and so summary and paraphrase are offered. As part of the effort to maintain a visible balance between the parties, statements of their contrasting positions frequently are juxtaposed. The difference between the judges and the media, as shown in the text, cannot be resolved by the collection and analysis of factual data; the claims are inexact and the task of definitive research unacceptably large and complicated. For that reason, the most reliable data arise in the debates. The summary of cases and the opinions of journalists enable the reader to consider and evaluate this best evidence.

The courts and the press alike are entitled to our respect. The quality of their work accounts for the satisfaction with which most of us view self-government in comparison with other kinds. At the same time, the work is done by human beings; friendly and helpful evaluation is always in order. Life under any dictatorship is unacceptable, including one imposed either by the courts or by the press on what news the public is to hear about crime and the courts.

The main purpose of this book is to help dispel misconceptions based on irritation and anger and to encourage peace between the courts and the press.

Acknowledgments

This study extends over many years, and the list of persons and institutions who have shared their interest in the subject is too long to insert here. My wife, Opal Dutton Gerald, was a full-time associate in the pre-1966 preparatory work. This study begins with Sheppard v. Maxwell, 384 U.S. 333 (1966) and the draft of the American Bar Association's Reardon Report in the same year. The College of Liberal Arts of the University of Minnesota, from its McMillan Fund, supported field study from which I derived rich perspective on the relations of the police and the press in the United States and the United Kingdom. Dr. George A. Graham of Fort Lauderdale, Florida, was supportive and considerate. Herbert C. Morton of Washington, D.C., has been an invaluable adviser since his student days. F. Gerald Kline, director of the School of Journalism and Mass Communication, University of Minnesota, studied responses of mock jurors to prejudicial information. David L. Graven, while Professor of Law at the University of Minnesota, joined in a national study of the accommodation of working journalists to the American Bar Association standards of criminal justice (fair trial and free press). My associates at the University of Minnesota in the Graduate School, the College of Liberal Arts, and the School of Journalism, and the librarians at the Law Library, provided over many years time and support for study. Thanks to them and to all the many others who have helped me skim away the human passions that overlie the faith and fairness of the sturdy persons engaged in the fair trial controversy.

COPYRIGHT ACKNOWLEDGMENTS

Alfred Friendly and Ronald L. Goldfarb, *Crime and Publicity* (New York: Twentieth Century Fund, 1967).

Harold R. Medina, *Freedom of the Press and Fair Trial* (New York: Columbia University Press, 1967).

"Media and the Law," from "Talk of the Town," *New Yorker,* July 12, 1976. Reprinted by permission; © 1976 The New Yorker Magazine, Inc.

Paul C. Reardon, "The Fair Trial-Free Press Controversy—Where We Have Been and Where We Should Be Going," *San Diego Law Review* 4:2 (1967). Copyright 1967 San Diego Law Review Association. Reprinted with permission of the *San Diego Law Review.*

Note, Judicial Restraint of the Press—Nebraska Press Ass'n v. Stuart, 9 Creighton L. Rev. 693, 694-96 (1976).

The Spirit of Liberty: Papers and Addresses of Learned Hand, Third Edition, Enlarged, edited by Irving Dilliard (New York: Alfred A. Knopf, 1952).

"Florida Judge Evaluates Camera Coverage of Trial," *Editor & Publisher,* January 7, 1978. Reprinted from *Editor & Publisher.*

Howard Simons and Joseph Califano, Jr., eds., *The Media and the Law* (New York: Praeger, 1976).

NEWS
OF
CRIME

Introduction   1

PROLOGUE

Readers sometimes feel more comfortable when picking up a book if they can see, at the outset, the model or the pattern of discourse which the author has in mind to follow. This is a study of free press and fair trial, of an often one-sided conflict between the courts and the press over the control of news about crime. There are events in the foreground and in the background of the study which are of importance to the reader. The events in the foreground are generated by rules of court which restrict precise details of crime news, particularly news of pretrial events setting out as fact unofficial versions of guilt or culpability. The press—the print and broadcast media collectively—is opposed to some of the rules because they are relatively new, because they represent coerced changes in long-standing news reporting procedures, and because they impose conditions upon journalists which mock the power of the press and reveal the true limits of the First Amendment—the first freedom. The legal conflict is on the high ground of the First, the Sixth, and the Fourteenth Amendments. A lawsuit of constitutional character affects not only the issue in court but all those like it coming up in the future. Not only the administration of criminal law but of news reporting has been reshaped in less than two decades—an accomplishment truly revolutionary in view of the obstacles to change.

In the same time period, writers and readers have sought to divest language of unintended sexist connotation. Both journalists and lawyers avoid potentially sexist usage when discussing general acts and attitudes, and that surely is intended here also. The use of "he" in the general sense is for convenience only and is not indicative of roles according to gender.

In the background, events have to do with the way the revolution was accomplished by the professional bar and the inability of the press to make an effective response. It is not easy to keep this aspect of the study in the foreground without unacceptable disruption of the legal events. The reader is asked to keep both sets of events in mind. But it would be a serious distortion of reality if events were stated in a rigid court-press dichotomy. The real substance of the differences in opinion lies in the intellectual and humanistic values that characterize persons, not professions. The values that maintain democratic society, those which appear triumphant in this series of events, are well distributed among journalists and lawyers alike. The victories, such as they are, belong to individuals, not to either profession.

The bar is not a mere voluntary alliance of lawyers; it is integrated, for the most part, into the state and federal court system and some of the consultation among members leads to rulemaking which is legislative in character and affects the practice of law, the operation of the courts and the rights of litigants.

The rulemaking power is derived, by interpretation, from the judicial power set out in the Constitution under a loose convention which requires legislative consent. Before the reader raises a skeptical eyebrow at the words "by interpretation," let it be added that the extent and character of the Bill of Rights originated in Court action, too, but of a different kind.* Since the rulemaking power is shared with the legislature and the executive there is a possibility of conflict which, when it occurs, cannot easily be resolved. But the major branches of government are organically interdependent; more than one button has to be pushed before the ship of state moves through the political waters, and the Court button, when pressed in a constitutional crisis, energizes countervailing powers that legislatures and executives have to accept in a spirit of compromise.

The rules of court which appear in the foreground of this study have the effect of law and bind persons to the extent that they are, at the time, under authority of the courts. The events in the background tell us a lot about the ability of the press to perform effectively as a private agency defending the political integrity of democratic institutions. The American Bar Association generated the rules by study and discussion and recommended them to the state and federal courts. Since adoption

---

*In order to help the reader, the word court, standing alone, is capitalized throughout when it refers to the Supreme Court of the United States.

presumably is voluntary, affirmative action did not always take place. Nevertheless, drawing up the rules related lawyers and judges to each other in an organizational structure able to create court policy.

Journalists have a voluntary communications network in which they assert an identity of professional interest, but they lack legislative structure. They are governed by rules of shops in which they work and influenced by voluntary codes of ethics, statements of principle, which bind an individual only to the extent that he is already committed by conscience. Journalists were unready, in organizational terms, to act as partners in an action program with the bar to define fair trial and to apply the rules to all journalists. For reasons to be made clear in the narrative, they are not able to commit themselves to professional rule-making. Denied a partnership role, they had to become petitioners.

EXPLANATION OF THE PROBLEM

The conflict between the press and the courts is over what to publish, and when to publish news of crime. The operating convention in journalism is based on market competition, on the scoop. For that reason, the courts have been accustomed to a free-wheeling press that picks up news from the police and the prosecutors and prints or broadcasts it immediately. This is a natural flow of the news without much artificial restraint.

By contrast, the rules of fair trial are based not on nature but on law, a quite artificial construct. A prospective juror, so the legal theory goes, should be neutral in mind and spirit when he is sworn. As a juror he should hear only what the court decides is permitted by law. If he does hear anything else, he may no longer qualify as that artificial person, an acceptable juror, as defined by law.

The quick and easy method of making the news conform to the artificial requirements of a trial court, one still in use by British courts, is to issue orders restricting the press and to put editors in jail when they disobey, to fine them large sums, or both. With all respect to the mother country, this policy is censorship and the United States Supreme Court has outlawed it as a method by which the courts can control the content of the press.

In 1966, the American Bar Association (ABA) decided that fair trial rules had to be improved and it appointed a committee to accomplish that purpose.[1] This committee found that lawyers and law enforcement personnel were, in large part, talking to journalists as friends and giving them whatever information they could about crime. In so doing, they neglected or ignored the artificial rules of fair trial.

The Supreme Court already had made clear that the press could not be censored or enjoined. It was almost equally difficult to punish journalists afterward for crime news which prejudiced, or appeared to prejudice, pending cases. The ABA committee proposed rules which directly regulated lawyers and affected the news media largely by closing up their dependable sources of facts about crime. The ABA adopted the new fair trial–free press standards and asked judges to implement them as rules of court or otherwise. Hundreds of cases have tested the application of the standards and the ABA has revised them several times. Constitutional questions raised by the rules, mainly under the First and Sixth Amendments, have been tested.

The new format differs from past patterns of rulemaking by judges for journalists. With rare exceptions, past efforts at control had resulted in conflict between one judge, frustrated by the tumult of publicity or criticism around a difficult criminal case, and his most visible tormentors, a journalist or two. The judge would demand that the journalists be silent and let him try the case in court, not in the papers. When journalists, as proud partisans of the First Amendment, refused they were sometimes tried without a jury and punished for contempt of court.

By 1966, when the ABA committee was appointed, both the bar and the media were organized in several national professional and trade groups. In view of the democratic temper of the society, the ABA consulted with journalists and with others before drafting its standards and making an effort to enforce them. When journalists discovered that the consultation was genuine, and not a polite cover for arbitrary behavior, they responded somewhat unsurely but with determination. They matched the ABA committee for committee and, facing a large and wealthy professional organization, they hired lawyers to coach them in the martial arts of lobbying the local, state, and national judicial establishment. Publishers previously had been active lobbyists on business matters, but this response was new to journalists as a group. Heretofore they had tried to make do with the editorial voice, sometimes indignant and often shrill, when confronting judges who, in the journalistic in-house metaphor, were "trampling on the First Amendment." Of course, they had hired lawyers previously on occasion to help them with lawsuits.

Courts, for the most part, move slowly and deliberately, and cushion their power with rules of fair play; they also wield the force of government. They define freedom of speech and press and the rights of individuals before the law. They originate the rules of criminal procedure through their quasi-legislative processes. In conflict with the media they tend, in an extremity, to reject legislative restraints and to sit in their own cases. In the criminal process, they have the last word.

There is not much doubt that the press is an underdog in the face of so formidable an opponent. The odds in 1966 were that it would lose. But the courts use reason in their processes and discussion provides an opportunity for a range of judicial opinion to assert itself. The press has gained as well as lost in the long dialogue over fair trial; among other changes, it has come to rely less on emotion and more on reason in its efforts to persuade the legal establishment.

The goal of the courts is to assure a defendant—especially one accused of a crime which, by nature, startles or revolts society—that he will get a fair chance to prove his innocence, or, if not clearly innocent, an equally fair chance to establish the limits of his liability. The media are not much interested in routine cases of crime such as robbery and assault and do not ordinarily report them.

Perhaps a couple of examples, by way of introduction, will help demonstrate why concern for a fair trial arises in the news.

Two Illustrative Cases

The Federal Bureau of Investigation decides to stage a series of stings, identified by the code name Abscam, to test the honesty of certain public officials because it had doubts that they would earn a passing grade. Rum afflicted some, greed motivated others among the chosen. Using disguised actors and hundreds of thousands of dollars of government money, the bureau dangles bribes before—among others—a United States senator and five members of the House of Representatives. Unknown to the public officials, they are photographed and their voices are recorded as they react to the possibility of receiving money from an Arab immigrant. The FBI approach borders on incitement to crime and entrapment and the Department of Justice drafts formal accusations with caution. Documents have to be duplicated and moved back and forth from desk to desk.

Some insiders apparently thought the news was too good to keep;

others were fearful, perhaps, that the voters wouldn't hear the news in time. The best and biggest story, with names and pictures, appears in the *New York Times*,[2] and NBC network cameras get exclusive pictures by being outside the right house at the right time. Soon all the other carriers of news have the story, too.

The United States attorney general, sworn to uphold the law, watches helplessly while the news ripples across the television screen and into print. Law enforcement on this scale is politics, as well as police work, and with the press the proper time to publish is *now*.

The Sixth Amendment promises every person a fair trial by due process of law. That is, the accused will not be victimized by official acts outside the law. Instead, these accused officials are tried by law enforcement insiders in the media. The journalists who took the story are among the finest and most ethical the profession affords. Their code of behavior attaches no guilt to getting and spreading the news. Some of them will be threatened with arrest if they do not tell where they got the story. A federal prosecutor and several officers will admit that they talked discreetly and legally to friends and official letters of criticism will go into their personnel files. But a journalist who got the story early will be cited for contempt and face jail unless she answers questions in court.[3]

From Abscam let us turn to homicide. Let us assume, for example, that two men are walking in the street. Pausing in the doorway of a bank, one says to the other, "Wait here while I cash a check." The speaker walks to the teller's counter, draws a gun and demands money. Loot in hand, he turns to find a policeman in line behind him, a surprise for which he is not mentally prepared. He fires his gun and the helpless officer is killed. More police rush in, but the gunman and his companion cannot be found. The police publish pictures from the bank's automatic cameras and ask the public to help find the gunman. He is arrested.

What about the other man? A woman customer finds the likeness of a youthful offender in the police file of persons previously arrested, a picture two years old, and she is willing to testify that he was seen with the killer. A second arrest is made.

The man with the gun is charged with murder. How shall the other man be charged? Eyewitness identification under the circumstances is unreliable. The police and the prosecutors interrogate both men, hoping they will accuse each other. It is important to the community's self-respect that the second man not be tried in the atmosphere of the case against a police killer, but the two could go to trial together unless the public defender, acting as their attorney, can obtain separate trials.

The prosecutor finds his decision far from easy. Who can he believe? His decision may have to be reviewed in a pretrial hearing as jurors gather for trial. Will journalists, when they report the hearing, catch the nuances, the doubts, the differences? Will the news stories be limited to the facts which can be admitted in evidence, or will the juvenile record and the identification rumors be published? If they are, will the stories reach and bias prospective jurors?

This is one of the central problems of law enforcement, infinitely varied by personalities and circumstances. Its most important element is reasonable doubt, a doubt the Constitution entrusts to a jury, not to anyone else. If the media tilt before trial toward the police theory that both men are guilty, fairness become tougher. Few cases are solved by policemen who give first priority to the presumption of innocence and it may be that the media will be influenced by the police suspicion and their hatred of cop killers. Perhaps the media, if they share the fury, will help the prosecutor resolve his doubts.

These two examples are common in the annals of law and journalism. The rules tell the police to keep their opinions to themselves, to be silent about the evidence and their belief in guilt until they testify in court. Journalists are not compelled at this stage to be considerate of the artificial legal rules. They are constrained by habit to publish and let the defendants take the consequences. If a pretrial hearing should take place, the contraband evidence may still come out. If so, who broke the rules? A policeman, or a prosecutor, in all probability, but who can take time to locate the right one in a crowd? The court would simply have to postpone the trial or move it out of town.

The cases demonstrate that the subject is complicated and that the system—the police, the prosecutor, the lawyers, the judges, and the journalists, living together in the institution of law enforcement—needs brief explanation before the discussion continues. This is written for laypersons who may wonder why human beings caught up in law enforcement behave as they do.

Police and Prosecutors

According to popular conception, police work under discipline, but it is self-discipline for the most part and out of sight of superiors. The public has little opportunity either to define the limits of police action or to see to it that all persons are treated fairly. It is the assignment of police physically to control persons suspected of criminal conduct and to risk retaliation in response to force, to see bodies of victims broken by violence, to interview grieving family members for details of incidents, to accompany accused persons to court, and to testify against them. The veteran police officer knows not only the person he accuses today but a throng of others who must be dealt with. Police soon come to have opinions about claims of innocence and guilt and degrees of punishment and would prefer to see these opinions supported by the prosecutors and the courts. When justice, as they see it, miscarries, the officers cannot avoid heavy hearts.

Prosecutors, according to popular conception, are bound by the law, but law commits them to tasks of interpretation which carry wide discretion. They administer not only humane canons, but are workflow officers whose judgment is clearly conditioned by limitations of time, money, and personnel as well as by the law. Prosecutors are aware that courts are saturated with jury trials and can handle no more, that court delays unfairly keep many accused persons waiting for trial.[4] It is clear to them that justice cannot be evenhanded unless trial judges are neither vengeful nor weak, and they are aware that no prosecutor can expect public support, or be elected to higher office, unless well known in the community. This means the prosecutor must deal with the press. One of his conscious conflicts is in his duty of discretion sworn to the court and the desire of the media to obtain evidence from the police, from witnesses, and from his office staff that, when published or broadcast, may compromise fair trial.

Two Judges Evaluate the Media

The conflict in the standards of the judiciary and the press have been noted; and the attitude of judges toward the danger of publicity and what should be done about it are far apart. At one end of the spectrum is Hubert L. Will, a U.S. district judge in Chicago; at the other is J. Skelly Wright, chief justice of the District of Columbia circuit. The distance between them shows that the judicial institution is not of one mind.

Judge Will said many years ago that acceptance of freedom of the press as a "kind of necessary nostrum for every ill of democracy, regardless of whether or not it proves an appropriate and effective ministration, has created a situation which makes the press's treatment of criminal trials and certain of their antecedents a significant threat to the fair administration of criminal justice by the courts." He says he shares with others a vision of a noble place for a free press in society but, in his judgment, the press generally misinforms or fails to inform the public fully. The press slants, misquotes, unfairly interprets. Its defects are those which indicate a lack of "thoroughness and accuracy, or professional competence and integrity." These faults produce an inaccurate and incomplete picture of what happens in the courtroom. Even when the press is reasonably thorough and accurate, "which is seldom," says Judge Will, it encroaches too often upon and "subverts the constitutional right to a fair trial by an impartial jury." As he views it, news of crime is written and printed for its lurid or curious appeal, for its shock and entertainment value to readers, listeners, and viewers.[5]

Judge Wright thinks the press tells the community what it needs to know. "The police, the district attorneys, and the courts perform perhaps the most sensitive functions in our society, the public generally has a right to know the manner in which these functions are being performed. And I submit that the very fact that the people will know how these functions are being performed will insure a more acceptable performance." He continued, "Lord Acton has said, 'Everything secret degenerates, even the administration of justice.' I could not agree with him more. . . . If the press has access to police headquarters and other sources of information concerning police work, the probability that that work will be conducted with respect to rights of the accused and the public is increased immeasurably." Judge Wright thinks press coverage will deny trial by an impartial jury "in only a precious few cases, and the dismissal of those cases as non-triable would be a small price to pay for the benefits we all receive—the public generally and persons accused of crime in particular—from disclosures made in the press with respect to the goings-on in police stations, district attorney's offices, and courtrooms throughout the country."[6]

Law and Journalism Contrasted

There is a quiet, cool current of altruism and public service identifiable in both law and journalism. Judge Will is an idealist. His views arise not in petulance but in fear that the media are corrupters of the beloved system. The rules instruct him to provide a speedy and public trial by an impartial jury. The persons who come before him are in grave peril. They may be deprived of liberty by a loose system of paper handling which makes it easy for the media to obtain information with which to try defendants ahead of their day in court. Above all else in a free country, a citizen is entitled to a fair trial.

Judge Wright is also an idealist and his eye is fixed on the same star—the good society. But he came to the bench out of the turbulence of Louisiana politics. To him, corrupters are persons who administer the law by the same ax-grinding rules common to county politics. He does not want to lock journalists out, he wants to bring them in to watch the corrupters and report the news of their activity.

So, two judges with the same high concern for truth and fairness express concern for the media in quite different ways. The journalist, for his part, is an idealist too. He believes in justice, even to the point of being impatient with the artificiality of trial procedures. He hates secrecy and suspects corruption when he is denied access to the facts, especially the grimy ones.

The ideals of any one of the three are not always easy for the layperson to see in today's confused scene. Ideas cast by each of the disciplines intimately affect self-government and have to be tested. The "facts" asserted by partisans in a dialogue about justice may undergo major change over time or even disappear. But the values dealt with in the theory of criminal law are fundamental. They affect the citizen's right to speak, to assemble, and to write; to have a fair and public trial by an impartial jury upon criminal accusations; and to have access to learned counsel when in need.

Fair trial under law means fair treatment at the time of interrogation and arrest; it means opportunity to confront accusing witnesses in court, to have access to the power of the state to obtain favorable testimony, and to have as jurors persons without prejudice who are able to reach a verdict on the law and the evidence brought out in court.

Justice, freedom, truth—tenets of the democratic state—are large and sometimes overriding concepts which arise in the frame of reference of what is yours, what is mine, what is right, what is wrong. Conflict between individuals over space for living gives them meaning. Law and journalism try to personalize these values, but they do not always succeed because the task is difficult. The two disciplines greatly differ in methodology. The legal process considers the arguments and, limiting the questions narrowly, tells antagonists who come before the bench what to do. The techniques of careful argument, discussion, and review succeed because judges are permitted to use coercion to end the discussion. Perhaps the reasoning process of courts gains prestige because it carries mandatory power.

The primary—indeed the only—tool of journalism, by contrast, is rhetoric. The wordsmith is not helpless if he can tell the people the facts and persuade them to act. The contemporary journalist, however, judging by what he writes on the topic, feels that institutions created to make us free are used for partisan and selfish advantage—to let out the news if it helps "us," to bottle it up if it hurts "us," to ladle it out if it hurts the opposition. A journalist is dependent on sources and the game is to make him the prisoner of those "in the know." The worst fate for a journalist is to be a pawn in the game of power: to be given a half truth as fact and to be denied the other half, to watch corrupt officials pose as servants of the state and, in the vacuum of the facts, to be rewarded for their treachery; to see the system of justice work for the rich and the crooked and against the common citizen, as if it had been designed just that way. In moments of frustration, the process of fair trial seems to the journalist to shield the crooks and shame the state. At such times the reporter may take a secret grand jury report—journalistic contraband, in the eyes of the court—and turn it into news, into facts he thinks the people ought to know. This action puts the heat not only on fair trial, but on the hypocrites.

Persons of high purpose and low tap the journalist's phones and subpoena his long distance phone bill in order to harass his sources, to fence him in. He has to hire a lawyer to keep himself out of jail while he does the day's work. The state, it seems to him, searches not so much for truth as for journalists who know something that will give the district attorney a lead, or to help the defense impeach an adverse witness.

If the journalist succeeds in getting a statute passed for access to official records, so as to make news gathering easier, the opponents attempt to restore the old restrictions by developing an artificially cultured new tort called "invasion of privacy."[7] While it is intended for a number of laudable purposes, the clear fact is that a privacy law limits access to facts—to news.

These struggles amidst bureaucratic infighting show that journalism and law are structural parts of the cultural apparatus by which society gets its work done. This structure exists not only in the folkways but in the close daily workings of journalism, business, law, and government. These institutions have grown up together in the democratic state. Everything a journalist writes about a public official, whether printed or broadcast, has political impact. It increases or decreases the prestige and credibility of the persons concerned. Journalism is thus linked to politics and the economy, a system which permits competition—a form of warfare which calls forth various rules to help the system survive even when the soldiers perish. Freedom of speech and press are necessary to the survival of the system but the power to guarantee freedom resides in judges who, as Judges Will and Wright demonstrate, are not persons of like mind. How could this be? Are not judges creatures of the same law? Yes, but according to Chief Justice Hughes the law from day to day is what the judges say it is. Conditions change, statutes change, the law changes and courts must depend on the media to make the reasons for change clear to the public.

The power of publicity thus helps judges maintain their independence. Legislative tampering with time-honored legal rules and the assignment of inadequate budgets can hurt court effectiveness. Political influence on some judges and some juries can render episodes in the criminal justice process corrupt. This danger is always with us and was increased, perhaps, when the states moved largely to popular election of judges between 1820 and 1860, marking a departure from the life tenure enjoyed by federal judges. Sporadic conflict between the press and the courts is worse today in state than in federal trial courts. Federal judges are usually appointed because of political activity, but they enjoy considerable freedom from pressures. The press has an ever-present opportunity to influence legislative decisions and, in the states, to participate in the nomination and election of state judges.

Improvement of Courts

The trial judge whose work rules put him in conflict with the media may look overwhelmingly powerful to those who do not wear the robe. But judges are ridden by routine and browbeaten by the glut of cases that move before them. They are hampered by unclear statutes and rules which tie them mercilessly to the book and to the appellate courts. The statutes are shaped in significant part by lawyer-legislators who show up later in court as attorneys to utilize their own handiwork. In a system where much is wrong, as well as right, judges can only do the best they can. Some of their problems are set out here in the language of distinguished lawyers to show their need for public sympathy and support, which must come largely through the educational gifts of the media.

Lord Bryce said in his classic work on American government in 1910 that "popular election, limited terms and small salaries have tended to lower the character of the judiciary; and in not a few states the state judges are men of moderate abilities and limited learning inferior (and sometimes conspicuously inferior) to the best of the men who practice before them. Nevertheless, in most states, the bench is respectable in point of character, while in some it is occasionally adorned by men of the highest eminence. . . . Corruption seems to be rare, but instances of subservience to powerful political groups sometimes shake public confidence."[8]

Improvements since he wrote, although slow in coming, have been implemented particularly by the multiform committees of the bar and cooperating groups. Even that effort has not always succeeded quickly. The Supreme Court held in Klopfer v. North Carolina that the right to a speedy trial, guaranteed by the Sixth Amendment, applies to the states.[9] The following year, 1968, ABA adopted its Standards of Criminal Justice which advised that delays in criminal trials should be granted only "upon a showing of good cause and only for so long as is necessary." Eight years later investigators found little or no impact from the ABA standard in 72 percent of the state courts and the District of Columbia.[10]

The presidential commission on law enforcement and the administration of justice concluded in 1976 that "the inertia of the criminal justice system is great. More than 30 years ago, the [George W.] Wickersham Commission described the scandalous way in which justice was being administered in many of the country's 'lower' courts, and urged that they be abolished; few of them have been abolished and many of the remaining ones are still a scandal."[11]

Justice Lewis F. Powell, Jr., in a speech to the ABA in 1976, commented on the dilatory pace of legislative reform: "Much of the expansion [brought about by the Warren Court] was a reaction to the sluggishness of the legislative branch in addressing urgent needs for reform."[12] Professor Caleb Foote says criminal justice is "like a bargain basement, viable only if 80 to 90 percent of all defendants plead guilty." He continues: "Plea bargaining is the heart of the system and, rightly or wrongly, it is believed that if most or all poor defendants were released pending trial instead of being jailed, the rate of guilty pleas would drop, the court would then be unable to handle the increased volume of trial and chaos would result."[13]

The burden of reform in this context has fallen largely upon the professions of law and government because the press, unfortunately, has not found a way to make the technical subject interesting. The state is not as yet able to try all citizens fairly, to maximize the search for truth, and to minimize influences that distort the search.

Given the resources at its disposal, the legal profession's effort at reform has been steady and persistent.[14] Yet this effort has subordinated individual rights of lawyers, as citizens, in order to enforce standards of practice and procedure set out by ABA and adopted by the courts. Study, analysis, and recommendation flow constantly from bar association committees, but even the most thoughtful of reports does not get sustained attention from the media and the legislatures necessary for remedial action.

The forces of reform, both liberal and reactionary, which are surprisingly strong in the legislatures and the courts, often strangle efforts to make changes by rule or by litigation. The pace of change, in view of public distress, seems intolerably slow.

Judges, lawyers, and law enforcement officials maintain a small-scale esoteric periodical press by means of which they communicate with each other. But persuasive communication between judges and the legislatures, in significant part, and between judges and the public, is through the mass media. What judges have to say to the community must first be said to journalists, which in turn is relayed to the voters and the legislators. Judges feel that they cannot take part in controversy with journalists, or anyone else, without losing their essential integrity. A judge decides cases on the law and the facts, as defined. A political antagonist argues about both law and the facts and appeals to the electorate to make a final decision. Nevertheless the leaders of the bar and bench in recent years have come to feel, as Judge Wright does, that given the problems of law enforcement a free press is a valuable ally. Government is obtuse; only free and inquisitive mass media that accept an adversary role can help keep the law enforcement establishment open, efficient, and constitutionally fair.

Many of the asserted inefficiencies of the courts arise from determined efforts to humanize justice and to be fair to the poor as well as to other defendants. In these areas, press understanding and sympathy are in scarce supply. United States District Judge William J. Campbell of Chicago, after conducting criminal cases for thirty-two years in a large metropolitan court, says much of the delay is recent. The reason is restatement of criminal law by the Supreme Court in terms that often require up to eight proceedings amounting in time and work to separate trials.[15] Motions to suppress evidence, attacks on validity of search and wiretap warrants, laborious editing of grand jury transcripts so that defendants get pertinent material but no more, tests of the validity of warnings given prisoners under interrogation and of procedure in the police line-ups, says Judge Campbell, at least double the time formerly required for trial.

If a confession is ruled valid, severance of codefendants and separate trials are required if the confession incriminates persons other than the one who gave the statement. Moreover, Judge Campbell says, when by law a prior conviction must be used to weigh or otherwise affect sentence in the case before the court, federal judges must, in effect, retry the first conviction, by way of a full hearing, to assure that no rights of the defendant were violated in the first case.[16]

The curative powers of the writ of habeas corpus, long confined to prisoners, have now been extended to persons who have not yet begun to serve because, under Peyton v. Rowe,[17] "a prisoner serving consecutive sentences is 'in custody' under any one of them for the purpose of his habeas corpus petition. . . . Petitions requiring a complete retrial daily increase in alarming numbers in federal court," according to Judge Campbell. Federal trials are never concluded and the guilt or innocence of a defendant no longer has anything to do with the administration of justice, he feels.[18]

Journalism's Credo

When, for the sake of balance and fairness, we turn to journalists, we find they, too, have a history and a sociology that influence their attitudes and condition their performance. Lawyers, judges, and journalists are organized into many groups based on role assignments: trial judges and managing editors, prosecutors and editorial writers, law schools and journalism schools, chief justices and executive editors, institutes for legal and for journalistic research—the organization and consultation make role definitions and standardization of practice possible.

Proud of their freedom, journalists accept no standard of professional preparation. Most of them are college graduates but anybody can practice journalism who can get a job or who has the money to run his own business. There are no entrance requirements and no exit requirements; the creed of the journalist respects ethical performance but rejects group sanctions. Licensing to obtain responsible performance, or for any other reason, is regarded as a form of government control certain to result in tyranny. Institutions of professionalism, such as councils on standards of practice, are highly controversial. At this writing a National News Council is struggling to achieve acceptance and there is only one press council in the states, an unofficial body, that carries complaints filed with it to the point of finding fault and giving publicity to its opinions. This contrast in the professional obligations of law and journalism can be understood better after the record of their extensive competition and conflict is laid out on these pages and discussed in the context of the concluding chapter.

Journalism remains free because the legislative, executive, and judicial powers were distributed to three separate yet coordinate branches of government. The change from the model of the British Parliament enables judges to hold legislatures and executives to constitutional standards in the course of the day's work. If a statute is held invalid, as not in accord with the Constitution, it will not be enforced by the courts. When actions of an administrator are disputed under law, they are reviewed by a court with power to approve or to overrule them under Constitution and statute.

The same tripartite structure was adopted by the states. The fragmentation of political power and constitutional protection by the courts accounts for the exceptional prestige and influence attained by American journalists. After 1941, if a journalist found himself cited for contempt for his writings about courts he could appeal to the Supreme Court of the United States, if necessary. When his conflict is with a statute which state courts mistakenly support, the same appeal route is open.

Journalists, for the most part, refer only ceremonially to their calling as a profession. "It is not [a profession]," says Alfred Friendly, a former managing editor of the *Washington Post*.[19] "And a very good thing, too, for the sake of freedom and diversity of expression. Those who wrote the First Amendment understood the danger that would ensue if everyone who was allowed to put words to paper for public exposure had first to undergo some sort of professional training, examination, qualification, and perhaps licensing.'' Bill Green, former ombudsman of the *Washington Post*, describes the work standards in the *Post* newsroom, a rigorous training, examination, and discipline among employees. On the basis of this description, what Friendly must mean is that the neophyte, acolyte, soldier, and journeyman must be responsible to his own system and to no other.[20]

Howard Simons, one of Friendly's successors as managing editor of the *Post*, thinks the journalist has constitutional status equal to the judge on the bench. That is to say the journalist knows society's needs as well as judges and should not be compelled to subordinate his judgment to other imperatives. Inspired by his view of the First Amendment, Simons writes on this subject more as a poet than in the manner of a man sensitive to the balance of forces in the community. Driven by his belief, he accepts no barrier to his faith.

When a court orders Richard Nixon, despite the president's high place in the Constitution, to surrender his voice tapes and thus potentially to convict himself out of his own mouth, the court is described as a hero entitled to the appreciation of society. When a court, applying the same reasoning, declines to adopt the journalist's poetic vision of the First Amendment, Simons writes that ''society is threatened.''[21] ''Judges and journalists do not believe each other's rhetoric,'' he says. ''The words one speaks are not the sounds the other hears.'' If the government has secrets, as in the Pentagon Papers affair, let the government keep them safe. If they come into the hands of journalists, ''we and we alone should make the decision as to what and when to publish.''[22]

If a trial court instructs lawyers, witnesses, parties, and law enforcement officers not to give information to the press, and one or more of them violates the order, ''under no circumstances should the press be subject to contempt for publishing information obtained from someone subject to such restraints.'' Simons explains:

What are the limits on . . . a journalist's right to obtain information [particularly for the aggressive investigative reporter hot on the trail of official wrongdoing]? . . . Reporters should, of course, be guided not only by a sense of legality, but also by a sense of decency and ethics. Reporters should not steal information [or] commit crimes—for example, threaten blackmail—in the course of obtaining information. But like all moral codes, the statement of these general principles is far simpler than their application in a complex, harassed and competitive life of a journalist. What is elegant in theory can be elusive in practice.[23]

Howard Simons repeats that the journalist, not a judge nor any third party, should make the critical decisions on what to print. If the public wants the best contribution to self-government the journalist can make, there can be no countervailing interpreter of his decisions. The fate of the First Amendment must be in no other hands.[24]

Although lacking power to incarcerate or coerce, journalists seek both security and influence for themselves by generating predictable responses to words and symbols. They assume major responsibility for enforcement of moral judgments in politics, but seldom attempt to formulate a creed by which the community is to live. Instead, journalists raise an alarm when officials appear to take public property for private use, or, in corrupt pursuit of power, break the democratic covenant to conduct the public's business by open rather than covert procedures. This journalistic activity is direct intervention into the security and progress of persons with political and economic power. Curiously, this intervention is rarely or never accompanied by confession of partisan or other political motive. The public, unless it has sources of information other than the press, is unaware of the political impact of an incident of news reporting and is left to assume that journalists are motivated only by what they term "the public interest."[25] Talent in use of accusatory words, coupled with wide distribution of their message, leads journalists into danger. The First Amendment, as they interpret it, is both their shield and their lance, but to make its sanctions effective for them they seek protective alliances with powerful economic interests and adopt supportive mercantile roles as purveyors of information, entertainment, and advertising.

Much information published and broadcast is not solicited by journalists but is volunteered by persons and agencies who want attention. The literature of political campaigns deals with publicity and propaganda but we put it aside to consider the journalist who has authority to define news, exclude items that do not meet his standard, and emphasize others which give him professional satisfaction.

When the journalist faces persons who do not desire to give him information he requests unless they can control the way it is presented to the public, he plays a role which is frankly described as adversarial. Upon approaching a public official who is suspected or accused of some breach in performance etiquette, the journalist says, "I am here to help you inform the public. You need me; you can trust my skill and sympathy. Let me help you tell your story." When the official is confused, undecided, or reluctant to talk, the journalist adopts a wheedling tone:

"Your reputation is at stake. You have been accused. Tell the whole truth. In this way—and only in this way—can you silence your critics and defeat your enemies."

These words seem to promise that when the public knows the whole truth it will understand and absolve. To be sure, if the official is wrongly criticized, or accused, some who hear his story may well support him. But if he blames others, while defending himself, the journalist who advised him to tell the truth will seek out the other persons mentioned and ask them for comment. A build up of controversy ensues and the journalist now firmly is committed to an accusatory role. He asks, for example, "If your supporters did not cast fraudulent ballots in your precinct, who did? . . . Do you know Slick Wardheeler? . . . Is he not your brother-in-law? . . . Slick, as everybody knows, likes baseball. Did you give him a season ticket to the Met? Where did you get it?"

There are two likely responses the public official can make to this line of inquiry: (1) obtain access to a mass medium which is friendly, sympathetic, and patient enough to tell a complicated story; (2) remain silent and reply to charges only when compelled by political exigencies or by criminal trial. In this day of one-newspaper towns and one-minute slots for news stories in the broadcasting media, a friendly, cooperative, and patient medium is hard to find. Accusation seems to journalists to deserve more emphasis than defense. The public official may find silence forced upon him because there is no way to tell his story.

The journalist, for his part, refuses to accept silence as a defense. He addresses himself seriously to the conscience of the community: "The people have a right to know. . . . The truth must come out. . . . Officials who meet in secret conspire against the public interest. . . . There ought to be a law." State and federal laws in fact do require disclosure of public business. Using them, the journalist operates in an alliance with the state. He is, in effect, an agent of the government in tracking down crime. Or has government become his agent? At least he is allied with those members of government sympathetic to his demands and is partisan in the sense that some persons will be helped and others will be hurt when official inquiry brings controversial allegations into the open.

Pride Inspires Both Sides

This description of two leading intellectual groups influential in public affairs omits the crucial factor of pride: the pride which commits lawyers and judges to fair trial for accused persons who need it most; and the pride which commits journalists to get and publish or broadcast news at any cost in the belief that, in this way, they can best serve the needs of the democratic state.

Pride, for lawyers and judges, means the establishment of social control through orderly processes. Pride commits journalists to reject all controls except those of conscience. Not all journalists respond to the same ethic and there is no way for them to develop a consensus. Lawyers put their ideals to work in structures of law and order. Journalists are privileged persons in this structure because judges, striving against corruption, have made them so. The political assignment of journalism is to keep public servants and special interest groups, whether their purpose is greed or lawful service, from unjust enrichment or irresponsible use of political and economic power.

If the dispute between the two groups could be kept in the narrow frame presented here, the danger of damage to either the courts or the press would be minimized. But the dispute rapidly spreads to the point where some journalists, in reporting crime news, compete with the courts for public approval, offering journalistic substitutes for constitutional rules and statutory procedures which the courts are obliged to follow. These attacks undermine authority and create a dangerous rivalry which, carried to its natural limit, means loss of liberty for the press and public and a court system which rejects the ancient ideal that justice must be seen in order to be trusted and approved. As explained at the outset, the press is an underdog in competing with the courts but enough cases have now been decided that the dog has shown surprising strength and usefulness. An account of these developments follows.

Conflict and Bargaining 2

Judges on the bench deal with working journalists from a tradition of authority recently naked but now clothed in restraints provided by the higher courts. (Bridges v. California, 1941.) But juries as well as judges are affected by the flow of news and, in order to protect defendants, the courts felt compelled at certain critical points to make the news conform to the time schedule set out in the rules of fair trial. (Sheppard v. Maxwell, 1966.) Protection of defendants must begin well ahead of trial, and the American Bar Association formulated standards to guide the release of news by the whole of the law enforcement establishment. (The Reardon Report, 1966 and 1968.) The news media felt gravely threatened when deprived of their customary access to sources of news. In the discussion which ensued, both the press and the bar made efforts at reconciliation. These included local bar, bench, and press councils, Socratic dialogues by leaders from both camps, and efforts at scholarly research to measure the impact of news on the fairness of criminal trials.

THE PATTERN OF CONTROLS

The introduction sought to show that relations between journalists and trial judges who live and work together in democratic interaction are characterized by tension and, at times, by rivalry for public support. The Supreme Court of the United States is the referee designated by the Constitution and it decides how far the rivalry between judges and journalists over control of crime news can go. For many decades, when disputes over press criticism went to court, some judges on the bench treated the journalist as an outlaw, cited him for contempt, and decided whether and to what extent the critic should be punished. In the somewhat enlightened present, when a judge sets out to punish a journalist for written or spoken criticism, other judges try the case and tend to see the dispute in quite different and dispassionate ways. Over time, rules for use of a court's contempt powers, well established in common law, were changed because they were basically in conflict with evolving judicial ideals.

Every time a judge fined or jailed a journalist for criticism of a court, or for publishing news forbidden by court order, the community uproar was unpleasant and difficult for the judiciary to deal with. When the journalist emerged from jail he was more likely to be greeted as a hero by his fellow citizens than as a criminal who deserved punishment. One of the precepts of jurisprudence, not mentioned often, is that if punishment does not lead defendants to reform there may be something wrong with it. Sending unrepentant journalists to jail for writing the news, or commenting upon it, and watching the community take them to its heart was not, in the calculus of judicial happiness, a productive exercise of authority.

The Supreme Court, fortified by a rising sense of fairness, finally restrained the trial bench in 1941. The case came from Los Angeles where a complaint against the *Los Angeles Times* had been initiated by an outraged and, by today's standards, somewhat pompous bar association. The *Times* had offered unwanted advice to trial courts for years and had been slow to accept either their criticism or their wisdom. For that reason, the bar association had a backlog of newspaper grievances ready for use in filing a complaint if and when it seemed likely to succeed. That likelihood appeared when Harry Bridges, the labor leader, sent a telegram to the U.S. Department of Labor at a time of community tension saying his longshoremen would walk out if a Superior Court judge issued, as he had threatened to do, a no-strike injunction. The *Times* reported the message fully while the judge pondered his course of action.

In the season of anxiety, the bar association and the trial court came to a meeting of minds. Bridges and the newspaper were cited for contempt, Bridges for threatening to violate a court order with a strike and the *Times* for editorials and news stories, not all related to the strike, which the court held to be obstructive. The bar's case seemed to be on firm ground except for one obstacle deemed insignificant at the time, but important in a democracy: A state statute forbade the court to punish speakers or writers for constructive contempt, that is, for what had been written or said outside of court. Similar federal and state statutes had been overridden by other courts, including the Supreme Court of the United States. Assuming that the statutes expressed political experience and the popular will, the courts were saying that a legislature could not advise or instruct a court about discipline of its citizen critics.

One of the justices of the California Supreme Court disagreed with the contempt sanction against the *Times* and Bridges, and when the case got to the U.S. Supreme Court on appeal his views prevailed, five to four. It was a tough decision for the judicial establishment to accept. The U.S. Supreme Court had to repeat its instructions to trial judges in two other state cases before the challenges subsided. But no one can say the spirit of the judges in the minority does not strongly survive.

The opinion of the Court left the way open for trial judges in subsequent cases to use the contempt power to restrain the press if they could show a clear and present danger that comment would disrupt the court's process. No such showing acceptable to the Supreme Court has been made. Over the long run, other changes, particularly a requirement that contempt cases be assigned for trial to a disinterested judge, reduced the frequency of crises like the Bridges case.

The theory of the high court in terms of public policy is that the court system is deemed to be strong enough to conduct its business in the normal hubbub of the community and that it gathers public sympathy and support in doing so. Reasonable men are capable of turning their backs upon a disruptive journal and, in times of public danger, will do so.

The Sheppard Mandate

The Bridges case,[1] in which the new policy was expressed, dealt with the impact of news and comment on judges, not juries. The ABA standards, which appeared in tentative draft in 1966 and were approved two years later, were formulated to deal with control of the flow of news so as to avoid juror bias. The leading Supreme Court opinion on the subject, Sheppard v. Maxwell,[2] also appeared in 1966 and both the standards and the case decision influence trial procedures. The opinion of the Court, however, is controlling and attempts of the trial courts to interpret it have caused the press the most trouble.

Evidence that the Sheppard opinion signaled a fundamental shift begins with the fact that the contradictions in the opinions and the recommendations on due process took more than a decade to clarify. The ten years Dr. Sam Sheppard spent in prison before he was given a new trial and acquitted saw the appellate courts abandon their apathetic attitudes toward the effect of news reports on trial and, at the prodding of the Supreme Court, begin to review claims of prejudice more carefully. This examination began to bring an end to an age where trial by newspaper was commonplace. What follows is a description of the case according to the Supreme Court opinions.

The trial. The objectionable characteristics of the case arose from the action of the *Cleveland Press*—now out of business but once the kingpin of the Scripps-Howard group—and, to a lesser extent, of other newspapers. The journalists took part as advocates in the entire criminal process: investigation, coroner's hearing, grand jury consideration, pretrial hearings, jury selection, trial, and punishment. The Court said that during the pretrial period "virulent and incriminating publicity" about Sheppard and the murder made the case notorious. The media, according to the court record, systematically reported police charges according to a double standard. The police standard permitted individual investigators to float lies and fanciful fabrications which were presented in the media as fact. At one point, a front-page picture of Mrs. Sheppard's bloodstained pillow was published after being retouched to show the alleged imprint of a surgical instrument—inferentially her husband's. The cruel hoaxes or myths never got on the trial record because there was little or no truth in them. But the police and the newspapers helped get them into the minds of the community.

The second standard is due process of law according to the Ohio statutes. Legal standards were put to one side in the enthusiastic effort to send Sheppard to prison. If the hard evidence, as it appeared, was inadequate to support indictment and trial, the newspaper response was to load editorials and news stories with pretrial, police-inspired assertions of guilt. Sheppard was pictured as a rich playboy literally getting away with murder. The coroner, the *Press* said, lacked the courage to hold an inquest. Smarting under the scorn of the newspapers, radio, and television, the coroner told his staff, "Well, it is evident the doctor did this, so let's go get a confession out of him."[3] The coroner questioned Sheppard while he was sedated in his hospital room. The hospital was operated by the Sheppard family and the police considered its staff biased. Sheppard was suffering from severe pains in his neck, a swollen eye, and shock. After this interview, and on the same day, Sheppard was interrogated by a police chief and two police officers. One of them demanded that he take a lie detector test which, because of its lack of scientific validity, is not admissible in evidence without the consent of the defendant and the court. Moreover, the hostile police would administer and interpret this or the equally subjective truth serum test. Sheppard refused both tests. The police publicized Sheppard's refusal and one of the officers told the doctor, "I think you killed your wife." The doctor was denied the support of counsel at hearings because the Supreme Court had not yet decided the series of cases culminating in Miranda v. Arizona, 384 U.S. 436 (1966), which made access to counsel at this stage a constitutional right. Sheppard submitted to extensive interrogation, but the newspapers said his family kept investigators away. Sheppard's effort to defend himself in the press was buried by accusative stories.

Presumption of guilt. After the way was prepared by publicity, the coroner held his inquest in a school gymnasium to accommodate newspapers, radio, television, and the curious public. The hearing lasted three days. Sheppard's lawyers were present but were ordered not to participate. When the chief counsel offered a written statement it was refused and the lawyer was forcibly ejected from the room. The newspapers dug up evidence of an extramarital affair, long since over, and others were manufactured for the occasion by volunteer accusers. Susan Hayes, the "other woman," was brought back from California for journalistic exposure.

Still, there was little evidence upon which to base indictment and arrest. The Court said that after widespread publicity failed to bring legal action, the newspapers directly demanded Sheppard's arrest. Thus challenged, the police arrested the doctor and took him for arraignment to his suburban village city hall "where hundreds of people, newscasters, photographers, and reporters were waiting for his arrival."[4] Sheppard asked for time to call his lawyer but the request was denied and he was immediately bound over to the grand jury. Two weeks later he was indicted on a charge that he murdered his wife.

After the media gossipmongers shredded Sheppard's reputation, the doctor fought back with counterpublicity. Letters he wrote to his small son from jail were published in the same columns as the accusatory stories. The community feeling was churned to anger and Sheppard's repeated cries of innocence were treated as whimpers of guilt.[5] Journalistic fancywork took his statements apart looking for discrepancies. The newspaper cuttings alone, according to the Court, filled five large volumes. The radio and television coverage could not be measured. The case, prepared in this way, went to trial two weeks before the general election at which the trial judge was a candidate to succeed himself and the prosecutor was running for the office of judge.

Journalists dominate courtroom. The courtroom was little larger than some outsize living rooms, twenty-six by forty-eight feet. Twenty reporters sat at a table inside the bar of the court. Others occupied all but fourteen seats in the public benches. Sheppard's family was assigned the remainder. The journalists came and went as they pleased. They took over all office space on the same floor as the courtroom, and a broadcasting studio was set up for them next to the jury room on another floor. A television station interviewed the trial judge, with his help, as he was about to enter the courthouse. Photographers worked in the corridors; they published pictures of jurors, witnesses, counsel, and the defendant. During twice-a-day recesses, the journalists took over the courtroom itself. The jurors were not sequestered. The media photographed the jury seated in the box and made individual pictures of jurors in the jury room. Such pictures appeared more than forty times in the Cleveland papers alone, giving publicity to the jurors in the atmosphere of accusation and guilt which helped persuade them to send Sheppard to prison.

"All of these arrangements with the news media and the massive coverage of the trial continued during the entire nine weeks of the trial," the Court said. The jurors themselves were constantly exposed to the news media. All but one of them testified in voir dire[6] that they had read about the case in the Cleveland papers or heard broadcast accounts.

Justice Tom C. Clark, in his opinion for the Supreme Court, laid down exhortations, advice, and rules without clearly distinguishing between them. Many of his points had to be litigated and are reported in the pages which follow. The Court's specific finding was that journalistic disturbance in the courtroom as well as massive, persuasive, and prejudicial pretrial publicity inspired by the police, prosecutor, and coroner denied Sheppard a fair trial. Witnesses were not insulated from each other. Publicity created a punitive atmosphere but the Court blamed that on officials; the behavior of the media was protected by the First Amendment. The attorneys and officials who inspired the publicity, however, were subject to court authority and administrative regulation. They should have been curbed, since control is prerequisite to fair trial.

The traditional remedies by which to combat the spirit of a hostile community are change of venue, continuance, questioning of prospective jurors in the voir dire, admonishment of jurors to avoid reading or talking about the case, and jury sequestration. Yet, in this case, voir dire was not used effectively, warning to jurors was perfunctory, and the other remedies were not used at all. The jurors were sequestered during deliberation but continued to make unsupervised telephone calls at will. Simply put, the trial judge did not assert control and, in the vacuum, the police and the press took over. The flood of sensational rumor and opinion led to infamous unfairness, an epic of trial by newspaper. In response to Sheppard and other cases, the Supreme Court and the organized bar wrote rules which could prevent similar abuses, a task to be done, no matter how careful the planning, through trial and error.

ABA TRIAL STANDARDS

The ambiguities found in the Supreme Court's Sheppard opinion were noted almost at once at the 1966 American Bar Association convention. A law teacher on the program asserted that the Court had invited judges to regulate the press through rules of court to be enforced by use of the contempt power. Justice Clark, author of the Sheppard opinion, responded shortly afterward at the same convention to deny that the Court intended such drastic measures. "I am not proposing that you jerk a newspaper reporter in the courtroom and hold him in contempt. We do not have to jeopardize freedom of the press," he said, adding that in his opinion the press had made our democracy work. But he did not want it to prejudice cases.[7]

Criminal law administrators were not only faced with mistaken impressions about the Sheppard Mandate but the remedy proposed at about the same time by the organized bar, through ABA's Reardon Committee, was even more complex and difficult to interpret. The task of interpretation is carried out through interaction of the several parts of the judicial establishment. Final authority to interpret case decisions and the rules lies with the Supreme Court, when and to the extent that it makes itself clear in its opinions. Judges interact with the public primarily through formal opinions; when they make speeches they tend to prefer general topics. Below the Court is a body of judges, lawyers, police, prosecutors, and litigants in both state and federal courts who manage the business of civil and criminal justice. They work through administrative and judicial committees, the ABA, the state and city bar associations, and several special institutions created for that purpose. After they analyze their problems and compare experiences they settle on recommendations for legislative and judicial action. At several points the actions of the facilitating groups described cross over into law, particularly through legislation and rules made by the courts for the conduct of business. Rules of criminal procedure, for example, are drawn by commissions and committees of judges but they also are adopted by the legislatures. The ethical rules of bar associations are part of the private sector, but are meaningless without sanctions which come from legislation or rules drawn by the courts. The contacts between the private and official system are multiform and when an association appoints an unofficial committee, ABA's Fair Trial and Free Press Committee for example, its recommendations have no more effect than *Robert's Rules of Order* until adopted and enforced by a willing court and law enforcement officers.

After adopting the standards in 1968, the ABA asked courts to implement them. The rules pertain to all three levels of government and can take effect in each only by an act of will. The ABA compelled nobody but it did write a charter into which authority could be introduced. The same conditions apply in each of the states and, except for the Constitution, there is little compelled uniformity among the states. Some state legislatures and high courts adopt ABA rules, some do not. The reader should distinguish between ABA recommendations and the binding rules which legislatures and high courts establish. ABA is not a paper tiger; it is a powerful and thoughtful deliberative body. But courts and legislatures move to the ABA's tune by choice, not by force.

On the federal judicial level, the rule-making body is the United States Judicial Conference, over which the chief justice presides, and it also has a mind of its own. It follows the ABA to the extent that it is impressed by the ABA's logic. The Justice Department makes administrative rules binding its employees. But district attorneys, when trying cases, are subject to the authority of the courts. The legislatures, the state high courts, and the law departments—all three—can and do participate in the complicated discussion, revision, and enforcement process. Under these conditions the development of ABA standards can be discussed from the committee stage in 1966 to the present, apart from cases in state and federal courts for the same time period which are to be described later. They are related but the ABA's rules, as such, are not controlling.

The Reardon Committee

The ABA committee was made up of outstanding talent. Justice Paul C. Reardon of Massachusetts, the chairman, was a former chairman of the ABA Section of Judicial Administration. Grant Cooper of Los Angeles was a past president of both the American College of Trial Lawyers and the Los Angeles County Bar Association. He had served as an assistant public prosecutor for twelve years. Chief United States Judge Edward J. Devitt of Minnesota had handled a series of widely-publicized and politics-related criminal cases. Robert M. Figg, Jr., was dean of the University of South Carolina Law School. Ross L. Malone of Roswell, N.M., and Robert G. Storey of Dallas were former presidents of the ABA. Judge Bernard S. Meyer of Mineola, N.Y., was a distinguished judge of the New York Supreme (trial) Court. He had studied the topic systematically and had published a widely discussed statutory proposal as a guide to fair trial. United States Judge Wade H. McCree, Jr., of Detroit, later U.S. solicitor general, sat in a district with a heavy docket of criminal cases. Abe Fortas, later associate justice of the Supreme Court of the United States, and Daniel P. Ward, state's attorney, Cook County (Chicago), were originally members of the committee. Lewis F. Powell, Jr., later associate justice, appointed the committee as president of the ABA.

The news control standards can be summarized, perhaps too briefly, in this way: Before an arrest, and while the search for suspects is under way, release of news is not greatly impeded unless the pursuing officers identify their quarry in terms that would impute guilt and create fear and prejudice among the people. But once a specific person is identified in a warrant or is arrested, the lawyer, the public official, and law enforcement employees are told not to release (1) past criminal or arrest records of the accused; (2) any purported confession or statement or to report that the suspect had declined to give information; (3) any news of examinations or tests taken or refused; (4) any probability of a plea of guilty to the charge or to a lesser charge; or (5) any opinion as to guilt or innocence, as to the merits of the case or of the evidence.

Information which can be freely released includes the following: (1) the fact and circumstances of arrest; (2) resistance, pursuit, and use of weapons; (3) the identity of investigating and arresting officer(s) and the length of the search; (4) a description of the physical evidence taken, the charges filed, and information about any stage in the investigation, including a denial of guilt by the persons held.

The federal and state rules of criminal procedure provide that a person shall not be held for trial unless the prosecution presents evidence at a preliminary hearing or arraignment to justify a trial. If highly prejudicial evidence is heard, with or without rebuttal, it cannot be kept out of the news media if the hearing is public.

The ABA standard assumes that the Constitution permits a defendant to waive a public hearing in favor of a closed session in the judge's chambers or elsewhere outside the view of the public. This standard provoked serious disagreement and litigation, not only between the media and the courts, but between members of the legal establishment. The disagreement continued when the Supreme Court, after more than a decade of delay, approved the standard in principle.

The closure-reform model. The controversial ABA recommendation for closure was not new or unsupported. Precedents for closure existed in New York, California, Arizona, Montana, Idaho, Nevada, North Dakota, and Utah. These states had adopted versions of the Field Code, dating from 1850 and named for David Dudley Field, a New York lawyer and legislator who disliked what he called "trial by newspaper." The Field model called for mandatory closure on motion by the defense but criticism caused the New York legislature to repeal the mandatory provision and to place discretion in the trial court. To indicate the kind of controversy which attended closure, the Arizona law caused a political uproar when a judge, sitting as magistrate in a closed pretrial hearing, dismissed for lack of evidence charges of land fraud against a public official. The state supreme court divided bitterly over closure and held the statute unconstitutional in 1966.[8] After long disuse in California, the Field statute was upheld by the state supreme court in 1960 and again in 1982.[9]

While the Reardon Committee was at work, the British were in the process of closing preliminary hearings for the first time. On the basis of a commission report, the British Criminal Justice Act of 1967 provided that the pretrial proceedings be on the basis of written rather than oral evidence. Publication or broadcast of such evidence was made unlawful. Even the right to remain silent under police interrogation was under heavy attack in the House of Commons at the same time it was given constitutional form in the United States. In effect, the two systems were moving in opposite directions at the same time and the British influence on the Reardon Committee, resulting from contacts which the committee reported, was against the American flow.[10]

On the authority of court rules based on the ABA standard, section 8-3.2, pretrial hearings of several kinds can be moved to the judge's chambers, thus excluding the public. Testimony crucial to guilt or innocence need be heard only at the trial itself in open court. Evidence offered in private or ruled inadmissable does not reach the media. The standard, to discourage abuse of secret proceedings, calls for a verbatim record of closed hearings which is to be made available after completion of trial or dismissal of charges without trial.

Journalists, commenting on closure, said that news is a perishable commodity and that law enforcement must be open if the people are to have confidence that justice is being done. They apparently mean that a transcript of a hearing released days or weeks after trial has no news value and will not be reported. "Thus, the inevitable effect of restricting the reporting of the crime news of the day will be to deprive the average citizen of his only way of obtaining the facts necessary to appraise his community's law enforcement activities," said J. Howard Wood, publisher of the *Chicago Tribune* and then president of the American Newspaper Publishers Association.[11]

Judge George C. Edwards, Jr., United States Court of Appeals, Sixth Circuit, had a similar view. "When we give thought to the problems posed in past (and present!) history by prosecutions corrupted against the public interest by organized crime or by such pressures as those of the Ku Klux Klan in some states, the dangers become obvious," he explained to a Connecticut law forum.[12]

Judges who supported the ABA standard said that allegations in the media attributed to a public official "have a ring of authority and authenticity." As a consequence of extreme statements (including reported confessions), the ABA committee said, "defendants sometimes are arraigned in the presence of hostile crowds in the courtroom."

Information from extrajudicial sources released during the trial, if it reaches the jury, is treated as grounds for a motion for mistrial. For that reason, the ABA wants information published and broadcast during trial confined to the court record.

Modified Federal Rules

The ABA standards, after two years of study, were substantially approved by the United States Judicial Conference. Each U.S. district court was advised to adopt them as local rules.

The conference also felt that federal marshals, bailiffs, clerks and court reporters were clearly subject to authority of the court and could be bound by a local rule. It did not recommend any direct curb or restraint on the mass media for dissemination of potentially prejudicial material. The conference noted that the Supreme Court had not as yet authorized exclusion of the press from preliminary and other public hearings held outside the presence of the jury, and it did not adopt the closure policy. At the same time it recognized as lawful the common practice of conferences at the bench and in chambers which could not be heard by the public.

In one other respect the conference departed from ABA standards. It left rules for access to criminal records in the hands of the attorney general. Justice Department rules already had been drawn and they did not flatly bar journalists from receiving and using such records. But the records, as made available, are considerably edited: Federal convictions only are shown, not state convictions or arrests and trials where no conviction was obtained.[13]

Administrative Rules for Secrecy

The ABA committee took strong objection to media reporting of plea bargaining, that is, the secret conferences between a defendant, his attorney, and the prosecutor which ordinarily result in submission of a negotiated plea of guilty. Bargaining downgrades the procedural safeguards and the courts along with it. Yet 90 percent of all cases are settled in this way without jury trials.[14] The objection to publicity is that incriminating information comes out which, by terms of the approved procedure, never gets on the record, is never rebutted, and might not be proved true if it were. The ABA objected equally to news accounts of previous convictions and of arrests ordinarily inadmissable in evidence, but the media insisted that these were on the public record and could not be kept out of pretrial stories. The difference of opinion ran through both federal and state court establishments.

The cogency of the ABA objection to reports of extrajudicial confessions was clear to all. Journalists generally eliminated pretrial reports of self-incrimination in all but a few sensational cases which, because of competitive media pressure and disorganization of law enforcement agencies at the time, were not kept secret.[15]

Prosecutors passed the ABA rules on to their staffs and to police, sheriffs, and other law enforcement personnel. The ABA recommended that internal disciplinary sanctions be provided to deal with breaches of the rules. The policy also was linked to the desire of the police and prosecutors to avoid continuances, changes of venue, difficulty in obtaining jurors, mistrials, reversals, and new trials. Yet court use of the exclusionary rule, rejecting evidence illegally taken, also put pressure on the police. If statutory support was not available, the standard then called for a local court rule binding on law enforcement people. This recommendation has been controversial from the start.[16] In 1978 the ABA came to the position that the separation of powers screened police from discipline based on rules made by the court. Alfred Blumrosen suggests that rules of criminal procedure might have to be revised to cover police offenses to which the contempt penalty might be applied.[17]

The problem of persuading policemen to inform on each other, or to confess to giving information to journalists in violation of a general rule, or of forcing the media to identify informants, transcends judicial rulemaking powers. The ABA also asked legislatures to deal with administrative employees who leak news to the press: "It does not appear that law enforcement agencies around the country are effectively regulating themselves on this matter."[18]

On the road to implementing the Reardon report, the ABA committee dealt formally with its journalistic adversaries. It gave a full hearing to news representatives at the Hawaii convention in 1967. Officers of the major journalism business and professional associations appeared before two ABA sections and before Justice Reardon's committee. Few changes resulted, however, and six months later the standards were presented to the House of Delegates and approved.

ABA Explains Its Purpose

Chairman Reardon and other ABA leaders, in response to expressions of media anxiety, offered reassurance. They rejected charges that the rules gagged the press. They recognized the indispensable role of a free press in our democracy, including the independence of the bar and the courts. They look upon the First and Sixth Amendments as coequal, not incompatible, they stated, and the bar seeks no special advantage. Journalists and lawyers alike depend upon freedom of expression. ABA said it asks no more than to reconcile fair trial and free speech in conditions of highly competitive news coverage.

Journalistic Opposition to the Rules

Before adoption of the standards, the journalistic defense was that police and attorneys, as in the Sam Sheppard case, readily provided the news to which the ABA objected. After the rule change, the press establishment argued that the First Amendment was being eroded. The courts were tying the hands of journalists in the reporting and editing process, it was argued, and the Constitution does not countenance the suppression of news of trials. Only the media should decide what to print and broadcast.

The attitude of the courts, the journalists said, is based on subjective judgment of the effects of news. Is this displeasure of the courts to be substituted for editorial freedom? If the courts use change of venue, continuance, and sequestration of juries, there will be no occasion to interfere with the free flow of news. The media representatives said they have discontinued pretrial mention of confessions and exercise discretion at other critical stages of a case. They are conscious of the tensions of a big story and are cooperative. But even if they make mistakes occasionally, the journalists said, their overall record is good and they do not deserve punitive treatment. The public's need for news is immediate. The flow of information should not be impeded, hampered, or delayed.

Investigative reporting that uncovers political corruption and solves crimes must not be curtailed, journalists insisted. The standards impose restrictions on reporting and televising of such events as political demonstrations on the street which result in criminal charges.

Who will watch and report on the activities of the police if the press no longer can deal with them legally? When hearings are secret and parts of trials are closed, the press says it is challenged to find out and to tell the public what went on. The standards encourage individual judges to control the press and to punish lawyers and police who give information. When terror or deep public anxiety result from a series of crimes and police catch and identify the person(s) responsible, is not the public entitled to know at once? How can ABA ask the people to wait for the time of trial to learn that the danger is over and that the police have done their work? Press leaders promised that journalists would use greater care not only in pretrial news but during trials when hearings to suppress evidence could get through to jurors.[19]

A DISTINGUISHED DISSENT

The most influential voice from within the judiciary to disagree with the Reardon standards was Circuit Judge Harold R. Medina, who, as a trial judge, presided over the nine-month trial of the executive committee of the Communist Party of the United States under the Smith Act.[20] Judge Medina chaired a study committee representing the Association of the Bar of the City of New York, operating under a charge quite similar to the Reardon Committee. Its recommendations were similar and parallel but Judge Medina and a committee majority spoke strongly of avoiding use of the contempt power to coerce journalists, police, lawyers, or prosecutors. It insisted that media behavior be judged not by "reasonable tendency" to interfere with a fair trial but by the stricter standard of clear and present danger. All persons concerned, Judge Medina's committee wrote, must recognize that neither the "public's right to know" nor the right of the accused to a fair trial is absolute, "for they conflict and must be reconciled in a manner calculated to cause the least injury to either value." He continued:

The administration of justice, and of criminal justice in particular, touches the operation of American democracy at the quick. It is highly desirable and is an undoubted part of the constitutional mandate itself that the processes of law enforcement be open to the public view, both for the purpose of protecting the innocent and bringing the guilty to boot and for the purpose of exposing incompetence, venality, or corruption on the part of those who arrest and prosecute and those who may sit in the seats of judgment. But there is, of course, no overriding policy consideration that favors the disclosure of facts at a time that will hamper investigation or make it more difficult either to acquit the innocent or to convict the guilty. . . . [21]

Frank S. Hogan, veteran district attorney of New York County, a member of the committee, did not agree that the First Amendment precluded direct control of the news media for the calculated purposes of fair trial. He favored resort to legislation which, he said, could be constitutional and a greater use of the court's contempt power.[22]

The ABA committee soon moderated its proposed use of the contempt power both with respect to journalists and lawyers. Years later, when the Nebraska courts used the ABA standard to threaten the media with contempt of court, Judge Medina, as an individual, strongly reiterated his opposition. "The prospect, in the pretrial period, of judges of various criminal courts of high and low degree sitting as petty tyrants handing down sentences of fine and imprisonment for contempt of court against lawyers, policemen, and reporters and editors is not attractive. Such an innovation might well cut prejudicial publicity to a minimum. But at what a price!" He said the press should stand on the First Amendment and "fight like tigers every inch of the way."[23]

Because of the selective nature of perception, the press has not given equal attention to other aspects of Judge Medina's views, but mainly to his dislike for the coercive features of the ABA standards. Judge Medina holds that lawyers, police, and others in law administration should not give the media information which, in effect, leads to prejudgment of cases, that trials should take place in the courtroom and not in the media.[24]

On other cardinal points, Judge Medina's committee was against abuses by the media: "Specifically, when crimes of violence occur, in particular those of murder, assault, rape, and robbery, creating widespread apprehension and at times holding the community in a grip of terror, the public demands to know what is being done to apprehend the perpetrators." In the committee view, the media exploit these pressures to force illegal disclosures of evidence. "In some instances, insinuations or accusations of nonfeasance or malfeasance [by police] begin to develop and to maintain momentum." To counteract this pressure the police share what they know with journalists. When an arrest is made, journalists in turn help publicize the police success story, ahead of trial, to the public.[25]

The journalists, through use of prior criminal records of suspects up for trial, help the police vent their impotence and frustration about the frequency with which offenders on bail or parole commit new offenses. The courts and the prisoner rehabilitation services can only hang their heads in anguish as their efforts to change criminal behavior and return prisoners to a peaceful life in the community are submerged by a tide of publicity true, perhaps, as to one individual but untrue as to the others who make it back to the law abiding world.[26]

The Medina committee would stop these and other excesses of publicity by the force of the canons of professional ethics for lawyers and by noncoercive bar, bench, and press committees to help the media achieve standards of fair trial.

ABA GOES BACK TO OPEN COURTS

New Rules for Fair Trial

In the summer of 1978, ten years after adoption of the ABA standards, Justice Michael R. Imbriani, sitting in the Criminal Division of the Superior Court for Mercer County, New Jersey, was ready to start a trial in which prominent politicians were defendants. The details reveal it to be a sad but routine confrontation between political figures and the law. The thirty-three counts against four persons—James Joyce, Wayne DeBellis, Morris Hacker, and Miles Burke—were allegations of embracery (trying to influence a jury sitting or about to sit), perjury, obstruction of justice, misconduct in public office, and conspiracy. Before the trial could begin, Judge Imbriani had to hear a motion to bar from evidence recordings of conversations by some of the indicted persons. The defendants and the prosecution asked that the hearing be closed to the public and to the media.

Judge Imbriani was sitting with scores of court decisions dancing in his mind and judicial conferences on the same subject ringing in his ears, guiding him, and perhaps confusing him, as he pondered whether or not to close his court. If he did so, a clamor would arise that he was violating the First Amendment. Questions of even more concern to him might be worded this way: Was he closing the court to favor the defendants? How could he prove that he worked openly in the interest of justice, not in the interest of politicians in trouble?

Standing for Journalists in Court

Unlike such hearings in 1965, attorneys for the *Trenton Times* and the *Trentonian* were in court as intervenors of record permitted to state the legal grounds, as they perceived them, against closing the hearing. It had taken weary years of litigation, a treasure in court costs, and decisions of the U.S. Supreme Court to make such intervention accepted procedure. In 1965, journalists usually appeared in court in such matters, if at all, to show cause why they should not be cited for contempt for circulating stories on closed hearings which they had obtained clandestinely.

Joyce and his codefendants, pushing for a closed hearing, said the voice record included "statements which are inadmissible in evidence, unkind comments about one or more public figures who are not parties to the litigation, and some statements which generally may be categorized as indecent." That kind of material, they lamented, would get too much publicity which, in spite of precautions, would reach the jurors and prejudice them.[27]

Precedents for a Ruling

Judge Imbriani remembered the admonition of the higher courts to seek "alternative solutions" before closing his court. Like other judges in such a situation, he longed for peaceful power to persuade journalists to give the jury a little more elbow room. He told the reporters that in another New Jersey jurisdiction journalists recently agreed to stay out of the hearing and to receive a copy of the recordings if they were admitted in evidence at the trial. He asked the journalists in Trenton if they would do as much.

No, they said; a journalist and only a journalist should decide what to print or broadcast. From the point of view of the defendants anxious for a fair trial, this rejection pictured the First Amendment as a device the press could use at will to blow away Sixth Amendment due process guarantees.

By now Judge Imbriani and others like him were hardened by the rhetoric of antagonists who had exchanged similar views in court. He was listening, instead, to the law as explained by higher courts at the time. He considered scheduling the evidence hearing after the jury was empaneled so he could have some control over what jurors read or heard. How could he be sure the jurors would not read or view the stories in the media? If he tested them by questions, and it turned out that some had heard prejudicial allegations, would he have to declare a mistrial? If so, would double jeopardy rules keep the defendants from being tried again?

The judge next considered closing the hearing, as the ABA rules suggest in cases of clear and present danger. His state supreme court had just laid out the rules for closure, warning of First Amendment complications, and Judge Imbriani did not think the case could legally be closed.[28] He could bring in a jury from outside the jurisdiction, or transfer the trial elsewhere, or continue the case until the publicity died down. But each of these alternatives, in one way or another, denied Sixth Amendment rights claimed by defendants.

Judge Imbriani said at the outset that he feared an explosive collision of the First and Sixth Amendments, but no one had shown evidence that giving the journalists their head would, in fact, prejudice the case. He decided to rely on voir dire, to examine each juror carefully for prejudicial taint. He said, later, that of the 101 venirepersons examined only 3 had read or heard about the case. The evidence hearing lasted six days and the media had reported it fully each day. Several newspaper accounts, he said, "bore what some would term sensational headlines."

The ABA Committee Pattern

The panorama of Judge Imbriani's thought, reconstituted here from the concentrated factual substance of his opinion, must be strikingly like that of the members of the ABA Legal Advisory Committee on Fair Trial and Free Press when, after long consideration, they recommended changes in the 1968 standards. The committee, now under the chairmanship of Judge Alfred T. Goodwin of the Ninth Circuit, solicited comment on rule changes during the summer of 1977. The record shows that Judge Goodwin received only limited help from the media. Proposed revisions were sent to the ABA House of Delegates and, with the exception of a controversial new standard on use of cameras in courtrooms, were adopted.

Adoption means no more now than it did in 1968. ABA proposes but the Supreme Court of the United States may not agree. If it does not, the ABA standards lack vitality. Judge Goodwin's standards reflected a wholesome new emphasis on open courts and open proceedings. The committee quoted Justice Brennan: "As 'pure speech,' public comment about law enforcement, the trial of criminal cases, and the administration of criminal justice enjoys the strongest possible presumption of First Amendment protection.''[29] The committee agreed. "Indeed," it said, "in the vast majority of criminal cases, extrajudicial statements by trial attorneys have no impact at all." It added that the original committee's failure to take account of this fact is the central weakness of its report.[30]

In implementing its views, the committee proposed that comment by lawyers, and by inference the comment of the news media, be judged by the "clear and present danger" test instead of the "reasonable likelihood" test used in the Reardon rules. It is assumed that a court rarely, if ever, can act to restrict comment under the clear and present danger guide. It was used in the Bridges case[31] and in two other cases, Craig v. Harney[32] and Wood v. Georgia,[33] where the pressure on the court was greater.[34] On the other hand, the reasonable likelihood test is vague and permissive. It enables the judge, rather than the attorney, to enjoy latitude. The Tenth Circuit, in 1979, had approved punishment of two minority political agitators for remarks they made in Spanish to their followers. The finding revived memories of earlier political citations for seditious libel.[35]

The two opinions that stirred judicial interest most were in the Seventh and the Fourth Circuits. Judge Luther M. Swygert, for the Seventh Circuit court, gave the protection of the clear and present danger test back to lawyers,[36] at least to those in his circuit, and inspired Judge Goodwin's committee. But such liberty was not supported by Judge John D. Butzner, Jr., and Chief Judge Clement N. Haynesworth, Jr., in the Fourth Circuit. They directly rebutted Judge Swygert and took time to praise the minority judges in Bridges.[37] The United States Judicial Conference, faced with the necessity of choice, said the Seventh Circuit opinion conceded that government attorneys could not comment with impunity on such matters as a defendant's prior criminal record, the possibility of a guilty plea, a confession, examinations or tests or a refusal to take them, information about potential witnesses, opinions about guilt or innocence, the evidence, and the merits of a case. Therefore it chose to use the reasonable likelihood language in its guidelines but withheld approval of incorporating the same language in the Rules of Criminal Procedure.[38]

Journalists recognized their common interest with lawyers in the matter and were intervenors in the Hirschkopf suit together with the American Civil Liberties Union.

There is also the question of whether rules to govern the dissemination of information by attorneys should be general and applicable to all trials, or whether special rules should be drawn for a particular case. Silence orders for a particular trial, while recognized, present two difficulties: It is hard to cover all contingencies without becoming vulnerable to attack for overbreadth and vagueness. Such orders tend to forbid practically all communication, and in some jurisdictions even prevent raising timely questions about due process.[39] The Judicial Conference still approves special orders.

The standards, Part II, 8-2 through 8-2.3 (Police and Judges), retain all of the previous safeguards against prejudgment of accused persons. The committee said these precautions have been the least criticized of the 1968 standards. However, the court's authority to place general limitations on the speech of law enforcement officials in the executive branch, in order to enforce these rules, continues to be in doubt. The debate over administrative rule enforcement is perhaps outside the scope of this work, but its outlines are found in the statement of the committee.[40] So that all criminal justice employees can see, the vital prohibition against release of confessions or plea bargains is separately set out and emphasized in the revised standards.

A preference for openness. The Supreme Court's ruling in the Nebraska Press Association case (see below) has its effect on Part III, 8-3 through 8-3.7 (Trials), of the standards. The ABA, reasoning from First Amendment premises, says the presumption now is "strongly in favor of open judicial proceedings and unsealed records." The burden is placed on the party moving to exclude the public to demonstrate necessity, under the clear and present danger test, and the ineffectiveness of alternative procedures. Prior restraints are prohibited. The standard of what to do goes beyond the Nebraska Press Association opinion, the committee says, but is neither radical nor unwarranted. The standard favors openness: "Except as provided below, pretrial proceedings and their record shall be open to the public, including representatives of the news media."

The first recourse of a judge dealing with the threat of publicity is to appeal to journalists to be fair to the defendants but, as Judge Imbriani's experience shows, this plea often falls on ears turned to stone by years of dispute. Two other recourses are to consider a defendant's offer of proof of clear and present danger that the publicity will destroy, or has destroyed, a fair trial. "First, as a general proposition," the Goodwin committee says, "the need for prior restraints will always be a highly conjectural matter in light of the alternative procedures available to a trial judge''—those alternatives Judge Imbriani detailed in his opinion, plus similar steps, severance of defendants, additional peremptory challenges, sequestration of the jury and admonitory instructions to jurors.[41]

Who can close the court? The cases make clear, the committee explains, that the right to an open public trial may not be accepted or rejected at will by a defendant. "Many courts have recognized that the public generally has an overlapping and compelling interest in public trials. . . . The transcendent reason for public trials is to insure efficiency, competence, and integrity in the overall operation of the judicial system.'' The openness requirement is also included in the Sixth Amendment but has since been limited by Gannett v. DePasquale, which is discussed later.[42] The committee is aware of the flat rejection of prior restraint in the first paragraph of the standard and acceptance of a case-by-case treatment of it in standard 8-3. The reason, apparently, is that adversarial case-by-case procedure is more likely to make lawful discriminations than the one-party citations under standard 8-1. The leading cases are against prior restraint and somewhat tolerant of due process considerations leading to limited closure of the court or sealing of records—that is, delaying media access to evidence for a time, as when a preliminary hearing is closed.

The Trials standard (8.3-2) provides the following:

> The presiding officer may close a preliminary hearing, bail hearing, or any other pretrial proceeding, including a motion to suppress, and may seal the record only if
> (i) the dissemination of information from the pretrial proceeding and its record would create a clear and present danger to the fairness of the trial, and
> (ii) the prejudicial effect of such information on trial fairness cannot be avoided by any reasonable alternative means. . . .
> Whenever, under this rule all or part of any pretrial proceeding is held in chambers or otherwise closed to the public, a complete record shall be kept and made available to the public following the completion of trial or earlier if consistent with trial fairness.

Neutralizing prejudice. The committee approves the use of voluntary fair trial–free press councils to help achieve the aims of the standard and says they exist in twenty-three states. The criticism of voir dire, which began in the Reardon Committee, is continued. The reliability of voir dire is suspected because the subtle effects of pretrial publicity so far cannot be determined. Prospective jurors are unable to appraise the state of their own minds. Courts which fail to question venirepersons individually reduce the voir dire to a kind of lottery. The number of peremptory challenges, if increased, can help stabilize the jury selection process.[43]

The ABA limits sequestration to notorious cases where the likelihood of material leaking through to jurors is high, and suggests that one way to take public pressure off jurors might be to withhold their names "so long as that information is not otherwise required by law to be a matter of public record." The exception respects the need to prevent jury tampering by either side. When the jury is not sequestered, the standard encourages exclusion of the public, in circumstances of peril to a fair trial, from "any portion of the trial that takes place outside the presence of the jury." Such an act would be tested by clear and present danger and by the availability of alternative means, but resistance at this point is rugged. Greater stress is placed upon admonitions to jurors before and during trials than in the 1968 standard.

Standard 8-4 (the Contempt Power) brings forward, without substantive change, the 1968 provisions for limited use of the contempt power. The committee says contempt should be used only when material knowingly distributed during trial goes beyond the public record of the court, or is designed to influence the jury's determination of guilt or innocence; or, when a person violates a valid judicial order not to disseminate information from a closed hearing or a sealed record. Journalists are not subject to contempt for disseminating information obtained through the misconduct of others unless they are guilty of bribery, theft, or fraud.

THE TOWN MEETING REMEDY

The Cry for Fair Trial

Like a cry for freedom to publish, the tradition of fair trial arose in countless encounters between individuals and the law over the past millenium. One can only understand the need for protection if he or she stands handcuffed and alone while those who carry out the force of the law have their way. It is enough to be one against a thousand

and to know the poverty of physical resources. It is worse to raise one's voice in pleading to ears that do not hear, to cry out for fair treatment to soldiers of the law who handle captives coldly as if they were mere pieces of paper, putting some on this hook, some on that hook, and exclaiming in despair that there is more work than they can handle today.

Truth and justice. Grant B. Cooper of California, as a member of the Reardon Committee, says the law seeks to develop the truth about each defendant and to confine trial to the charge authorized by law. Hearsay is not permitted. Only those who saw, touched, or heard may directly accuse and if none of these is on hand, conviction may be had only if the texture of circumstance pointing to guilt is complete beyond a shadow of doubt. A person accused may stand silent in the courtroom, as a matter of right, and escape impeachment as he does so. Tales of previous arrests and misdemeanor convictions may not be reiterated in court ahead of the jury's verdict. The opinions about complicity, guilt, or innocence are limited to those expressed by qualified experts. A confession may not be presented in court until it is affirmatively shown to be offered freely and voluntarily by a defendant who is aware of his rights to stand mute and to have the timely help of learned counsel. The evidence must meet the tests for relevance. If it is seized by criminal strategem or deceit, or if it is not traced to the defendant according to claim, it may not be mentioned in court. "At every recess courts admonish jurors not to form any opinion or discuss the case among themselves or with any other person until the case is submitted to them [for collective judgment]."[44]

There are other safeguards, but these mentioned show the basis of anxieties which afflict court and media relationships. The free press, operating outside all of these rules, can avoid disruption of fair trial only by an act of its own uncoerced will.

So that all may see. The court must be open so the captive person can be seen at all times in the hands of those who can torture, corrupt, or befriend. It must be closed to rumor, avarice, conspiracy, error; it must be open to truth and temperate with mercy. These conditions are implicit in the compact of government. The obligation of the citizen to obey and support government rests upon its adherence to these principles.

As an observer of the process of justice the journalist, historically, is one step in rank below the scrivener, the writer of documents. Raised now in rank and prestige by the marvel of mass communication, the journalist selectively observes the events of law enforcement and sells an account of them to the public. Earning a living in this way, he is independent of the authority of the system yet in every other way a part of it. His work with words is confined to the news media, and in all respects he is a true middleman, standing between the court and the community, between the defendant and the jury, rendering a commercial report for a fee.

The Press-Bar Council

The main fair trial–free press contentions arise in the middleman role. The bench, bar, and press council functions here as an educational device to keep the changing generations of lawyers, judges, law enforcement officers, and journalists aware of the convention of each of the principles in the council. It is a substitute, on the one hand, for reaching out by the legal system to silence the journalist, a powerless individual unable to resist the authority of the court. On the other hand, it is a social instrument by which the judges and journalists explain to each other their respective roles and functions. The council seeks an equilibrium in the narrow area of prejudicial publicity by teaching law to the journalist and journalism to the judge. The teaching relationship is voluntary. We have long taken for granted that a horse may be led to water but not forced to drink.

The first bench, bar, and press councils were formed in Massachusetts and Oregon. The Massachusetts council was based on formal rules of fair play for the accused person but it did not attract membership from the competitive metropolitan Boston papers and broadcast media. It still works well outside the cities. The Oregon council chose such a low profile that it was difficult for observers outside the state to assess its impact. The Oregon council promised little more than that the component members were willing to talk about fair trial when they had something to say. Yet it turned out in 1977 that a founder and former member of the Oregon council, by now a federal circuit judge, Alfred T. Goodwin, was chairman of the ABA Legal Advisory Committee on Fair Trial and Free Press. He was instrumental in introducing the conciliatory spirit of the Oregon plan into the Standards of Criminal Justice adopted by the ABA and the courts.

In addition, the people in Washington state and California developed the basic Oregon idea in individual ways. California's bench, bar, and press council seems, on its face, little more than an agreement to talk about basic principles of fair trial and free press but, as explained later, the talking produces some cooperation. The temperament of the Washington state leaders gives definition, drive, and reputation to their work. One of them, an unassuming missionary, Hu Blonk, for years managing editor of the *Wenatchee World*, taught members of the Associated Press and lawyers who would listen about the Washington council.[45] The justices of the state supreme court and the editors and lawyers who formed the council put energy in a statewide effort to develop the council's presence and to encourage its use. The result was a transfer of conflict between the media and the judges outside court for settlement by straight-forward principles of conflict resolution.

Paul Conrad, executive secretary of the Allied Daily Newspapers of Washington, one of the founders, is a lawyer and he thinks the council survived the impact of conflict because two leading newspapers were represented on the council by their lawyers. This strength enabled the council to negotiate informally with judges and avoid punitive action against the media. It is not training in law but a willingness to negotiate on points of view that makes for success of a council. The media in most other states have access to competent lawyers but no councils. On one occasion when the Washington council got to the scene too late to conciliate an aggrieved trial judge, the state supreme court officially took a liberal view of the First Amendment but privately was severe with journalists who operated outside the council's guidelines.[46]

Well ahead of the ABA. The Washington council drew up its standards of reporting criminal news ahead of the Reardon Committee. Organization began in 1963. The provisions of the two sets of rules are remarkably alike. The main difference is that the Reardon rules were announced as from the high bench in a context of authority and coercion. The Washington rules were drawn by a committee representing only itself. Justice Charles F. Stafford, one of the council leaders, says:

[L]eadership and participation by the Chief Justice and the [state] Supreme Court was vital to the project. It is doubtful that anyone other than a Chief Justice of a Supreme Court, acting on behalf of that court, could have attracted so many leaders from the top ranks of the news media, the bar and trial bench. The very nature of his position added a note of importance and urgency to his invitation to join in the formation of the committee.

Most of those who responded to the call were leaders of their organizations, papers, or corporations. Although their response was willing, I would be less than candid if I did not admit that some came out of curiosity and many, if not most, arrived with a "show me" attitude. Yet, when they were presented with the importance of the undertaking, suspicion was overcome by cooperation.

At the first organization meeting in February of 1964, the committee chose the Supreme Court, acting through its Chief Justice, as the vehicle through which the committee would be formed initially. Thereafter, all member organizations were to be equal partners with an equal voice, represented by their own men. This removed any question of slanted studies or domination by any one group. Furthermore, it allowed the work product to filter from top to bottom in each represented group for more rapid acceptance.[47]

The chief justice at the time of council organization, Richard B. Otto, was the first chairman. He and his successors have indicated in this way their view of the council's importance. Justice Finley says "it is most significant that the entire program has operated without the necessity of legislative sanction or mandate, without any exercise of the rule-making power of the Supreme Court, and without any other court, administrative or other official orders or proclamations being issued."[48]

A broad program. The Washington council prepared guidelines for civil, criminal, and juvenile courts. It formed a task force on access to public records and another on use of cameras in the courtroom. It learned at the outset that a large committee representing the entire state did not assure understanding of the council program by people in the state. The committee organized seminars around the state so that judges, lawyers, journalists, and law administrators could be reached. Judge Stafford noted that the seminars also reached law and journalism students: "These open-minded young people are still searching for new ideas. They have yet to form occupational prejudices. Thus, it is with this group that we hope to make our greatest contribution."[49]

When the American Society of Newspaper Editors sent a committee to Hawaii in an effort to persuade the Reardon Committee to modify its standards, some Washington council members were invited to explain their organization. Blonk was given the assignment of describing the council's work with the juvenile courts. Journalists attend the sessions of juvenile courts, he said, but rarely do they publish or broadcast news stories. The prevailing ethic is to punish a juvenile by admonition and forgiveness and to put the parents or guardian on notice that help is needed. If the family help is not adequate, he continued, the state has to step in. One out of six male youths in Washington is referred to court at some time or another. What is done with them in court can have a far-reaching effect. The judge can, to a degree, "determine whether more and more of our youth will be engulfed in delinquency."[50]

The Washington council chose not to argue the question of whether naming juvenile offenders in the media deters crime. Instead, it accepted joint responsibility with the courts for developing a public interest in and an understanding of the child. The council did not dispute control of juvenile court records but it insisted that the media could use names of defendants referred to trial for felonies, a position subsequently supported in part by the U.S. Supreme Court.[51] However, the guidelines bound the media to consider recommendations of the juvenile court. Blonk said the media have not agreed to a form of censorship—"a horrible word for us. We have just set up standards that allow us to do a better job for the general public and for the juveniles involved."

Blonk agreed with Judge Stafford that teaching the values of fair trial and free press to young people is important. He continued his work by helping to persuade the law teachers in the Association of Law Schools and in the Association for Education in Journalism to set up a joint committee and to arrange joint programs.[52]

Neighborhood spirit. An active member of the council at the outset was Robert C. Finley, later chief justice, an imposing figure customarily comfortable in committee sessions without his jacket, his extrawide and extralong galluses showing his innate caution and conservatism. As a young man in the Big Band era, Justice Finley had been a professional musician and he still played his clarinet in informal company. His music and his friendly demeanor created a wide circle of friends useful in council affairs. After his death, friends held a memorial wake for him in a small night club. A journalist played the guitar, someone from the audience took the piano, and the current chief justice, Robert Hunter, sang the lyrics Justice Finley liked. Justice Finley had played his clarinet at gatherings of the same group on happier occasions.

This was the atmosphere in which, over the years, tension drained out of fair trial and free press in Washington state.[53]

Operation of the Council

The Washington council has thirty-three members consisting of two judges of the state Supreme Court, four trial judges representing the Superior Court Judges Association, two judges from the courts of limited jurisdiction, five members of the state bar association, six representatives of daily newspapers divided among the papers according to size, two representatives of weekly newspaper editors, one faculty member from the University of Washington School of Communications, and two representatives each from radio broadcasting, television and the wire services. After experience, members were added from the prosecuting attorney, sheriff, and police chief ranks, the state parole board, and the federal courts.[54]

The journalists in this company talked about the First Amendment in the same terms as their counterparts in other states but in the give-and-take with the committee members they lost some of their customary aggressions. They came to believe that the courts wanted fair trial in full view of the public. Rigidity of attitude based on habit gave way as they found that the joint interpretations of the First and the Sixth Amendments were not greatly different from their own.

One of the most difficult conflict situations facing a council, the courts, and the press is a hearing on a motion to suppress evidence, such as a purported confession. The tradition of open courts persuades journalists that closure of the court is a violation of the First Amendment. Yet if the proceedings are published there is great risk that members of a jury venire standing by for the trial may become prejudiced. If the report of a confession reaches them trial delays are almost certain. If the defense asks for a change of venue the judge will be put under additional strain, particularly if he decides to go ahead with the jury selection process. The council plan calls for journalists to be told about the sensitive hearing in advance so they have time to think it over before the motion comes up in court. They do not learn of the problem through an oral order from the judge to hold up publication of testimony until the next day, or indefinitely. Instead, the news will come from a representative of the council's Fire Brigade and they are not coerced to delay publication. If they delay the story, they do so because their judgment of the best interests of the community persuades them to do so. If they publish or broadcast, the decision is still theirs. If a trial judge permits a lawyer to talk him into closing the court to keep out the public, or if he issues what amounts to a censorship order to journalists, the Fire Brigade will be on the phone and in the judge's chambers asking for delay until consultations can be held. In the bench, bar, and press council consultation, the judge will learn what the prevailing law is with respect to his action and he may or may not decide on a different course. At least he learns that there are no imperatives higher than the First Amendment although other considerations at the moment may be of equal importance.

In this manner, the council provides time for judges and journalists voluntarily to think through a course of action before precipitating a conflict difficult to handle or a case hard to win. The heart of the council plan is that in Washington, as in other states where judges and journalists have a working understanding, delay in publication of incriminating evidence heard in open court can be arranged by mutual consent. Journalists are willing to accommodate an urgent need to assemble an impartial jury, yet no lapse occurs in public inspection of court proceedings. It is not the First Amendment which gives way. Instead, news is defined to give priority to information heard during trial, not to that in a pretrial hearing on the eve of trial. If there is a public interest in hearing the pretrial evidence it is fulfilled when the matter is heard by the jury or when it is published after the jury is sequestered or after it reaches a verdict.[55]

ABA sponsorship of councils. The American Bar Association encouraged the formation of councils after the Reardon report was coolly received by the press. Councils exist in twenty-three states but the degree of activity has not been measured.[56] Some of the councils are successful in spite of an atmosphere of indifference. California and New York, for example, formed councils and adopted guidelines. The two states together account for more than two million serious crimes against persons and property each year, a substantial part of the criminal case load. Some of the newspapers in each state have patterns of writing and editing based on rough commercial competition, yet both states chose to accept important elements of the ABA guidelines. New York papers look upon a prior criminal record as in the public domain. Some papers print them at will, even on the eve of jury selection in publicity cases, and one of the consequences is partial closure of proceedings and the sealing of evidence and records until they are produced in court. But the council exists and obtains cooperation.

California is as reluctant as New York to tie the hands of journalists or judges with guidelines. Its statewide council is valuable, though, because it is a forum for public policy discussion with respect to the institutions of justice and the press and not as a grievance board. The articles adopted are not guidelines but a statement of principle. California has been plagued with court-press conflicts stemming from areas where the bar and bench consultants have not been able to reach a consensus.

Nebraska's council guidelines were incorporated by Judge Hugh Stuart in his order restraining the media in the Simants case discussed below. This action was set aside by Justice Harry Blackmun in an opinion in chambers and was also criticized by the U.S. Supreme Court. The sudden transformation of voluntary guidelines, which were couched in vague and imprecise language, into coercive rules in Nebraska caused a reaction against councils nationally. Combined with the Court's opinion in the Nebraska Press Association (Simants) case, this action significantly reduced pressure for compliance with guidelines and damaged the council idea nationally.

Remedy centers on the court. The fact that guidelines were used in less than half the states, and indifferently followed in some of these, has kept the center of activity in the courts and in the ABA. The ABA accepted Judge Paul H. Roney's recommendation, as chairman of the Legal Advisory Committee on Fair Trial and Free Press at the time, to allow the media to argue against a motion for closure and a right to quick appeals when a constitutional claim comes under consideration. This plan, when judges are willing, fosters discussion of the standards. According to Hu Blonk, the Washington council opposed Judge Roney's rule on the ground that conciliation through councils was a better idea.[57]

At any rate, when a court grants standing to a journalist to argue a closure motion, the council, if any, is bypassed. A ruling by the court is binding on the parties. Jack Landau, director of the Reporter's Committee on Freedom of the Press, sponsored the rule with Judge Roney. *New York Times* lawyers, and perhaps others, said this remedy led journalists to surrender the constitutional claim to open courts. Landau responded that ordinary due process, when applied, provides adequate protection for the media.[58]

Ford and ASNE Seminars

Meanwhile, another movement has been under way since 1974 to bring jurists and journalists together in Socratic dialogues designed to scrub away rigid attitudes and promote consideration and mutual respect. The dialogue model was developed by the Ford Foundation in cooperation with the American Society of Newspaper Editors (ASNE). After proving themselves, the dialogues found ready cosponsors among newspapers, broadcasters, and foundations. Through 1978 more than sixty seminars had taken place under ASNE sponsorship and a dozen more had been arranged directly by other sponsors working with the Ford Foundation.

The dialogue is intended to dispel extreme ideas about the First Amendment, as some journalists see it, and the Sixth Amendment, as some judges and lawyers see it. When situational dilemmas are presented which are intractable in the logical framework of professional ethics, the participants try to seek a compromise that is least threatening to their respective ideals. This is the same process followed by successful bench, bar, and press councils. Such a council, however, solves a court-press conflict on the spot; to that extent it is efficient. When the attitudes break up during the dialogues, the derived concepts must still be transferred to a court-press conflict situation.

Fred Friendly, former CBS News vice president and the Ford Foundation's media adviser, recommended the dialogues to the foundation when he sensed "a death-grip confrontation [between the media and the courts] that threatened to destroy the First Amendment's guarantee of a free press." Friendly told the *New Yorker*: "A few years ago, I realized that the press had a big chip on its shoulder. It wanted a confrontation on the free-press issue. It wanted to fight all the way to the Supreme Court *every* attempt by *any* court to limit its total freedom to do as it pleased. I found that journalists had come to feel that the First Amendment was a trade symbol belonging only to them, instead of being a right belonging to everyone. Judges, on the other hand, turned out to have a low—a *very* low—opinion of journalists in general, and regarded them as creatures out of 'The Front Page.'"[59]

Range of discussion. Major responsibility for ASNE's part in the seminars fell on the Ethics committee, chaired at the time by Robert P. Clark, then executive editor of the Jacksonville, Fla., *Times-Union* and *Journal*. The case studies presented problems in libel, privacy, gag orders, confidential sources, checkbook journalism, grand jury secrecy, and intrusion in newsgathering methods. The dialogue series, which has now ended, was conducted by Professors Arthur Miller and Charles Nesson of Harvard Law School.[60]

Link to councils? The dialogue format was designed to appeal to top executives in law and journalism and the record shows that the target group was pleased. The seminar series spread to regional and small-city settings. The format appealed to participants because the seminars usually were confined to one day. There was, however, no visible arrangement for passing the new attitudes along to members of the news staffs who actually use the information every day.

The bench, bar, and press councils, by contrast, require a continuing commitment of time for some key individuals. One of the rigid attitudes the seminars did not undertake to adjust is rejection of the council idea by many editors and proprietors. The ideal educational arrangement would turn the seminars toward development of councils so the inter- mixing of minds and attitudes, which is so sincerely sought, could continue regularly in the councils.

Scholars Look for Roots of Prejudice

Scholars joined in the effort to develop a theory by which prejudicial crime news could be identified and controlled. They recognized this step as a key to resolution of the conflict between the courts and the press. If the type of news that causes prejudice can be identified, the hope was that all concerned can turn toward a search for remedies. But the causes of prejudice so far have escaped identification in objective form. One reason is that the major research effort which might have dealt with the problem, along with a general study of juror deliberation, was stopped by a political uproar when it came to public attention. This study was carried on by Harry Kalven, Jr., and Hans Zeisel of the University of Chicago Law School. The basis of the complaint against their work, apparently, was that the secrecy of jury deliberations was being violated. This assertion was plausible only in the most indirect and impersonal way. The juries overheard dealt with civil and com- mercial, not criminal, cases. The observation was undertaken with the knowledge of the judges concerned. No juror was identified, nor any litigant, and no trial was compromised. But it was a new idea even for trusted professionals to make a confidential voice record of jury delib- erations for analysis, and some ancient prejudices were challenged. Not the least of these is a superstition that, where the great American jury is concerned, we are better off not to know how it works lest we come to distrust it. As a result of legislative and bar association action, lis- tening in on juries for the time being became unthinkable.

The original Reardon Committee found itself largely dependent on opinion with respect to the critical questions of when and how news reports prejudice jurors and require protective actions. Some of its sources were learned conjectures which applied assumptions to trial publicity without specific empirical connection to jury behavior.[61] During the first years of the controversy, much of the published material was self-serving. The Reardon Committee, in spite of the national impact of its study and recommendations, was understaffed and underfunded. Its terms of reference were based on the assumption that law and procedure were basically good and would work satisfactorily if extraneous media interference could be reduced.

The leading journalists consulted by the ABA were not unwilling on occasion to accept accolades for their ability to influence readers. Now, under attack on the assumption that ordinary news reporting prejudiced cases before and after they got to court, they tended to deny that jurors could be influenced by what they had read or seen in the media. The human ability to remember was all too short, they said. Let a little time elapse, and recall is lost. Besides, journalists repeatedly argued, a juror can and will accept the facts and instruction of the court and reach a verdict on the evidence, uncontrolled by prejudice.[62]

Twelve years later, the same committee under Judge Goodwin's chairmanship still was in search of hard facts about the impact of the media on jurors. The media are all-pervasive and affect jury selection after change of venue and continuance, the Goodwin committee assumed.[63] Its lack of faith in the screening which takes place in voir dire, the committee explained, arises in

(1) inadequate understanding of the way pretrial publicity influences the thought processes of prospective jurors; (2) the tendency among a significant number of prospective jurors to underplay the importance of exposure to prejudicial publicity, and to exaggerate their ability to be impartial; and (3) persistent concern about the ability of attorneys and trial judges to discern bias, particularly at the subconscious level, even when the prospective juror is being completely candid. Although these empirical and perceptual limitations cast doubt on virtually every fair trial/free press policy choice, this doubt is certainly more intense in connection with voir dire than other procedures.[64]

Social scientists have tried to help with these problems but inhibitions against observation of actual juries force researchers to work with inadequate simulations of trials. Yet even the best aspected studies are flawed.

The most ambitious of the systematic studies which simulated juries was developed by Allen H. Barton, director of the Bureau of Applied

Social Research, Columbia University, and Alice M. Padawar-Singer. The research was encouraged by Judge Bernard S. Meyer of Mineola, N.Y., who, as a trial judge and member of the ABA Reardon Committee, frequently expressed a desire to see such studies made. When the study was undertaken he cooperated in some of the procedures.

Padawar-Singer was able to use courtrooms and jurors drawn for service in two New York jurisdictions, but had to substitute a three-hour voice tape for the trial. No suitable film or videotape was available. Time for jury deliberation was limited and more juries than expected could not reach a verdict. Voir dire was used only in part. In order to generate and measure prejudice, news stories of a prior criminal record and of a disputed confession were covertly introduced to some juries but not to others.

Padawar-Singer, who directed the field work, reported conditions which distorted her study as well as the many achievements. She used thirty-three juries, but all were not handled alike. For this reason, she said, she could not test her data for statistical significance. She made a voice record of the deliberations, with permission, and the indications here, she said, were that the jurors who had read the criminal record story were affected by it. She had essentially two types of juries. In the first, forty-seven out of sixty contaminated jurors voted accordingly; however, thirty-three out of sixty in the control groups also voted "guilty." In the second, in terms of jury types, six out of ten who saw the stories voted to convict; in the others, the spread was two for conviction and thirteen for acquittal.[65]

Other studies of simulated juries were not as well financed but they each exposed test groups to two or more versions of the evidence, as did Padawar-Singer. From them it was determined that prejudicial news reports, even when printed and broadcast only once, are in fact considered in jury deliberations. Prejudice increases with the quantity of exposure to biased materials. The jury verdict follows closely upon exposure to the extrajudicial materials and the experiments do not test the journalistic theory that jurors forget media publicity when it is separated from the trial. For their part, journalists have not shown how much time lapse is required. One study director, Rita James Simon, shows greater rejection by jurors of some news reports and greater reliance on authorized versions of evidence introduced at trial. The studies, taken together, do not deal with the phenomenon of the "publicity trial"—the central problem in the fair trial controversy.[66]

The late Chilton R. Bush of Stanford, Fred S. Siebert of Michigan State, and Walter Wilcox of the University of California at Los Angeles, all journalism educators, contributed studies to a volume which approached the problem differently. Siebert contracted with National Opinion Research Center (NORC) at the University of Chicago to interview trial judges, hoping for significant improvement over the kindred effort by the Reardon Committee. The NORC chose a national sample of 545 judges and obtained interviews with 483. It said its survey results are within five percentage points of the true values in the 4000-judge universe. This study destroys the myth of a monolithic attitude on the part of judges about juries and about the remedies for publicity.

With specific reference to voir dire, only 11.8 percent of the judges in the Siebert study handled questioning alone in selecting a jury, and 61 percent thought that separate and individual questioning was not necessary. This puts them in disagreement with a third of the sample and the ABA committees, which look upon questioning of a juror, while others in the venire are present, as increasing the chances of prejudice. Voir dire is regarded as effective by 44.3 percent of the judges and as moderately effective by 35.6 percent. Nearly 82 percent of the judges admonish jurors not to read or listen to the media about the case under trial but 27.9 percent believe the admonition is not complied with. The respondent judges said jurors are sequestered in about 22.5 percent of the widely reported felony trials before them and occasionally sequestered in about 1.9 percent. In 40 percent of the cases, jurors who say they have learned about the case from published reports are accepted. In another 10.8 percent of the cases such jurors are seated half of the time.

The media have insisted on access to criminal records of arrested and accused persons, yet 86.3 percent of the judges think publication of such records is inappropriate. As to publicity about confessions, 96.4 percent of the judges are opposed. Objection to reports of a polygraph test is almost as high, 93.7 percent. A parallel situation is presented by media coverage of evidentiary hearings. Reporters are present in 73 percent of the cases and not present in 25.4 percent. However, the question posed to the judges may have been confusing. A related query found 51.3 percent of reporters admitted to hear arguments on the admission of evidence.[67] This does not mean they were free to report what they heard.

Wilcox surveyed the writings of behavioral scientists on the subject of influence of the press on jurors. He found that the scientists had not yet dealt frontally with the problem often enough to provide the insight judges and journalists want. ''Behavioral science theories, principles, concepts, postulates and experiments, by themselves or in limited combinations cannot [yet] be expected to yield definitive explanations. Only the potent effect of publicity about prior criminal records seems to persist throughout the search,'' he found. It also gets through to the jury in spite of safeguards.[68]

Comment

This chapter has dealt with the theory of information flow in criminal cases. The Sheppard Mandate, read with appreciation of the importance of keeping courts open to the public, remained on the level of theory for years while trial judges applied it in varying ways. The ABA's plan was straightforward political theory: given the needs of the community, this is the way things *ought* to be done.

The theory can be understood by remembering its roots in the community. The American judiciary, unlike its British prototype, resembles the yeomanry more than the royal household. It obtains respect through work, not through rank, and its motivation is a fierce professional pride based in a sense of duty. Pride is fed by learning, experience, and tradition. The concept that the law is master and that all are equally bound by it contrasts with the spirit of the lay committee. Naturally a jurist prefers to have the fair trial rules made by members of the profession, not by a lay committee, as in the council plan. What good is learning and experience when those who possess it must submit to the rule of a committee of laymen?

When it came to organize bench, bar, and press committees, the American Bar Association left very little leeway to its lay committees. The standards of fair trial were those given by the Reardon Committee. The lay journalists were chosen to help explain the standards to other journalists. They had limited influence on the substance of the standards, which eventually became rules of court, that is, law. Several hundred journalists volunteered for the councils and accepted the subordinate educational role with good will. They believe in fair trial, short of closing courts, and they have tried to make the ABA rules effective. They were against prior restraint and refused to accept it, whatever the argument.

The councils had to educate as many judges as journalists. In spite of the leveling of ego which accompanies rise to judgeship in county politics, some judges act in excess of their powers. Were they mere members of a committee, a kick in the shins under the table might bring them around. But as judges they are entitled to due process and review followed by tactful correction of error.

The cumulative wisdom of due process and review was available to the Reardon Committee in 1966, but the members misread the professional wisdom with respect to the influence of publicity on a defendant's case. Its members went too far in depriving lawyers and journalists of freedom of speech and press, of the opportunity to represent clients in the forum of the community as well as in court.

The ABA also misread community tolerance for summary contempt procedures applicable to both lawyers and journalists and backtracked on that score before it could get its final text approved. It made further changes when it realized that its premise on the effects of the flow of news was overbroad. When it asked judges to decide whether to delay trials by estimating the effects of public opinion, judges ignored the suggestion and continued to rely on their ability to impanel a jury.

Judges were asked to assume that, in keeping news from the press, they could lay down binding rules for police and law enforcement officers. This effort proved to be strained and was abandoned in favor of self-administered rules originated by the agencies concerned. ABA criticism of voir dire caused counsel and judges to give more care to questioning and seating jurors. Publicity to one side, this effort improved trial quality.

On one vital and controversial point, the ABA has held to its recommendation that pretrial hearings and portions of trials be closed to the public if there is a clear and present danger that testimony to be heard, if disseminated by the media, will deprive a defendant of a fair trial. In so doing, it modified its test by which prejudicial information is to be judged, thus liberalizing the rule. This recommendation raises the question of what is the best public policy: (1) to keep the courts open to the public and to take the consequences of public foreknowledge of disputed elements of culpability in the defendant's case, or (2) to close the courts and allow a defendant to face a jury which presumably has no foreknowledge of the disputed evidence? This question goes to the heart of public confidence in the courts and the ability of judges to adhere to moral standards based on professional pride. To let a defendant's wishes determine the policy decision on this point is to say that the dangers of the flow of news are greater than the continuing dangers of corruption of courts that meet in secret.

Journalists are outnumbered on the Washington state bench, bar, and press council, which is viewed here as a prototype, and there are some risks of paternalism. This risk is offset by the fact that influence flows both ways in a relationship based on the dynamism of events where the individuals are able and willing to learn. The risk is less to freedom of the press than might be expected. Printing and broadcast of news of suppression hearings, and other hearings occurring close to the time of trial, is a problem in few cities and fewer cases. Most journalists already respect the wishes of the courts in such matters and there is no nationwide risk that the media will compete with the courts by substituting publicity for due process of law.

If there is weakness in the Washington state plan it is that it substitutes trust for coercion, a step much admired in our society but underused. The standing now granted journalists in court when closure, sealing of documents, or other motions are heard means that crisis assignments normal to council operations are now handled by the court under due process rules. The councils are further weakened by a U.S. Supreme Court decision which, for the first time, authorizes closure of pretrial hearings under the Sixth and Fourteenth Amendments. The educational tasks of the councils remain but the courts have reasserted their monopoly with respect to critical bar-press relationships. What remains is to look for evidence of the extent to which they have weakened the cooperative relationship fostered by the councils.

Trial Standards in Use 3

The conflicts presaged by the new rules of court restricting the flow of crime news come into play in this chapter, which moves from theories to practical remedies for possible prejudice of trials. A number of terms come into the narrative which are new to some readers, perhaps: continuance, or delay of trial; change of venue, that is, transfer of trial to a new community; voir dire, a courtroom procedure by which jurors are examined and selected after being tested for bias and general alertness; and sequestration, the system of putting jurors in around-the-clock custody during trial. These safeguards against the effects of prejudicial news are supported by the media, as well as by the courts. The object of the courts is to protect a defendant even at heavy expense and personal inconvenience to jurors. The object of the media is to maintain maximum opportunity for news dissemination at minimum risk of juror contamination. These goals, expressed as rules of court, had to be tested by the bar and press, through discussion and litigation, and a number of representative cases are explained here. The judges have not been of one mind and have made some changes of their own volition in the Supreme Court model. They also have sharply limited the use of contempt powers to coerce journalists. Prejudice, when it arises, is shown to be the joint error of law officers and journalists.

JOURNALISTS OPPOSE CONTROLS

Fred Graham, CBS News Supreme Court reporter, said early in the national discussion of fair trial and free press that an obvious reform could stem the flow of prejudicial news. What was required, he said, was for the lawyers and judges to use their codes of ethics to curb publicity-hungry state judges, prosecutors and law enforcement officials, as had been done in the federal system. The state officials, or at least some important ones, were close to politics and the press had a justified fear of their political ambitions and legal powers. Even for a purpose as important as fair trial, journalists could not turn their liberty over to the judges.[1] As it turned out, sentiments similar to Graham's prevailed in the American Bar Association and in the Supreme Court, and cases show how the Court moved directly to make such controls possible and how the American Bar Association fair trial rules implemented the Court's opinions.

Before presenting the cases, however, the attitude of journalists must be made a bit clearer. As mentioned earlier, Judge Skelly Wright said that society needs the press to keep law enforcement personnel under inspection. The reward the journalists expect, as he was wise enough to see, is access to news of crime—news which appeals to the average person as the most interesting and exciting in the paper and on television. People are exposed to news which is, so to speak, good for them, and is quite often impersonal, because they find it near items of more elemental appeal. It is not a new development. The ancient lore and the songs of medieval times, like the mass media today, did not neglect the violent human-interest story. The new development is that there is less violent content in the press now than in the past.

Another noted journalist, William B. Monroe of NBC, has explained that, as in the frontier tradition, the journalist does not want to be hemmed in by arbitrary controls. In dealing with crisis situations in the pretrial stages of crime stories, he says, the journalist needs freedom to ask questions if he is to help relatively powerless individuals caught up in community passion or conflicting evidence.

There is a strong case for keeping the press free to investigate incidents of local police abuse of civil rights, of false arrest, of holding prisoners without hearing or bail, and without access to an attorney. Yet this cannot be done lawfully if a judge, for his own reasons, has issued a "no publicity" order. Along with other journalists, Monroe would not hesitate to use the criminal records of persons in the news because he thinks such facts cannot be remembered long enough to prejudice a jury. Like Judge Wright, he would prefer to dismiss a few defendants who had to be freed because of pretrial news in order to preserve freedom of action, to retain the investigative momentum he draws from freedom of the press.[2]

Since a free press makes free government possible, the journalist's demand for elbow room should not be put down as self-serving without more evidence. The 1979 text of the ABA standards (8-3.1) prohibits direct restraint on the media: "No rule of court or judicial order shall be promulgated that prohibits representatives of the news media from broadcasting or publishing any information in their possession relating to a criminal case." This text expresses the U.S. Supreme Court's heavy presumption against prior restraints on the press.[3]

Leon Jaworski, the Watergate special prosecutor, says he embraces a bold press, a fair and responsible one to be sure, but "fearless and militant in exposing wrongs, injustices and above all else, the misuse of power and the abuse of public trust."[4]

Extra Workload for Judges

Jaworski is an outspoken political conservative, and all journalists might not accept his definition of "fair and responsible." For example, he believes the media should observe silence near the time of trial.[5] But the conflict over fair trial has placed emphasis on this key phrase, above all others, in evaluating the handling of crime news. While journalists constitute a learned profession—and there are among them some lawyers who, like Graham, are somewhat at home in both professions— they are not learned in the law. Understanding of the law requires an ability to distinguish detail and shades of meaning, a skill which comes from analyzing the cases. A fair journalistic judgment of court procedures is not possible without knowledge of what it costs, under the rules, to repair the damage of prejudicial information transfers from the media to a jury, or to potential jurors. That understanding comes from the cases. Equally important is the increase in the work load of the courts caused by these transfers. The cases in this chapter show why rules have been developed to reduce the delays and the extra work. Some of them also show how well the new rules have worked. The purpose of this book is to help dispel misconceptions based on irritation and anger and to encourage understanding between the courts and the press. In the few instances where the courts are still at the mercy of the flow of news, only an informed and voluntary journalistic definition of "fair and responsible" can protect a jury.

While the neglect of the fair trial problem must be charged first to the courts and the legislatures, the difficulty of getting the consent of the press must not be ignored. The problem was put off because it is intractable. Frank G. Raichle, a former president of the American College of Trial Lawyers, says that until recently the courts felt so helpless in dealing with the flood of publicity that they ignored it.[6] Changes of venue were denied on the ground that publicity was everywhere and the Supreme Court, for its part, heard only seventeen cases from 1807 to 1966, asking for new trials as a result of failure to obtain change of venue, and it refused to review at least twenty-three others.

Rule 21 of the Federal Rules of Criminal Procedure authorizes a judge to remove trial to another district if necessary for fair trial. Continuance of date for trial is implicit in authority to fix a court calendar. State rules are essentially similar. When it comes to jury selection, federal Rule 24 tells the court it can examine jurors directly for bias or ask counsel to suggest questions. State rules vary considerably. The federal rule also fixes norms for the removal of venirepersons deemed unsuitable for service without further proof of bias.[7]

The general determination to act was generated by cases like Irvin v. Dowd,[8] and by the season of introspection which came upon the courts as a result of the assassinations of President Kennedy and Lee Harvey Oswald. The judicial establishment did not see how, in the face of the crush of rumors and the flood of hearsay identifying Oswald as the President's assassin, that he could have received a fair trial. The commission to study the President's death, headed by Chief Justice Warren, criticized the press as well as the Dallas law enforcement officials. It was this report which generated not only a fair trial study by the ABA Reardon Committee but a general study and restatement of criminal law and procedure.

Irvin v. Dowd, decided in 1961, intensively reiterated pretrial claims of guilt by the media circulated to whole communities. It is credited for preparing the Court to take an interest in Sheppard—which it had ignored at time of trial—and helped increase the justices' concern to the point where they would treat the problem as one of constitutional dimension.

Irvin was accused of six murders and several robberies so violent that the media, the police, and the populace joined in indignation. Although the community did not resort to the use of the traditional rope and tree, the spirit of lynching existed. Other communities experience similar hostility upon occasion and courts are tested when they insist on providing due process in the pretrial stage.

Irvin's criminal record, beginning with his juvenile crimes, came out in the media. He had written fraudulent checks, had been courtmartialed in the Army for being AWOL, convicted for burglary and arson, then paroled and rearrested for violating terms of his release. The press said he had confessed to twenty-four robberies, and that the method used in some of them was strikingly similar to that used in the murders of which he was accused. Police and the media kept the public advised hourly of efforts to get Irvin to confess and they reported, finally, that he had confessed. Thereafter the media used a condemnatory epithet, "confessed slayer of six," in writing about him. Irvin asked for a change of venue and his case was transferred to an adjoining county where the publicity and the public attitudes were similar. He was denied a second change of venue to a more remote county on the ground that the state law did not permit it.

The trial court labored four weeks to obtain a jury. A venire of 430 persons was first examined; 268 of them admitted prejudice and were excused and another 103 were excused for objections to capital punishment. The court examined 355 other persons, 233 of whom said they had formed and expressed opinions of guilt but were willing to swear they could reach a fair verdict on the evidence. A jury was seated despite evidence in the voir dire that four of the members said Irvin was guilty. The prosecutor trying the case was sworn as a witness by the court and allowed to testify that Irvin had confessed murder to him. Irvin did not testify and no written confession was admitted, but the prosecutor, on summation, pleaded with the jury to accept his second-hand version of a confession as valid evidence. His testimony was a violation of trial rules. Irvin was convicted and sentenced to death. The Supreme Court, however, reasoning solely from the communitywide prejudice spread by the press, granted him a new trial. After another change of venue, Irvin was convicted a second time and sent to prison. His crimes were grave, but the community's belief, based on pretrial publicity, that he needed no other trial also violated convention. The judicial system draws its support in substantial part from public faith in its integrity, a faith which cannot survive a lack of concern for fair trial.

Juror impartiality. The Supreme Court's anxiety about pretrial news in general was obvious. Justice Frankfurter, relishing the opportunity, denounced press behavior and warned that continued encroachment on fair trial would bring drastic controls. However, with reference to the difficulty in finding a jury, the Court said "It is not required . . . that the jurors be totally ignorant of the facts and issues involved. . . . To hold that mere existence of any preconceived notion as to the guilt or innocence of an accused, without more, is sufficient to rebut the presumption of a prospective juror's impartiality would be to establish an impossible standard. It is sufficient if the juror can lay aside his impression or opinion and render a verdict based on the evidence presented in court."[9]

As a precedent, the Irvin case caused trial and appellate courts to exert greater care and to be more receptive when claims of prejudice were presented. The case thus set new constitutional standards for continuance and change of venue in publicity cases.

A precedent which had similar procedural impact arose in Louisiana. The defendant, Rideau, was captured after a bank robbery and quite freely confessed to the sheriff while in custody and before arraignment. Taking advantage of the talkative prisoner, the sheriff put Rideau on television and the two discussed the crime. Rideau confessed his guilt to the listeners and the station thought it such a good show that the film was run twice more during the day. The Supreme Court held that prejudice generated in this way by an official is so conclusive that change of venue and continuance of trial are automatic. No amount of care in jury selection could cure the prejudice.[10]

Juan Corona: A Big Publicity Case

Most of the troublesome characteristics of a big publicity crime are found in the Juan Corona mass murder case in Sutter County, California. There was a flood of news about multiple murders, some of it bordering on fiction, but also including vital evidence seeming to prove Corona's guilt. The journalists found enough hard evidence, in applications for search warrants, and in the return on these warrants, to convince them of Corona's guilt. Local officials in the essentially rural community were overwhelmed by the crush of visitors. When they could not provide new facts readily, the journalists went out on their own to gather information for their stories and to track down unauthenticated reports.

Juan Corona made his living as a middleman contractor supplying migrant labor to farmers. His clients had few local roots and were known mostly to him. For that reason, their disappearance from time to time did not come to attention. Curiosity as to the cause of a shallow indentation in a field near Yuba City led to the discovery of the first body, a hacked and lacerated forty-year-old man. The next discovery, eight miles away, was of eight similarly slashed bodies. After charges were filed, the public defender represented Corona until the appointment of Attorney Richard Hawk. The judge had acted, too late, to seal documents and to impose silence on law enforcement officers, court employees, and attorneys.[11] This delay, while perhaps unavoidable, was enough to enable the reporters to run with the story.

Corona's attorney, in trying for a change of venue, assembled elaborate exhibits of television film, newspaper cuttings, and several volumes of transcribed oral testimony—all evidence of the work of the media. He commissioned a commercial public opinion survey of community information and followed it by a survey to evaluate the first study. There was a collection of affidavits giving personal views of citizens on the improbabilities of a fair trial in Sutter County. Another survey was commissioned by the prosecutor. In the circumstances, the county picked up the bill for most of the work.[12]

Ethical rules strained. The appellate court, considering the application to force a change of venue, expressed indignation about the pretrial publicity: "The prosecution may never offer the 'evidence' served up by the media. It may be inaccurate. Its inculpatory impact may diminish as new facts develop. It may be inadmissable at the trial as a matter of law. It may be hearsay. . . . It may have come to light as the product of an unconstitutional search and seizure. If it is ultimately admitted at the trial the possibility of prejudice still exists, for it has entered the minds of potential jurors without the accompaniment of cross-examination and rebuttal."[13] The court said an ethical breakdown had occurred and blamed both the bar and the press. It accused the press of profit seeking and observed that some of the law enforcement people were basking in the sunshine of publicity, perhaps for the first and last time.[14] The California court, in an unusual action, mandated a change of venue.[15]

Jerry Cohen, a reporter for the *Los Angeles Times*, interviewed thirty members of juries, including some of Corona's jurors. No juror told Cohen that he had been influenced by what he read before trial. This is not surprising since jury selection and the juror's oath are intended to screen out those who have formed opinions. Cohen said nearly all

of Corona's jurors had read or heard about the case in the media during
the trial. "Some received information inadvertently; others couldn't
resist the temptation to peek at a newspaper or television newscast. One
went home every evening and read about the trial in his local newspaper." Quite a bit of material came from Hawk, the defense attorney,
who said he hoped the information would reach the jury. After the trial,
Hawk was fined $4200 and sentenced to seventy-four days in jail for
ignoring orders of the trial court.[16] Corona's second trial, moved to
Hayward, Calif., lasted seven months and cost the state $4.3 million.
Corona was sentenced again on December 15, 1982, for a series of life
terms.[17]

The Aaron Burr Trial as a Model

The courts had worked out a philosophy over the years and a procedure for handling such cases. Most of the procedures were discussed
and confirmed in the 1807 treason trial of former Vice President Aaron
Burr, who had killed an American hero, Alexander Hamilton, in a
petulant duel. The importance of Burr's case, in retrospect, makes the
trials of Irvin and Corona mere sideshows in a village carnival. Chief
Justice Marshall, as presiding justice of the circuit, chose to sit as trial
judge in the case. Burr had been accused of raising an armed force to
make war against the United States in the Louisiana Territory. A great
deal of information about the case, including two affidavits by distinguished prosecution witnesses, had been printed and circulated.

As a politician, Burr had been making friends and enemies all his
adult life. His adventures in the South and West had touched enormous
public interest and made him, as a defendant, even more controversial.
Only the fact that he was a lawyer, and was supported by experienced
counsel, enabled him to use the strict definition of treason in the Constitution and the trial rules based on the common law to secure acquittal.

Burr said he had no hope of getting a jury whose members had not
read the principal charges against him by government witnesses. Federal
District Attorney George Hay believed there "was no single man in the
state qualified to become a juryman, who had not, in some form or
other, made up, and declared an opinion."[18] Hay did not like the
questions about personal prejudice Burr asked of veniremen; instead,
he wanted to test jurors with this question: "Have you formed and
expressed an opinion on the point at issue; that is, whether Aaron Burr

is guilty of treason?'' In this way he sought to distinguish between Burr's reputation and the actions of which he was accused. Burr, for his part, said he hoped to identify and reject veniremen who had spoken openly against him or whose biases stemmed from political differences or personal enmity. In court, Hamilton Morrison, a venireman whom Burr had not suspected of prejudice, volunteered that he harbored resentment because of the death of the man for whom he was named. Burr challenged and Morrison was excused.

After two days of argument, the chief justice ruled that, in a capital case, the court ought to obtain jurors with "perfect freedom from previous impression," but if that were impossible, the duty of the court was to obtain as large a portion of impartiality as possible. "It is too general a question [Marshall said] to ask whether [a prospective juror] has impressions about Colonel Burr. The impressions may be so light, that they do not amount to an opinion of guilt; nor do they go to the extent of believing that the prisoner deserves capital punishment.''[19] Marshall continued: "I have always conceived, and still conceive, an impartial jury as required by the common law, and as secured by the Constitution, must be composed of men, who will fairly hear the testimony which may be offered to them, and bring in their verdict, according to that testimony, and according to the law arising on it. This is not to be expected, certainly the law does not expect it, where the jurors, before they hear the testimony, have deliberately formed and delivered an opinion, that the person whom they are to try, is guilty or innocent of the charges alleged against him.''[20]

The chief justice also held that an opinion formed and expressed with reference to part of the question before a court had to be evaluated for importance. If the question deals with subsidiary or peripheral matters, it may not disqualify a juror, but if it deals with an essential part of the case—if it goes far toward a decision of the whole case—the venireman is unacceptable. "The question must always depend on the strength and nature of the opinion which has been formed," Marshall explained. In closing, he came back to a point he had made before, and which Burr and his counsel resisted: Where communitywide prejudice exists "the rule must perhaps bend to it, but the rule will bend no further than is required by actual necessity.''[21]

The Marshall rule requires interpretation and was under test as long as the higher courts would hear appeals. The Supreme Court for decades showed little sensitivity to publicity as a ground for granting a new trial, continuance, or change of venue. The lower courts, accordingly, brushed aside complaints about publicity. The appellate courts, by the 1890s, would not question jury selection unless gross error by the trial judge could be shown. The burden was on the defendant to show that jurors were prejudiced. If a defendant failed to exhaust his peremptory challenges, as in the spectacular Haymarket riot trial,[22] the presumption was that he could not successfully allege bias on application for a new trial. Consequently, continuance or change of venue was not easy to obtain.[23]

Fair Trial for the Notorious

Turning from Burr's case to the present day, the rationale of juror selection has not changed much. The Marshall rule, which seems reasonable enough, can be stretched upon occasion to somewhat unusual limits, as shown by the case against Jack Rowland Murphy—"Murph the Surf," as he was known in the press. Murphy had been associated with many criminal events, including theft of the spectacular sapphire, Star of India, from a museum. Fair trial idealists would think unbiased jurors hard to find. Murphy had recently been tried for murder and found guilty; now he was to be tried for an attempt to rob a wealthy Miami Beach woman in her home. In addition, two other murder charges against him had been given wide publicity.[24]

By the time the robbery charge came up for trial, Murphy's lawyer deemed him crazy and he asked for a sanity hearing. Murphy was held incompetent to stand trial. The prosecution, however, asked for another sanity hearing and Murphy was found competent. As the robbery trial progressed, Murphy was denied a change of venue and the court found a jury without much difficulty. Indeed, the Supreme Court found evidence in the record that the jurors had no actual prejudice against Murphy. His criminal record was not admissible at trial and jurors said they were able to separate the murder convictions from the robbery charges.[25]

The defense attorney's trial strategy, however, was a tribute to desperation. He identified Murphy to each prospective juror as a convicted murderer and notorious thief and, by leading questions, sought to obtain from each of them an admission that this information made it difficult to try his client fairly. Counsel offered no witnesses or evidence and did not cross-examine the state witnesses. After conviction, he asked for a writ of habeas corpus on the ground that the trial was unfair and the Supreme Court took the case on that point. Justice Brennan and Chief Justice Burger, in the minority, felt sympathy for the claim. In his dissenting opinion, Brennan said little weight can be ascribed to self-serving protestations of fairness by jurors in this case, as in Irvin.

Fair trial, as the Court interpreted it in Murphy, approves seating of jurors who are obviously troubled and confused by the command to be fair to a defendant in bad repute, a murderer and robber who, in a life interlude of involuntary cease fire, asks his enemy, society, not to try him again because he is so bad.[26]

SHEPPARD MANDATE RULES

The Sheppard Mandate suggests administrative controls to insulate trials from the impact of news which may prejudice them. Some of the rules involve delays in the time of trial or extra burden on the trial judge. The emphasis on administrative remedies is a consequence of the decision to leave the press free to enjoy its First Amendment rights while law enforcement people are constrained to follow the fair trial requirements of the Sixth Amendment. Conflict, when it arises, comes from press insistence that the First Amendment gives it access to news as well as the freedom to print and to broadcast. If the strategy is to work, the defendants must ask courts to resist press encroachments on the fundamental Sixth Amendment guarantees.[27]

When the flow of news reiterates an accusation of guilt to the extent that jury selection may be difficult, the trial courts routinely consider one or more of the following remedies:

1. Continuance, that is, delay, of a trial beyond its normal starting point in the hope that the passage of time will extinguish memories of prejudicial information.

2. Change of venue, removal of trial from the county in which the alleged crime took place, to another site where, it is assumed, persons in the jury pool are less likely to remember news of the crime.

3. Voir dire, questioning prospective jurors before seating, to ascertain the extent of information each has learned about a case and to permit the court to form a judgment as to each person's ability to be fair.

4. Sequestration of the jury during trial, which means the jury is put into custody and closely supervised night and day until the verdict is announced in

court. Sequestration can begin any time during the trial the court decides it is necessary.

5. Cautioning of parties, witnesses, and law enforcement employees not to go beyond the public record of the case in disseminating information. Jurors, and witnesses who have not yet testified, are told not to read newspapers, watch television news, or listen to such news on radio during trial.

6. Unless the defense has money to investigate beforehand, voir dire is the principal protection against seating a prejudiced juror. Jurors who have been exposed to prejudicial information after seating can be disqualified, or the court may order a mistrial if the prejudice is beyond remedy. In doubtful circumstances, the only way to enforce these rules is for the court to probe the juror's response to a prejudicial contact.

7. Grant of a new trial in the event serious error is found.[28]

All of these measures are under the control of the trial judge and are to be applied according to the court's understanding of the law.

Despite emphasis on the Sheppard Mandate, big publicity cases do not occur often. Chief Justice Burger has said that "In an overwhelming majority of criminal trials, pretrial publicity presents few unmanageable threats to this important right."[29] Judge Eric E. Younger, a member of the ABA fair trial and free press committee a decade after Sheppard, agrees that the big publicity case is not a major factor. Each trial judge in Los Angeles County, one of the busiest courts in the country, has about one chance in seventy of handling a publicity case in a given year and the average court in the country will never have one, he says. Judges, in an extremity, who must enforce rules against representatives of the news media, he said, find themselves in an uncomfortable role because the conflicts are usually sincere efforts to test First Amendment principles.[30]

Claude Sowle, former teacher at Northwestern and former dean of the University of Cincinnati Law School, said only a handful of cases arise in Chicago each year that involve fair trial issues. Most of the defendants are beyond help. Men such as Anthony Accardo and James Hoffa, as examples, had been in the headlines for years. "Can anyone seriously contend that a brief, selective, legislatively imposed pretrial news blackout in their cases would be meaningful?"[31]

The courts have not been able to provide statistical reports needed for clear analysis, but the national discussion turned up evidence that the media are not much interested in routine criminal episodes. Judge

Skelly Wright pointed out that "only a few precious cases" are involved.[32] For example, New York City reported 11,724 felony cases in January 1965, according to Clifton Daniel of the *New York Times*, and only 41 of them were mentioned in the New York *Daily News*, the newspaper in the city at that time which gave most attention to crime news.[33]

Each city has its own "tiny fraction" of cases which are singled out for publicity and the national total must be not insignificant. The ABA fair trial and free press committee suggests that the press is interested only in the cases which most severely test the fairness of the judicial process.[34] These figures seem to show it could hardly be otherwise.

Rigid Rules Overturned

Dicta in the Sheppard opinion, portions not necessary to the decision, sometimes lead judges who depend on them to overregulate the trial process. The language is sweeping and the ground covered is extensive. Yet the holding itself is interpreted quite narrowly. Evelle J. Younger, former California attorney general, was prosecuting attorney of Los Angeles County when Sirhan Bishara Sirhan, the assassin of Robert Kennedy, was tried. The trial judge relied on the untested ABA standards and the Sheppard dicta to enjoin silence on everyone he could connect to the trial, however remotely—court attachés, employees, public officials, grand jurors, and witnesses before and after testifying. A freeze was placed on reference to any and all court documents or "purported documents."[35] Younger found he could not communicate with the public, even though it was upset by the loss of a second Kennedy brother. The public, he felt, could suffer apprehensions during a period of artificial silence as upsetting as those in a storm or panic. Under the order, he could not even answer questions in terms free of prejudicial effect. In frustration, he tested the judge's order with a carefully hedged, noncommittal statement. As expected, the court immediately cited him for contempt. The court of appeal, however, agreed with Younger that, in the circumstances, the restrictions were unreasonable.

Younger said that, aside from the excessive caution evident in the order, the restrictions showed anxiety about jurors he did not share. "Jurors are conscientious, intelligent people who oftentimes bend over backwards to give a defendant a fair trial; they are not prone simply to decide cases on the merits of what they read in the newspapers," he said. The contrast between the chaos of the first Juan Corona trial and the tight control sought by Sirhan's trial judge is marked. Clearly the sensible regulation is somewhere in between and locating the golden mean is what makes a judge's job difficult.

In the Sirhan case there was little or no question of guilt although there was room for consideration of sanity. The assassin, in effect, had been captured by witnesses as the smoking gun fell from his hand.

Costs of Venue Change

Selecting a jury is time consuming. Chief Justice Burger says it has become a major component of litigation, consuming days or weeks. Yet judges feel that they must resist changes of venue because of the expense. Moving a state trial also moves the expense to the host county. In the metropolitan counties, the case load is on the rise. Criminal filings in Los Angeles Superior Court, for example, more than doubled between 1966 and 1969 and the court has been unable to keep current.[36] Justice Reardon commented in 1967 that a reading of collected fair trial cases does not provide "an adequate description of the endless days spent on voir dire at great private and public expense prior to the commencement of the trial where everyone in attendance from the judge down is wrung dry in interrogations based on possible juror prejudice emanating from dangerous publicity. Any judge who has gone through this either at the nisi prius [jury trial] level or in review of a record containing hundreds of pages setting out the process before a jury is finally seated is likely to hold strong views."[37]

Side Effects of Trial Delays

Judge Eric E. Younger said that "continuances are probably the most universally agreed-upon villain of the court administrative process, and one which, especially without the consent of the defendant, is expressly forbidden by statute in many states and, now, in the federal system as well. The last measure which a legal system conscious of its image needs is to attempt to create fairness in its most celebrated cases by keeping them around for long periods of time."[38] An example, not necessarily extreme, is a defendant in a rape and murder case who was not a participant but legally an accomplice. He spent fourteen months in jail while all the time asking for trial.[39]

In general, the lapse of time between the appearance of prejudicial news and the trial is assumed to have an effect on the ability of prospective jurors to remember details of a case and to set bias aside in considering evidence. At least seventeen states restrict venue changes in part because of the expense to the host county.[40] Donald R. Wright, writing both as chief justice of California and as chairman of the state judicial council, said the council recommends that the entire cost of conducting a transferred trial be borne by the county where the case originated. Judge Younger said the trial of Joseph Remiro for the murder of Marcus Foster, the Oakland superintendent of schools, cost Contra Costa County, to which the trial was moved, about $500,000.[41] Chief Justice Wright called for consultation between affected counties before a change of venue is granted and for a change of rules to permit the prosecution, as well as the defense, to ask for a change of venue.[42]

Standard of Juror Acceptibility

The ABA standard of juror acceptibility, 8-3.5 of the 1979 approved text of *Standards Relating to the Administration of Criminal Justice: Fair Trial and Free Press,* tries to establish a norm acceptable under the Sheppard and Irvin decisions. (The full text is in the notes for this chapter.)[43] The rule facilitates identification and rejection of a juror who is biased. The problem not only is to identify the person of doubtful reliability but to evaluate seemingly acceptable persons for flexibility of mind and fairness of spirit. If all persons could guard against impairment of judgment, as judges are trained to do, biased and prejudiced news reports would be less of a problem. The judge, when he takes time to face each venireperson, can only rely on what he sees and hears. By rule, some information in the mind of a prospective juror is deemed damaging beyond repair, such as reports of confessions. But the effect of information that tends to indicate guilt has to be evaluated by the quite brief and intuitive selection process.

The probability of change of venue or continuance grows when incriminating stories are attributed to, or inspired by, public officials. Hearings by the Congress and state legislatures near the time of trial regularly force continuance of trial but, eventually, use of voir dire enables courts to meet the Irvin standard. The reader may remember the trials of Dave Beck, the Teamsters Union leader, and his son were delayed by such hearings.[44] Two continuances are not always enough;

in sensitive cases mistrials may be declared because the trial court did not grant more.[45]

Voir Dire Distrusted

The Reardon Committee distrusted voir dire. It had before it such studies as that of Dale W. Broeder, who had interviewed 225 federal jurors and counsel in twenty-three cases. The conduct of voir dire, he said, was stilted, hurried, and routine. The venirepersons were examined in groups of twenty-two and the judges simply asked the group if the members could be fair and would they follow the law as the judge explained it?[46] The original committee standard, now abandoned in part, provided ''If a motion for change of venue . . . is made prior to the impaneling of the jury, the motion should be disposed of before impaneling.''

How should prospective jurors be questioned? In groups? If so, how many to a group? Individually? If so, by whom, the attorneys or the judge, or both? A criminal tax evasion trial in Milwaukee helps to illustrate this point. The *Milwaukee Journal*, through enterprise reporting, had brought Milton Margoles to public attention before his trial. Margoles sought to prove that he had been entrapped and the quality of his evidence turned on the effect of the news reports. The trial judge asked the venirepersons collectively if they had formed or expressed any opinion on guilt or innocence. Some said they had and were questioned individually; all but one of them were excused. This juror was seated when he said he had no question in his mind about the case.[47] Upholding conviction, the appeals court said the trial judge gave a ''strong statement of presumption of innocence'' to the jurors as a group and defense counsel joined in. Indeed, according to the appellate court, both the trial judge and the counsel commendably created an atmosphere conducive to candor by the jurors.[48]

A person skeptical of group questioning would say that the procedure demonstrates no more than that judges can warmly defend their own individual way of doing things. The procedure is formalistic. We have only their opinions to prove that the sitting jurors were free of bias. But in the Margoles appeal the argument over news reports was eclipsed by another fact: His defense counsel had consented to the method of examination. The Margoles jury was not sequestered.[49]

A heavy flow of news, from another perspective, made jury selection in the Patricia Hearst bank robbery trial a close case, and the trial judge, Oliver J. Carter, barred the press from voir dire. Judge Carter said closure encouraged utmost candor in response to questions and he assured the press he was merely following court rules.[50] He told the journalists, in response to their protests, that he was required to give a fair trial but they were not.[51] The alternative to closure was a gag order, and he had no taste for that. The judge gave the media a verbatim record of the voir dire after it was over, which showed that he had conducted the questioning personally from the bench. He said he did not want counsel trying to persuade jurors in advance how to vote.[52] There was no appeal.

An unusual level of publicity certainly characterized the case of Lieutenant William Calley, Jr. At a habeas corpus hearing in the U.S. district court, after his conviction for murders at My Lai, he was released because the court found his case had been prejudiced. The circuit court, however, found the publicity to be as much for as against him. Calley was returned to military custody and paroled shortly thereafter.[53]

Watergate Trials

The ninety-four separate criminal cases clustered around President Nixon's staff, including trial for illegal entry into Democratic Party national headquarters in the Watergate office-apartment complex and fund raising for the election campaign, presented the prejudicial news claims in varying degrees.[54] Herbert Miller, counsel to Nixon, argued that fair trial was impossible and he relied for this view on past cases in which congressional hearings turned up incriminating accusations.[55] He said the torrent of news condemning Nixon was greater than in Sheppard. Leon Jaworski, the special prosecutor, when questioned after it was all over, said he did not think the President could have had a fair trial if indicted. The one thing that distinguished the case from those of John Mitchell and others was the televised impeachment process in the House which condemned the President.[56] All of the Watergate defendants filed one or more motions for separate trials, delay, change of venue, or dismissal on account of the publicity, but all motions were denied.[57] Judge John Sirica, as trial judge, offered on occasion to transfer trials if he had trouble getting a jury. He did not.[58]

Sequestration of Jurors

Sequestration of juries, another of the Sheppard points, not only serves to protect the members against outside communication, but gives the media an opportunity for its normal handling of crime news. It is not always easy or desirable from the court's standpoint. The Juan Corona case, for example, drew large numbers of journalists in the pretrial stage. Recovered bodies of victims were counted and described serially in detail by the media everywhere. What can be accomplished by change of venue or sequestration in such circumstances? The trial court could see no reason for change; the whole of California was saturated with the news. However, the higher courts forced the trial to move anyway. At times, and Corona was one of those occasions, the evidence seems to be so clear, and the news, for all its sensationalism, so close to the evidence, that guilt or innocence has already been decided. In spite of the venue change, Corona had to be retried because of errors on the part of his counsel. The case shows that not only journalists but the whole law enforcement establishment needs to practice restraint.

Sirhan trial leak. In the Sirhan Sirhan case, sequestration took place too late to escape a severe prejudicial leak and only the court's prior admonitions appear to have saved the plea bargain. The defense did not claim Sirhan was innocent. Instead, the attorneys hoped to avoid a death penalty. On a three-day weekend, as the last juror was selected but before sequestration, the *Los Angeles Times* reported that the defendant probably would plead guilty to first degree murder and rely on testimony, particularly that of psychiatrists, to avoid the death penalty. The plea would avert a long trial, the *Times* said. This story followed, and obviously was based on, a plea bargain motion in chambers. Clearly, the newspaper had penetrated the secrecy of the judge's conference to obtain its exclusive story. All of the media repeated the story before the jurors could get back to be sequestered.[59]

The defense, fearing that the leak might jeopardize the bargain, and mindful of its duty to exhaust all remedies for the defendant in a political murder who already had been universally condemned by the public, moved for a mistrial. The judge conferred with lawyers for both sides to find out how the leak occurred but they convinced him they were not responsible for it. The judge then questioned all twelve jurors and six alternates in chambers and concluded that, in accordance with the cautions given them, the jurors had neither read nor heard about the main points in the newspaper article. Several had heard or read comments of a general nature, such as "a friend thought there was not going to be a trial." At least four had heard of the probability of a guilty plea and of a plea to first degree murder. But the jurors assured the court they could set aside these brief comments and decide only on the evidence. Mistrial was denied and Sirhan's fate was placed in the hands of the jury on the guilty plea. A motion was made for a new trial and denied—pure formality.[60]

The ABA guidelines, standard 8-4.2, provides that journalists who receive information, such as that handled by the *Los Angeles Times*, shall not be subject to contempt of court "unless the information is acquired by bribery, theft, or fraud." The informant, if subject to the court's silence order, is in jeopardy if his act creates a clear and present danger of influencing the jury's determination of guilt or innocence.

Jurors dislike the lockup. Jurors forced into sequestration may find some solace in thoughts of their good citizenship, but this comfort survives only with difficulty in a long trial in which witnesses and defendants exhibit little or nothing in the way of humanity, classic tragedy, or pathos to make them seem worthy of a citizen's sacrifice. Confinement is so unpopular with jurors that the identity of attorneys who move for sequestration ordinarily is withheld from them by the court. Sequestration means that persons of professional status or business responsibility usually cannot give time to jury duty. Moreover, sequestration involves expensive hotel accommodations, transportation, and security services, the latter applied with such rigor that resentment results.

Nevertheless, when adversarial feeling is high and the community is aroused, sequestration is necessary. The ABA standard, 8-3.6 (b), provides for sequestration "only if it is determined that the case is of such notoriety or the issues are of such a nature that, in the absence of sequestration, there is a substantial likelihood that highly prejudicial matters will come to the attention of the jurors."

Sequestration opens up another series of problems for the courts: how to isolate reluctant jurors from the outside world, how to select bailiffs who will not try to influence the outcome of the case, and how to obtain evidence that will shed light on motions for a new trial if it is alleged that a jury has been compromised. Ordinary news reports do not cause these problems. There is an extremist judicial position which would restrain the media from distributing inculpatory information which is outside the court record even during trial, but the weight of opinion gives this view little support.

State rules. State court rules no longer follow the common law requirement that juries be sequestered, after taking the oath, in all serious criminal actions. Abby P. Simms says thirty states by statute and seven by court decision require sequestration at the time the case is given to the jury. Trials on capital offenses are treated separately.[61] Federal jurors are sequestered when deliberation starts unless the judge finds reason to shield them earlier. The judge decides on sequestration after listening to advice from the parties, but juror attitudes incline him to depend on admonitions to avoid reading, or listening to broadcasts, about a case. Comments by judges indicates that they expect information to seep through the official screen and to reach jurors. Their real concern is with the probable effect of such seepage in a particular case and the reports here show that the judges go directly to jurors, when necessary, as in the Sirhan case, to make that determination.

How to avoid mistrial. What can be done, in the absence of sequestration, to keep lively and inquisitive media reports that go well beyond the record from reaching jurors and causing a mistrial? United States v. Pfingst provides some answers.[62] Pfingst was a former Supreme Court trial judge in New York state. The charge against him was that, before he came to the bench, he was a partner in a scheme to divert assets of two companies jointly owned while setting them up for bankruptcy. He appealed his conviction on the ground that the prosecutor planned and generated publicity unfavorable to him. The trial judge, Jack B. Weinstein, weathered the appellate attack and the circuit court praised his management of the trial. How did he achieve this approval? The publicity appeared six months before trial. Judge Weinstein checked the prospective jurors personally and disqualified the only one who remembered anything about the news stories. Moreover, as the jurors came in, and as they left each day, he eloquently pleaded with them to avoid any use of the media. When the prosecutor, unintentionally or not, violated the rules in questioning a witness, Judge Weinstein stopped him in midsentence and required an explanation and apology.[63] His action persuaded the higher court that he was fair.

Troubles in the jury room. Identifying the source, nature, and effect of information reaching a sitting jury creates a problem. Usually, assertion that extrinsic information has affected outcome of a trial is made after a verdict. But making a case for retrial means that one or more jurors will have to admit outside contacts or other illegal acts. The rules of investigation seek to protect the mental processes of jurors and to discourage inquiry into the relative impact of parts of the evidence. What must be the reaction of a court to reports that a juror has been offered a bribe or that newspapers and books linked directly to the case were in the jury room? What is to be done when a government witness operates a tape recorder in the jury room? Or when a jury discovers $750 in cash in a trial exhibit where the defendant is accused of illegal gain?

The cases present an array of jurors who introduce extrinsic information themselves into deliberations. The courts deal with these matters by formal inquiry into what information was given to jurors and by whom. Afterward, they try to decide whether a case was prejudiced. When jurors are called to a hearing it is difficult to explain to them tactfully what is at stake. Their own honor seems to be on the line as well as fair trial for a defendant. The trial court, nevertheless, has to inquire into the reality of prejudice.[64]

What happened to a jury when the members heard a newscast which told them, by innuendo, that a key witness did not show up at the trial today because she had been intimidated? Some of the jurors in the same case heard on the radio that the defendant was a three-time loser and was shielding the real culprit, a relative. When questioned, all the jurors assured the court they would be fair, but the court said rebuttal was impossible. The remedy must be a new trial.[65]

The rule is that "the evidence developed against a defendant shall come from the witness stand in a public courtroom where there is a full judicial protection of the defendant's right of confrontation, of cross-examination, and of counsel."[66]

Do not read the papers! Jurors who escape sequestration must monitor themselves when they go home at night and on weekends. Are they required to abandon all use of the media? The family has to cooperate if the juror avoids the media. One family which sought to help clipped out the trial stories before handing the newspaper to the juror. They put the clippings in a scrapbook for use after the trial closed, but the defense, which had the money to monitor the behavior of jurors, heard about the scrapbook and forced an investigation by the trial judge. All of this took place after the court admonished the jurors that, if they picked up a newspaper and found a story about the trial they were to put it down at once. If they watched television and trial news came on, they were to "blind themselves" to it. When one juror said she could not meet the conditions, she was excused. The others were faced with the human urge to ignore such taboos and read and watch anyway. The tactics used by Judge Weinstein strengthen the taboo but keeping the news and the trial separate take an act of will.[67]

Sequestration standard. The 1979 ABA standard regulating sequestration leaves room for judicial discretion; a "substantial likelihood" of prejudice is required to deprive jurors of their freedom to go and come during trial. The standard suggests that names and addresses of jurors may be withheld from the media as one means of protecting them against threats or intimidation, and the media have repeatedly, and futilely, opposed application of the rule. The point is that if they have the names they can help prevent fraud in the selection of jurors. The courts respond that publicity puts the jurors under community pressure, as in the Sheppard case. This pressure may have no relationship to the burden of evidence. Witnesses, too, may be sequestered when the community is abuzz with news that will not be accepted in evidence. The text of the standard is in the notes.[68]

Gag Rule by the Courts   4

The Supreme Court's 1966 decision in the Sam Sheppard murder case expressed many of the frustrations trial judges encounter in dealing with journalists. The case itself also showed journalists at work could not be blamed for the chaos that results when a trial judge mismanages his assignment. But when judges relied on the Sheppard opinion to coerce journalists on when and how to use information about criminal cases heard in open court, they met reversal. The Supreme Court, while deciding the case at bar, would not assign priorities to the Sixth Amendment or to the First Amendment. Instead, it insisted that one should be balanced against the other in light of the facts at hand. Judges make plain they also fear the consequences of secrecy and they are divided on the wisdom of the ABA closure standard for pretrial hearings. After thirteen years, the Supreme Court allowed closure of a state pretrial evidence suppression hearing. A year later, without disturbing the rule on hearings, the Court ordered that all civil and criminal trials be open. Openness is the historical practice, closure is the rare exception, the Court said, placing the burden on the moving party at a trial to justify closure.

THE PERIL: FAIR TRIAL V. THE NEWS

We are dealing at this point with a court system open to the public and, for that reason, unable to protect defendants against accusative information outside the rules, some of it generated by the news media.

When an accumulation of events stirred the system to action, the Supreme Court and the American Bar Association at about the same time began to prepare remedies. The Court acted by deciding to hear an appeal in the Sam Sheppard murder case after the defendant had been released by a federal judge on a writ of habeas corpus. The ABA acted by appointing the Reardon Committee to draft standards for fair trial and free press to be used by the courts.

Criminal news events of interest and importance stud the road by which the vulnerable court system traveled to fashion controls adequate to deal with the flow of extralegal information. The cases which arose tend to be associated with rich newspapers in large cities not because all news takes place there, quite the contrary, but because money and legal talent necessary for a good showing is found there.

Trial courts have fixed areas of geographic jurisdiction, but these lines mean nothing to the media. Journalists go wherever the news is. In the big cities, the jurisdiction of a court may end or begin in the middle of a busy street. The trial court has no real influence on the law enforcement officials across the street, or across state lines. The lawful rules a court can make to protect defendants from the spread of prejudicial rumors apply only in the district and almost never apply to the press.

Journalists, who are not restrained by artificial district lines, have little and sometimes no sense of obligation to help a court provide a fair trial to a person who clearly has perpetrated an atrocious criminal act. Journalists have always admired the ideal of a legal system that treats a criminal defendant as innocent until proved guilty but, until recently, there has been little or no mercy for the individual caught up in that system who is getting a bad press.

The trial rules keep juries from considering a defendant's past criminal record while weighing his guilt on other charges. Judges, at time of sentencing, and probation officers afterward, can consider the whole life. So can juries in some states where the law assigns them an advisory role, but that begins only after trial has settled the question of guilt.

Conflict between judges and journalists arises in differing social assignments: Judges are told to hold a trial to the narrow scope of the indictment and the law—this and no more. Journalists are to get the news. Any official interference with news, the journalists claim, is censorship.

Closure as a Remedy

The clashes between the press and the courts led to the inevitable showdown over fair trial in the United States Supreme Court. Our benchmark for dealing with closure of pretrial hearings, one of the serious trouble areas, is the ABA Trial standard, section 8-3, adopted to help the courts avoid publicity on critical matters of evidence until a jury could hear the testimony in the process of trial. Standard 3.1 in the original text provided the following:

In any preliminary hearing, bail hearing, or other pretrial hearing in a criminal case, including a motion to suppress evidence, the defendant may move that all or part of the hearing be held in chambers or otherwise closed to the public, including representatives of the news media, on the ground that dissemination of evidence or argument adduced at the hearing may disclose matters that will be inadmissable in evidence at the trial and is therefore likely to interfere with his right to a fair trial by an impartial jury. The motion shall be granted unless the presiding officer determines there is no substantial likelihood of such interference.

When this rule led to closing a court for a time it was outside the law. The Supreme Court had not approved it and it was a fundamental departure from custom. For that reason, the United States Judicial Conference, chaired by the chief justice, did not adopt the proposed rule in that form.

The conduct of lawyers in making public statements about a case was regulated but it was left to the state and federal judicial departments to supervise law enforcement personnel through administrative rules. In addition to this gray area in their authority, trial judges had to be guided by the Sheppard Mandate. It told them sternly to control the press, but it did not say how.

Judicial authority, no less than freedom of the press, is a cornerstone of political liberty. It is the constitutional tool used to fashion and maintain the basic civil liberties, including the freedom of speech and press. It is set out in the Constitution, particularly in Article III, sections 1 and 2, and is in part elucidated by Marbury v. Madison: "If then, the courts are to regard [that is, interpret] the Constitution and the Constitution is superior to any ordinary act of the legislature, the Constitution and not such ordinary act, must govern the case to which they both apply."[1]

Judges and journalists alike interpret the Constitution. "It is difficult for the press to understand that a frank acknowledgment by a trial judge that a Supreme Court opinion seems unwise does not entitle the trial judge to do it *his* way instead of the *Supreme Court's* way if there is a conflict," says Judge Eric Younger. "The reporter's only guide, in the last analysis, is himself. Most reporters in the United States have the highest standards but they should recognize that they, along with the reading public and their editors, serve as their own supreme court."[2]

The American Society of Newspaper Editors, at the outset of the national debate, formally acknowledged the necessity of media responsibility. "At the immediate pretrial and trial stages," the society said, "the press should recognize the sensitivity of the judicial process and should cooperate on a voluntary basis with the bench and bar in preserving the substance of fair trial. The press should not encourage and should be circumspect in reporting extrajudicial statements or activities calculated to influence the outcome of a case." They continued, "the press fully recognizes the judiciary's responsibility to insure a fair trial, insisting only that what happens in open court should be openly reported."[3]

In working daily with the courts, the media must read events at the same time as the judges and decide when to resist and when to yield to requests. There is no point in expecting journalists to agree to terms and conditions of censorship, and it will become clear that they did not realize, when making the above statement, that courts might be closed.

Justice Francis T. Murphy, Jr., of the New York Supreme Court, explained the attitude of journalists better than they have dared to put it themselves. Like them, he favored open courts, but he said it was up to the legislatures to "chart a new course for the media in the area of crime reporting, particularly as it pertains to cases in progress. Nothing short of such legislation will suffice. It is idle to speak of canons, principles, or guidelines for the press," he said, for, quoting another case, the press has no collective ethical conscience. It is not organized as a profession and the practice of self-restraint merely gives a competitive advantage to those who lack it.[4]

Rival Claims Confuse the Public

As far as the lay public is concerned, publicity in the mass media must have created two First Amendments—the one advocated by the press in its daily criticism and admonition addressed to the community, and the one held by the courts which permits limits on release of criminal information.

The views of the press as an institution are learned through policy statements of its professional and trade associations and the editorial opinions of the few newspapers with national impact. These organizations and newspapers have been mentioned frequently in these pages and differences in their expressed views have been identified. Their views, when adopted by other newspapers and broadcasting stations— as they are—result in a virtual monopoly in attitude passed along to the general public. This is not to assert that the media do not make an effort to be fair and balanced. But the bias of interest, and pervasive institutional interest at that, is not easily pushed aside.

The courts have no unified voice and even the First Amendment cases result in divided opinions in the Supreme Court, often five to four. Reported opinions show a rich diversity of views of the First Amendment.[5]

Are journalists to be trusted more than judges to decide their own cases? The mild answer seems to be that journalists lack the power to put people in jail. The public, at the very least, is being called upon to referee press-court disagreements and to influence legislatures in matters about which the courts do not have equal access, or even access in the due process sense, to the public's attention. The heroic stance of dignified silence, which normally characterizes the courts under criticism, does not mean they have nothing appropriate to say but, without access to a medium of mass circulation, lack an effective forum in which to state their case to the community.

If journalists and judges come to recognize the difference in the compulsions of law and ethics, says Judge Younger, the change "would go a long way to improving understanding."[6]

Court Orders Not to Publish

At least two lines of cases which grew out of Sheppard and the ABA standards concern us at this point: (1) challenge of court orders to journalists not to publish items of news heard in open court; and (2) challenge of orders closing courts or sealing documents, including grand jury reports, which are not yet entered in evidence.

Cases in the first category quickly attracted in both law and journalism the pejorative label "gag." Such cases arose because of difficulty in interpreting Supreme Court opinions and because a gross and cruel crime simply overloads the law enforcement community. When deaths are multiple, and accompanied by violent sex events, the airplanes of the media, bearing writing and photographic talent, are soon on the scene. When they come to a community that is unprepared for them the authorities not only have a multiple murder on their hands but a media event. Courts are torn between conflicting obligations to their rules and to the public's demand for news. Journalists are caught up in a fearful competition and, like the citizens of the shocked community, change character until the culprit is caught, the savage details of his crime reported, and his motivations unveiled.[7]

We can see these conflicting expectations in action by turning to a Philadelphia federal court case where Judge J. William Ditter, Jr., was trying Frederick Schiavo on a charge of perjury. The federal government had lost a valued informer and witness, Martin Alan Hess, when a bomb exploded in his car. Schiavo was under indictment charging conspiracy in Hess's death and under state first degree murder charges in New Jersey. The perjury charge was filed after he testified to a grand jury about Hess's death.

Susan Q. Stranahan of the *Philadelphia Inquirer,* as most professional reporters do, had notes about all these charges on hand while sitting in Judge Ditter's court during the perjury trial. She inserted in her story information that Schiavo was ''one of five men charged with conspiring to kill a government informer last August.'' Stranahan's routine was Ditter's inflammatory incident because he feared the information would reach the jury, prejudice the case, and bring about a mistrial.[8]

The judge called reporters aside in his court and asked them to keep his problems in mind if they should mention the other two indictments. This routine request by the judge was an inflammatory incident for Stranahan. She worked for a national company which had been fighting in court for freedom of the press at least since 1946 when its *Miami Herald* was cited for contempt in state courts and saved by the Supreme Court.[9] She consulted her editor and published the same information again. Ditter then ordered the reporters orally not to mention the two cases until the perjury trial was over. He warned Stranahan that she and her editors would face contempt charges if they disobeyed. They disobeyed. On conviction, they appealed and won, but Judge Ruggero J. Aldisert, in his dissent, explained the position of the *Inquirer* and its several professional allies who filed briefs in support. The basic argument of Stranahan and her editors ''in this appeal is clear and clean cut. They contend that no court may prevent the publication of courts news under any circumstances because such news is a matter of public record."[10] Judge Aldisert thought the requirements of fair trial took precedence and that the journalists should be punished for contempt.

How much of the *Inquirer*'s position was due to pure journalistic cussedness in dealing with courts? To what extent could the newspaper justify the claim that it was acting in the public interest? What is the purpose of keeping the courts open? Ostensibly, to permit the public to observe and to report that justice, under law, is being done.

Was Judge Ditter trying to hide the defendant's illegal activities? No. If so, the press anxiety might have some basis in the public interest. But that topic did not come up. Apparently the judge was doing no more than try to keep Schiavo's criminal record, which could not be considered in determining his guilt in the case, from being printed every day during the perjury trial. Ditter considered it a great probability that sitting jurors would see it and cause him or another court a lot of extra work.[11]

The press council option. Cases essentially like Schiavo's can be dealt with by bar, bench, and press councils, as outlined in chapter 2. A representative Washington state case of this category involves two defendants whose crimes took place in two states.[12] Thomas E. Braun and Leonard E. Maine were jointly charged with first degree murder and were on trial in Everett, Wash. The judge issued a gag order much like the one stated orally by Judge Ditter in Schiavo's case. On the second trial day, with several reporters in court, the jury was excused to permit a hearing on admissibility of evidence. The next day a colorful story in the *Seattle Times* told how the two men had been seized in a California hotel and, according to a witness now dead, had shot her companion to death and wounded her. She was left bleeding on the public highway. The story bore directly on the evidence to be admitted or suppressed; and so the trial judge summoned the writers and, after a hearing, cited them for contempt.

The reporters appealed to the state supreme court and that court faced the constitutional issue squarely, holding that collateral attack on the contempt proceeding was permitted. The contempt order, said the court, was void. The trial court could not, by prior order, forbid the reporting of court proceedings, and the reporters could not be found guilty of contempt for a news story about testimony in open court in the absence of a jury.

The matter would end here, a victory for the press, except for the bar, bench, and press council. Associate Justice Finley, once chairman of the council, reminded the journalists in his opinion that fair trial conflicts of this sort should be handled inside the council. If not, ample precedent exists for requiring journalists to prove that their actions do not constitute a clear and present danger to a fair trial. The justice appended the full text of the bar, bench, and press council rules, of which the journalists already had several copies, so that no one would miss his point.[13]

Use of criminal records. Justice John R. Starkey issued a gag order to reporters of the *New York Times* and the *New York Daily News* in the Robert Carson case. In so doing, he provoked instant legal response which helped acerbate the gag issue. Carson and his codefendants, who asked for a gag on the press, were charged with murder, kidnapping, robbery, and burglary, and were on trial in Kings County. They had previously been convicted in Nassau County. As they came to trial in Judge Starkey's court, the judge asked Dena Kleiman of the *Times* and Irving Liebman of the *News* not to mention the Nassau County convictions.

Two days later, however, Kleiman published a story about the previous convictions, noting that the events took place the same evening as the crimes for which they were being tried in Kings County. Carson's counsel objected to the story. The judge then orally restated his request as an order and said violation would carry a citation for contempt.

Judge Starkey's oral order brought the *Times* counsel to court to move that the order be vacated or stayed until appeal could be heard. The judge refused, asserting that he was basing his action on constitutional grounds. The *Times* then asked that the order be filed in writing. Judge Starkey declined; the order was already in the record, he said.

The *Times* appealed and, reasonably sure of its grounds, published other articles on the criminal background of the defendants. This action forced Judge Starkey to put his order in writing and induced the *News* to file a separate appeal. The Appellate Division held that Judge Starkey presumably had authority to issue such an order but he had failed to establish an adequate ground for doing so. He had not offered proof that the publicity would deny Carson and his codefendants a fair trial. Neither did he show that the danger could not be avoided or minimized by sequestering the jury or instructing the jurors to avoid information available outside the courtroom. Because the order placed the reporters in jeopardy, the trial court was obligated to give notice and hearing to the media along the lines recommended by the American Bar Association Legal Advisory Committee on Fair Trial and Free Press.[14]

THE PRESS IN CONTEMPT OF COURT

The Gag in Baton Rouge

Journalists go to jail like any other citizen when sent by a judge, but they do not accept the rulings which appear to conflict with the First Amendment and they ask the public for help. One of the most exasperating of many cases, for both parties, was when Judge E. Gordon West of Baton Rouge, La., issued a gag order and then fined journalists who still published the story.

The case before Judge West was United States v. Dickinson.[15] It hinges on events that Judge J. Skelly Wright might have described as "goings on" at the courthouse because the charges with which the court and the press were dealing originated when Frank Stewart, a VISTA worker, was accused of conspiring to assassinate the mayor of Baton Rouge. Were the charges based on fact or were they fiction contrived to discredit a civil rights troublemaker?

Stewart's lawyer, instead of resting his defense on avowals of outrage and innocence, asserted that the charges were trumped up and were motivated by Stewart's racial and political activity. But the trial court would not hear him on these points. So he raised the same question in the United States district court. There Judge West would not compel the trial court to consider Stewart's motion to dismiss the charges. Stewart appealed to the U.S. circuit court which overruled Judge West and ordered the trial court to hear the evidence on which Stewart based his motion. As Judge West, in response to this decision, made ready for a rehearing, the circuit judges seemed further away than the political tumult around him. His order to the trial court did not satisfy Stewart and the judge had to go through another cycle of appeal and remand. Reporters Larry Dickinson and Gibbs Adams of Baton Rouge, who were writing about the case for their daily newspapers, were in court as Judge West heard arguments during the second round. The prosecutor moved for an order requiring the reporters to be silent about the hearing and the judge, without hearing on that motion, granted the request. The penalty for disobedience was a contempt of court charge, resulting in a fine or jail, or both. The rule at that time, and subsequently changed, was that journalists were not parties to the proceedings, even though dragged in by the court, and therefore not entitled to argue the merits of Judge West's order.

A no-win media option. Accustomed since entering journalism to the belief that the Constitution forbids injunction against publication, the reporters and their attorneys may have least expected a federal judge to gag them and their newspapers. Their employers felt they had a choice: to accept censorship and take an appeal or, the quickest and most hazardous, to publish and plead First Amendment justification in defense. They chose to publish. In so doing, they said they were exercising not only their own rights but the rights of a civil rights worker who needed help to stay out of jail.

Judge West then carried out his promise, fining each writer $300. Meanwhile, as noted, Stewart's challenge of the good faith motive of his prosecutors was losing before Judge West a second time and was returning to the circuit court.

Judge West had cited local rules of court as authority for his order to the press to be silent. These rules had come down as a model from the U.S. Judicial Conference. They provide that in a widely publicized or highly sensational case where jury contamination is possible, the trial court is authorized to warn against extrajudicial statements by parties and witnesses which are likely to interfere with a fair trial. Also, the rules authorized the judge to supervise the seating of persons in the courtroom and to keep them from mingling with jurors and witnesses. Yet the Supreme Court opinion on which these rules depended plainly said, "Of course, there is nothing that proscribes the press from reporting events that transpire in the courtroom."[16] Moreover, no jury was involved in Judge West's court.

As journalists see it, Judge West had every opportunity to know that the rules did not authorize any court to originate, supervise, or control the content of news stories. The educational process by which one becomes a lawyer and then a judge makes clear, on historical as well as case-record grounds, the antipathy of the Constitution for prior restraints on expression. But Judge West is not alone among judges in misreading the Sheppard Mandate.[17] As the record unfolds, there will be reason to doubt his legal scholarship but not his sincerity.

The task of writing an opinion in the court of appeals fell to Chief

Judge John R. Brown. He reviewed the history of the contempt power carefully and plainly showed collegial courtesy in his analysis of Judge West's action and the conditions in which it arose. Judge Brown said the silence imposed by Judge West affected the political process and was of public concern. Maximum freedom of the press is required when a hearing involves basic rights: Was the charge against Stewart based upon reason or was it a gesture of intimidation, malice, or fear? What transpires in the courtroom is public property. The press had a right to be there. "Clearly, pervasive and irresponsible news coverage of a pending criminal proceeding can so inflame and prejudice a community that it becomes virtually impossible to select an impartial jury therefrom," Judge Brown said. "Newspapers, in enjoyment of their constitutional rights, may not deprive accused persons of their right to a fair trial." Was the publicity hurting or helping Stewart's case?

Wrong-headed judge wins. As to the journalists, the appeals court held the contempt citation unconstitutional. But they were still in Judge West's power. The order not to publish was in the nature of an injunction which cannot be disobeyed with impunity. Even Martin Luther King, Jr., had made the same mistake and had gone to jail. It is not enough that citizens do not have to obey an unconstitutional police order, or an illegal congressional subpoena, or even an illegal order of induction into the armed forces. When it comes to disobeying an unconstitutional federal court injunction, the fate of contemners is left to the judge's subjective determination as to whether their conduct was culpable, blameworthy, and deserving of punishment. The reporters should have immediately challenged the citation in court, Judge West had argued, and at least two courts were open for that purpose. If they had done so, they would have avoided sentence for contempt but it also meant that months of silence about Stewart's case could have occurred. It was publicity as well as the circuit court which kept Stewart from being further victimized.

Judge Brown carefully delineated Judge West's massive errors in law. Then, on behalf of his court, he put the question whether, in view of the clear error, Judge West should not graciously lift the contempt order.[18] But, of course, the reporters had ignored his order and, for that reason, were vulnerable.

Judge West stood his ground. He said that reporters were punished for "intentional, willful, flagrant and contemptuous disregard of his order without trying in any way to have the order, which obviously was issued in good faith, judicially reviewed.'' It was upon this action, he insisted, rather than a mistake in law, that the contempt citation was bottomed.[19] Judge West was upheld in the sense that the circuit court agreed as to the matter of law and the United States Supreme Court declined to act further.[20] The state criminal case against Frank Stewart was quietly dropped by a new prosecutor.

Panic in Nebraska

The concept of what a court is and what it can do under the Sheppard opinion came up for examination in the Nebraska Press Association suit against District Judge Hugh Stuart of Lincoln County, Neb., which had a population in 1970 of almost thirty thousand.[21] The argument before the Supreme Court shows that the state attorney general and Judge Stuart believed that direct prior restraint of the media with respect to evidence heard in open court was approved by the Sheppard Mandate and was necessary to assure fair trial of the mass murderer.

Judge Stuart was trying the case of State v. Simants[22] when the gag challenge came about. Erwin Charles Simants of Sutherland, Neb., population 850, shot to death six members of the Henry Kellie family who lived next door. The first to die was the Kellies' ten-year-old granddaughter, whom Simants raped and shot in the head, then Mr. and Mrs. Kellie and their son, and two other grandchildren, in unknown order, were killed. The autopsy report introduced in evidence said that sexual assault of Mrs. Kellie and her granddaughter took place both before and after death.[23]

Simants told his thirteen-year-old nephew about the shootings and asked him to telephone Simant's father. Later, he sent a note to his family. The father immediately went to the Kellie home, looked inside, and called the police and an ambulance. The elder Simants advised his son to turn himself in, but the son visited a couple of bars and then went into the woods until the next morning. He was arrested as he came home, or, as the sheriff told reporters, ''back to the scene of the crime.''

A press association reporter had called the Simants home and had verified the confession. But he did not release it, although to do so would have given him considerable advantage over rivals. Another press association reporter attributed report of a confession to the prosecutor

but, upon learning of his error, had to retract and attribute it to the
hearsay of an ambulance driver's husband.[24]

Thomas Abbey's record of newspaper and television stories, reviewed
in a *Creighton Law Review* article,[25] detailed the publicity events. One
hour after the murders, a television program was interrupted to warn
the community of shootings and asking the people to be on the alert.
Journalists came to the scene in force at once, some arriving by heli-
copter and plane. They wanted access to the Kellie home but were
refused. The set up headquarters, along with the police, in the city hall.
The news was released that Simants had been arrested and identified.

The day after the arrest, the press described Simants's personality as
a loner, an outsider, who cannot express his emotions easily. On this
same day, the newspapers reported previous arrests of Simants. The
Denver Post, a newspaper not covered by the Nebraska fair trial-free
press guidelines, reported statements Simants made to authorities. The
North Platte Telegraph, published in Lincoln County, reported the admission of guilt Simants made to his father. However, the other newspapers and broadcasting stations did not report any of the confessions
to the nephew, to law officers, or in the note to the family. The fact
that journalists had the information but did not use it is explained in
part by their respect for fair trial as expressed in the guidelines. Pictures
of Simants in jail garb—his own clothes had been taken for use as
evidence—were made at the same time of his arrest and arraignment.
This took place October 19, 1975. The preliminary hearing was scheduled for October 23.

The grapevine carries the news. In the small town the news media
were not needed to spread information to everyone interested. The whole
town knew that Simants had been guilty of sexual assault on a small
child and her grandmother, that he had shot and killed six persons, and
that he had admitted his guilt.

When the county court judge, Ronald Ruff, issued his gag order to
the journalists on October 22, in preparation for the hearing the next
day, he was trying to wipe out the news that had already been published
and to roll back human minds in Lincoln County to the point where
Simants could be regarded as innocent until the cumbersome legal system got around to giving him a trial. In doing so, he sought to follow
legal standards mired in the mud of unreality. The legal wagon was
still stuck the next day when he opened the preliminary hearing to

journalists, admitted the confession in evidence as justification for binding Simants over to trial for murder, and then reminded all present that the testimony was restricted and could not be reported under a threat of punishment for contempt of court.

Why did he not close the hearing? He did not think the law permitted it. The state supreme court, weeks later, agreed and interpreted the law—in the light of ABA standards—as permitting closure in similar future situations.

Judge Ruff also adopted the Nebraska fair trial voluntary guidelines as part of his restrictive order and ruled that in case of conflict between the First Amendment and the due process guaranteed by the Sixth Amendment, the First Amendment gives way.

What duty is owed the First Amendment? As soon as the county court had finished, the district court took over with Judge Stuart issuing a new restraining order. The journalists at once were granted permission to present their objections, but, in response, Judge Stuart changed Judge Ruff's plan very little, narrowing the terms by removing some ambiguities. The media, in alarm, took their plea to Justice Harry A. Blackmun, as circuit judge, in Washington, D.C., and, after waiting for the Nebraska Supreme Court to act, he made decisions which show that far more importance is attached to prompt action on First Amendment cases in Washington, D.C., than in Lincoln County, Neb., and the Nebraska Supreme Court.

Justice Blackmun treated the First Amendment rights as too precious to permit delay in lifting some of the restraint. His line of reasoning may be found in Freedman v. Maryland,[26] which said that courts must quickly decide cases which interfere with and delay motion picture exhibition. The burden to show that a film is entitled to a license must not be placed on the film exhibitor or distributor in censorship cases. Instead, the censor must take the burden of proof. The court is required to act within the "shortest fixed period compatible with sound judicial resolution." Justice Blackmun treated the Nebraska courts as subject to the same time limitations when applying prior restraint to reporting of events taking place in open court.

The Nebraska Supreme Court was surprised by the show of concern but failed to disturb its regular calendar of business. In the face of this response, Justice Blackmun issued an order lifting the Nebraska restraints except for the ban on publishing Simants's confession and his prior criminal record.

After Justice Blackmun's action, the Nebraska high court decided the case within two weeks. It adopted ABA standard 3.1 and upheld the gag order. The journalists appealed.[27]

Prior restraint rejected. The relative importance of the First Amendment in this case was given top priority at the opinion-writing stage. The Supreme Court decided unanimously that prior restraint should not have been used. The opinion for the Court was by Chief Justice Burger. The opinion the media would prefer is by Justice William J. Brennan and one they would find most hopeful was by Justice John Paul Stevens who said, as the newest member of the Court at that time, that the case was settled to his satisfaction by Chief Justice Burger's opinion, but if the First Amendment had needed his vote he might have given it.

Yet even Justice Brennan pulled back from an absolutist position—the media will have to give way come the critical moment when, on balance, the public's interest in national security or fair trial is greater than its desire to protect freedom of expression.

The chief justice wrote that the cases show "pretrial publicity—even persuasive, adverse publicity—does not inevitably lead to an unfair trial." The outcome of a trial is determined by a mix of factors, such as the capacity of the jurors, the tone and extent of publicity as shaped by attorneys, police, and other officials. "The trial judge has a major responsibility. What the judge says about a case, in or out of the courtroom, is likely to appear in newspapers and broadcasts." And the publicity can distort outcome of the case unless the judge is alert to mitigate its effects.[28] Chief Justice Burger reiterated that there is a heavy presumption against prior restraint. Even when temporary, such restraints "are the most serious and the least tolerable infringements on First Amendment rights." Prior restraint is an irreversible sanction and "[t]he damage can be particularly great when the prior restraint falls upon the communication of news and commentary on current events. Truthful reports of public judicial proceedings have been afforded special protections against subsequent punishment."[29]

The authors of the Bill of Rights did not establish priorities between First Amendment and Sixth Amendment rights, the chief justice said, and he found it unnecessary to do so now. "Yet it is nonetheless clear that the barriers to prior restraint remain high unless we are to abandon what the Court has said for nearly a quarter of our national existence and implied throughout all of it."[30]

Alternative measures suggested. The Nebraska courts did not show whether they considered measures short of a restraint order. Decisions of the Court, particularly Sheppard, had emphasized the use of continuance, change of venue, and careful voir dire examination and there is no finding that these measures would not have assured Simants a fair trial.[31]

Even if prior restraint were used, conditions are such that it probably would not accomplish its purpose. Newspapers and broadcasting stations outside the jurisdiction of the trial court would not be bound by a silence order. News travels quickly by word of mouth. "[P]lainly a whole community cannot be restrained from discussing a subject intimately affecting life within it," as noted by the Court.[32] Events that transpire in the courtroom are public property. The restraining order "plainly violated settled principles." The trial court knows now it could have closed the preliminary hearing but as long as the hearing is open the media cannot be restrained.[33]

MEDIA ACCESS TO COURT NEWS

Changing Rules for the Press

As was true of the gag cases, there are many access cases, some of considerable human interest, and a representative few can be mentioned as a preface to the cases of major impact. Access cases are those in which the news media feel that they are entitled to official information as a matter of right under the First Amendment. While the Supreme Court delayed deciding the matter for a long time, a 1980 opinion on the topic gave the media what they wanted.

The problem of access, as well as the right to print what is in hand, extends into every phase of the pretrial, the trial, and the punishment. Appellate courts bear the responsibility for clear statement of standards but press review of court performance can be felt in timely and adequate reports about the whole range of fair trial, such as representation by counsel, custodial treatment and arraignment procedures, police performance, use of electronic surveillance, questions as to the performance of prosecutors and trial judges, evidence discovery procedures whereby both sides prepare for trial, bail requirements, plea bargaining, sentencing, probation, and other post-conviction business. Society assigns high value to fair play in the treatment of accused persons.[34] But few will know who is treated unfairly unless the press points them out.

In this spirit, Walter V. Schaefer said, "The quality of a nation's civilization can be largely measured by the methods it uses in the enforcement of criminal law."[35] When secrecy orders and the requirements of social justice conflict, the issue of court openness comes sharply to the fore.

The Supreme Court of the United States said in 1948 that it had found no record of a criminal trial conducted in secret in any federal, state, or municipal court.[36] But judges did close portions of trials. Journalists working in a courtroom were given no opportunity to assert a claim based on the First Amendment when courts ordered them out. In part because of the energy generated by Judge West's holding, the appellate courts modified the mootness rule,[37] holding that on the constitutional issue of a gag or of access, even after the case closed, the injury survived and was capable of repetition. Therefore the closure issue still could be tried. A case in which a restraining order was served on the *New Orleans Times-Picayune* illustrates the point. The newspaper appealed to the federal courts but got no response for eight months. The case then was held moot.[38] First Amendment rights in this instance had been neglected by the high courts.

The ABA Standard

The ABA standard on closure of pretrial hearings is a Sixth Amendment matter until a court couples it with prior restraint of the media. The Trial standard, section 8-3.2, was adopted to help the courts hold off publicity on critical matters of evidence until a jury could hear the testimony for the first time in the process of trial. This standard, section 3.1, in the original text, provides the following:

In any preliminary hearing, bail hearing, or other pretrial hearing in a criminal case, including a motion to suppress evidence, the defendant may move that all or part of the hearing be held in chambers or otherwise closed to the public, including representatives of the news media, on the ground that dissemination of evidence or argument adduced at the hearing may disclose matters that will be inadmissable in evidence at the trial and is therefore likely to interfere with his right to a fair trial by an impartial jury. The motion shall be granted unless the presiding officer determines there is no substantial likelihood of such interference.

Lawyers, as well as journalists, have a First Amendment interest in orders closing trials and limiting comment on pending cases. The courts, while maintaining their inherent power for use in the event of violation of local rules, ordinarily looked to bar associations to discipline lawyers.[39] Both the Reardon and the federal standards left an individual free to speak in his own defense but, in practice, an attorney is a defendant's spokesman.[40]

Restraint of Demonstrators

Student antiwar demonstrators at Kent State University and the University of California at Berkeley were ordered to be silent, to seal themselves away from the public upon whom they were dependent for political support. At Kent State,[41] National Guardsmen, who had been summoned to deal with peaceful demonstrators, killed and wounded several students and spectators. A grand jury responsive to the common pleas court heard witnesses and made a report oriented as much to conservative politics as to homicide. The judges swore every juror and witness to secrecy and the grand jury then released its report blaming the unpleasantness on radical students and faculty. The press had to sue in federal court to get access to the witnesses. The judges defended the secrecy order, saying it affected only three hundred persons. The federal court replied that the error in this thinking was that the order kept everybody else from hearing what they needed to know. The secrecy order was set aside.[42]

The young demonstrators at Berkeley were a truculent lot. They had occupied a mostly vacant lot on campus as a protest headquarters. The place was dirty and the crowd was politically offensive to the community. Many of the squatters were charged with unlawful occupation and public nuisance. Status as legal defendants made them subject to lawful orders of the court, and the court apparently felt this cancelled their First Amendment rights, too. The papers and the airwaves had been full of antiwar cries for days but the municipal court, two days before trial, called for sudden silence on the part of the defendants. The court said its authority for the gag was in the Sheppard Mandate; this seemed, at the time and in retrospect, a doubtful discovery. Some of the protestors demonstrated anew and then sued in state court to protect themselves from reprisals by the municipal court. They lost in state courts and the U.S. Supreme Court was not interested in the case.[43]

After the long public uproar, what information did the trial court keep from whom?

Public Officials on Trial

Closing a court to hide evidence against accused public officials conflicts especially with public policy. Vito N. Pisciotta, a Pennsylvania common pleas court judge, was indicted on a charge of accepting bribes to protect interstate cigarette smugglers. Federal District Judge Louis C. Bechtle closed a hearing on a motion to suppress a recording which had been made public a month earlier. The *Philadelphia Inquirer* resisted closure, saying misconduct of public officials was of vital and immediate interest to the public. Judge Bechtle declined to amend his order but the court of appeals required him to do so and, after he complied, the paper withdrew the suit. In the trial that followed, Pisciotta was convicted of smuggling, conspiracy, and tax evasion.[44]

The tradition of open justice for public officials was equally important in the trial of Henry J. Cianfrani, a prominent Philadelphia legislative leader who pleaded guilty to charges of corruption, and shows the obvious need of the electorate to know about his behavior in office. News reports gave the case its First Amendment character. Cianfrani had served both in the state house and senate and at the time of indictment was chairman of the senate appropriations committee. He was charged with mail fraud and racketeering.[45] The indictment said he had placed friends on the legislative payroll with the understanding that they would not do any work and that he accepted money from students he sponsored for admission to state-funded graduate and professional schools.

Much of the evidence was gathered by two or three intimate friends of Cianfrani who had recorded their telephone conversations with him. In fighting admission of the recordings, Cianfrani's lawyers used the federal wiretapping statute in an effort to keep them from being admitted as evidence. The government showed that the tapes were made without inducements and the motion to suppress them failed. There was an effort to close this hearing and, when that failed, Cianfrani pleaded guilty and sought thereby to impound the voice tapes. The district court agreed with him, the circuit court did not.

The journalists, who intervened to argue against suppression of the tapes, said that the First and the Sixth Amendments give preference to openness which must be overcome before closure can be ordered. Much of the justification offered is familiar material to us by now. Chief Judge Seitz said that courts long ago recognized that justice must be open as one restraint of abuse of judicial power and against possible perjury by witnesses testifying in public. Publicity is of critical importance, he said, so that the citizens can pass final judgment on the proper conduct of the public's business.[46]

Getting the Court's Attention

The urban American ethic seems to be that selling sex is a crime while buying it is a gentleman's pastime. When the police get a list of customers from prostitutes a court battle usually ensues to keep it out of the papers. When the once-rich playboy Minot F. ("Mickey") Jelke was charged with forcing prostitution on young women the New York police obtained a list much wanted by the press. As the names of purported customers was about to be entered in the trial record the judge, Francis L. Valente, closed the court and, on appeal, the appellate court agreed with him. The press, it was held, had no standing to raise the issue.

Judge George Postel, another New Yorker, sustained a reversal trying to do somewhat the same thing during the trial of Carmine A. Persico, Jr., on charges of extortion and conspiracy. Persico was acquitted in spite of the fact that the papers printed his record of arrests and of the criminal charges placed against him from time to time. Judge Postel asked the journalists not to repeat the stories during trial but got no help. He then excluded the public from the trial and sealed the transcript until after the jury's verdict. The appellate division of the state supreme court found no fault with the order but the court of appeals reversed. Judge Valente was interpreting a statute, the high court said; Judge Postel was interpreting a rule of court legislative in nature. Rules, but not statutes, are subject to collateral challenge. Moreover, Postel's order directly affected the journalists, Valente's did not.[47]

OPEN COURTS: WHEN AND FOR WHOM?

Suppression Hearing Closed

Two Supreme Court cases round out developments in the discussion that began with Sheppard v. Maxwell and the drafting of the ABA standards in 1966. These are Gannett v. DePasquale[48] and Richmond Newspapers v. Virginia.[49] They were decided a year apart, the first in 1979.

The Gannett decision supporting the original ABA standard permitted closure of a pretrial suppression hearing under the Sixth Amendment. The second, Richmond Newspapers, held that under the First Amendment both civil and criminal trials presumptively are to be open and can be closed only when the need for a fair trial overrides the society's ancient commitment to open courts. The difference between them is that the Court says a hearing is not a trial and may be closed for reasons somewhat less substantial than those required to close a trial.

The issues in the two cases are intertwined but it is best to deal with them separately, at least in the beginning. In previous major cases, the Court avoided assigning a rank order either to the First or Sixth Amendment. In Gannett, it found itself reduced to a plurality decision because different weights were assigned by members to the concept of open courts. Under either the Sixth or the First Amendment all justices were willing to close pretrial evidence hearings on proof of necessity to save fair trial, but some were more reluctant to close than others. The Trials section of the ABA standards, particularly 8-3.2, which permitted closure on a showing of clear and present danger to fair trial, was upheld by the Court's Gannett decision. The press has no absolute right to attend pretrial hearings, the Court said, and it was not enjoined from publishing anything in its possession, but the clear and present danger favored by ABA standards was not applicable.[50] The United States Judicial Conference, following this reasoning, chose a test which makes it easier for a defendant, and the court, to justify pretrial closure.

Since 1966, motions to close had generated friction between judges and the media. It was not unusual for a jury to stand by, ready to be sworn, while the court had to hear and decide whether incriminating evidence had been legally taken and could be used. If the evidence was admitted the trial at times was virtually over. If the evidence was not admitted, the press would inform the public anyway and the judge would have to question each juror anew to see if the news reports had altered his fitness to serve. This was the situation the court confronted in the Gannett case.

The New York Court of Appeals in deciding that the hearing could be closed, as mentioned below, went against the weight of decisions.[51] The decisive factor was whether openness, the most important tradition in American jurisprudence, could be modified without making corruption of the judicial system easier.

Justice Stewart's opinion for the Court described the area of litigation: "While the Sixth Amendment guarantees to a defendant in a criminal trial the right to a public trial, it does not guarantee the right to compel a private trial." That can only be decided after a hearing. Justice Stewart had earlier warmly defended the claim of journalists to protect their sources: His opinions made him one of journalism's folk heroes. Whether Stewart, as a judge particularly popular with the press, took on the opinion-writing chore in the hopes of promoting moderate response is not now known. But his opinion has edges, points of defiance, as well as points necessary to state the law. One of these edges, mere dictum according to competent authorities,[52] was in his statement that the public has no right to attend either pretrial hearings or trials. Perhaps there is no significance to this dictum other than that the justices need a competent revisor of opinions to help them say what they collectively mean. But until the Richmond Newspapers case lifted their gloom, the journalists were in despair. Journalists, however, customarily interpret the First Amendment to suit their functional needs. If the Court expunged the traditional openness of the Sixth Amendment for the same reasons, who can cast the first stone?

Chief Justice Burger and Justices Stevens, Powell, and Rehnquist voted with Stewart, but Powell, no matter how he voted, clearly said he was thinking in terms of the First Amendment. The tests he constructed for closure came from the First Amendment cases. But he was willing to close a hearing when it seemed likely to the Court that news reports would prevent fair trial.

As the leading dissenter, Justice Blackmun argued that the Sixth Amendment and the First both guarantee open trials. A defendant must show that it is strictly and inescapably necessary to close a hearing in order to get a fair trial. In view of the fact that open trials are strongly supported in the Richmond Newspapers case the effect of the two cases is that, at last, the courts have worked out a regular procedure for dealing with press opposition to closure. When the courtroom is closed after a hearing, there is to be no news until the court releases a transcript of proceedings. This will not happen until the jury is sequestered or otherwise out of reach of the media.

Justice Blackmun says there are as many opportunities for the miscarriage of justice in a suppression hearing as in a trial. He wishes to apply the same safeguards to both. Secret proceedings threaten liberty. An open court subjects all participants—defendants, prosecutors, police, the judge, and the judicial processes themselves—to extensive public scrutiny. He thinks these processes should not take place in secret.[53]

Forty-eight of the fifty states require open trials in one way or another. Justice Blackmun interprets this virtual unanimity as evidence of a societal interest in openness which he values more highly than the literal wording of the Sixth Amendment. Justice Story, as one of the contemporaries of the development of the Sixth Amendment, said it incorporates the same definition of openness as the common law.[54]

The New York Court of Appeals had observed that the public may rightfully demand access to hearings on charges of political corruption. The Cianfrani case is important in this respect, although inferentially overruled by Gannett v. DePasquale,[55] because it shows how a political defendant can struggle to hide the thieving facts of his life from public view. Can the public respect a court which hides such unfaithfulness, Justice Blackmun asks? The searches and prisoner interrogations evaluated in hearings do not take place in public. The hearing usually presents the only opportunity the public has to learn about police and prosecutorial misconduct.[56] Justice Blackmun's test for closure of a hearing is incorporated in the narrative below.

Back to the Basic Open Trial

In the Richmond Newspapers v. Virginia case, the Supreme Court confronted a state statute that permitted closure of a trial and its decision brought First Amendment openness back in good order. Open access to the courts is a principle of the democratic covenant and access to news is precious to political freedom; it is the philosophical equivalent of the people's right to know.

The provision of access rights under the First and Fourteenth Amendments makes Richmond Newspapers a landmark, according to James C. Goodale who, as former general counsel to the New York Times, had sought to persuade the courts to this view. The term is somewhat blurred by nonjudicial definitions, but it had been introduced into the debate years ago by the American Society of Newspaper Editors.[57] Now it has meaning in a form that requires the states as well as the federal government to recognize it. Goodale thinks that, if lawyers nurture the phrase, the right of access will render unnecessary the Freedom of Information Act which, currently, some influential officials try to weaken.

All of the eight justices voting, including Chief Justice Burger, say the statute on which the trial court based its order is defective. It did not link closure, in the rare event it becomes necessary, to fair trial. An open court is the historical practice, closure the rare exception. He spells out qualities of Anglo-American civilization which explain the compulsion of openness to which the Court responded.

The process of understanding the chief justice's opinion is helped by recollection of contemporary efforts to restrain police action and the recent checks put on custodial interrogation. If a person presumed innocent must suffer—as those investigated, indicted, and tried in criminal courts must do—the process is infinitely fairer when it takes place in the public view. Civilization has worked for openness through the centuries and the courts today dare not rupture the pattern.[58]

Whoever wants to close a trial must show reasons that outweigh the rules of openness derived from cultural experience. "This is no quirk of history; rather, it has long been recognized as an indispensable attribute of an Anglo-American trial," the chief justice said for the Court. But, in necessity, trials may be closed. Then, as students of great words must, he quotes the irreplaceable and immortal Jeremy Bentham: "Without publicity, all other checks are insufficient; in comparison of publicity, all other checks are of small account."[59]

Justice Brennan, joined by Justice Marshall, concurred in the judgment and argued that "it is not necessary" to consider conditions which might compel closure.[60] Justice Stewart said the Constitution clearly gives the press and public access to trials, civil as well as criminal, thus correcting his error in Gannett; but the right must be balanced at times against other public interests to see if limitation is justified.[61] Justice Blackmun, who encouraged Justice Brennan to incorporate some paragraphs from his Gannett dissent into an amplification of the same points, still thinks the Gannett decision in error. The Sixth Amendment presumes open trials; closure is a rare exception.[62] Justice Rehnquist, discouraged by the resolve of his colleagues and their commitment to principles he did not share, twitted them with a quatrain from Gilbert and Sullivan and subsided in disbelief.

Development of Closure Rules

Cases since Gannett and Richmond Newspapers, including one in the United States Supreme Court, have established a pattern of response to motions for closure of pretrial hearings. The Third, Eighth, and Ninth Circuit Courts decided cases raising similar questions and agreed, in the main, on interpretation of rules of procedure. The courts blend in their thinking the recommendations of Justices Powell and Blackmun in the Gannett case. The Third Circuit Court says it was also influenced by the Supreme Court's Globe Newspaper decision. Powell's opinion gave sparse guidance for procedures. Blackmun's was detailed and couched in the mental processes of a trial judge; for that reason, and for its general usefulness in testing the reasoning behind motions to close, it has been the most influential.

Justice Blackmun at no point suggests that the Sixth Amendment, even though he reads it as compelling open courts, prevents a court from restricting access to a pretrial suppression hearing "where such restriction is necessary in order to insure that a defendant may not be denied a fair trial as a result of prejudicial publicity flowing from that hearing."[63]

But when it comes to action on closure he would, first, put the burden on the defendant to provide an adequate factual basis to support a claim of substantial probability that irreparable damage to a fair trial will result from a hearing in public (Justice Powell's language is "likely to be jeopardized by publicity.") Second, the accused should show a substantial probability that alternatives to closure will not protect adequately. He has in mind the traditional remedies of continuance, change of venue, voir dire, and so on, but he also thinks the court could instruct the parties to conduct an adequate public hearing without mentioning the substance of confessions or wiretap evidence. Third, the accused should demonstrate that closure will protect from perceived harms. Justice Blackmun would not close if significantly prejudicial information has already been released and closure would accomplish little or nothing. A high level of publicity, if it is factual, "is not necessarily inconsistent" with fair trial. Fourth, "any person removed from a court should be given a reasonable opportunity to state his objections prior to the effectiveness of the order."[64]

Justice Powell agrees with these points except for the "strict and inescapable necessity for closure" phrase Justice Blackmun uses in putting the burden of proof on the defendant.

Circuit court opinions. Chief Judge Collins J. Seitz of the Third Circuit dealt with a Philadelphia Newspapers, Inc., appeal from closure of a hearing for four of the Abscam defendants and sealing of the transcript.[65] The case was decided on the ground that the trial judge did not justify his decision to close. After making that point, the court discussed constitutional issues. In its view, the court says, the First Amendment forces the Gannett and Richmond Newspapers decisions into the same operating space. Under Gannett, the United States Supreme Court confined changes to the Sixth Amendment. That amendment was construed to be a charter of individual rights for persons accused of crime, including the right to be tried in public, so that a criminal defendant, upon a showing of necessity, can now exclude the public from suppression hearings. The First Amendment was set aside in this process, but it actually continued to be a dominant force because a defendant closing a hearing had to prove that fair trial depended on brief suspension of the public's right to access to all judicial proceedings.

It is not uncharacteristic of Justice Stewart, author of the Gannett opinion, that if he faced dislodging either the Sixth Amendment or the First Amendment from traditional usage, he might save the latter. Which is the better policy: to restate the Sixth Amendment right of open trial in terms of partial closure or to create a new and mischievous First Amendment limitation which might contain legal genes capable of malignant mutation? Whatever his intention, the First Amendment is now back in the biological broth.

Judge Seitz sought to raise anew—and will succeed if more courts join in—the question of whether there is any real constitutional difference between the rule in Gannett and that in Richmond Newspapers. He chose to say that, with respect to three pretrial questions, the law should be the same for a hearing or a trial. It is the First Amendment which requires access to pretrial hearings. If it is to be limited, let the proposed incursion be tested severely in advance and on the record; if permitted, a closure order should address the bare requirements. The Third Circuit would distribute First Amendment access rights in this situation only to pretrial suppression, due process, and entrapment hearings. Defendants must enter notice of intent to move for closure of hearings in the court docket, or calendar, so that the public can make timely response.[66] The court cites Rule C-4, the federal court version of the ABA standard 8-3.2, as requiring the action taken. The federal rule and the ABA standard differ somewhat, but there is little reason why state and federal procedure should vary greatly. The ABA calls for closure when there is a showing of "clear and present danger" to fair trial; Rule C uses the terms "reasonable likelihood." The Ninth Circuit opts for Justice Blackmun undiluted: "strict and inescapable necessity."[67] The federal rule requires the defendant's consent to close, following the Court in Gannett; the ABA standard does not, in fact it authorizes the presiding officer to move toward closure on his own initiative.

The Eighth Circuit, through Chief Judge Floyd R. Gibson, dealt with a similar matter. It had before it the appeal of Powers, a defendant who wanted to close his pretrial hearing. He argued that he was a government informer whose life was in danger. The federal prosecutor objected to closure since he was bound by Justice Department guidelines to consult with his superior before giving his consent. The trial court could find no danger to Powers's personal security. Citing the Gannett opinion, the Eighth Circuit Court held that, on appeal, a trial court order on closure "ordinarily will not be separable from issues to be resolved in the trial itself." There was no reason to delay the trial for an appeal.[68]

The court held that the trial court should require clear and convincing evidence that closure would effectively prevent the harm alleged and that there are no effective alternatives to closure. There must be proof that a threat to fair trial exists. Only in rare cases will it be necessary to exclude the press, and instances of partial closure will occur even more rarely. The court said there was no history of closed courts before the Gannett decision and only in the most exceptional circumstances should closure even be considered.

The Ninth Circuit Court opinion by Chief Judge James R. Browning, the third major decision in the group, dealt with closing of the voir dire and of an unannounced hearing during the trial on the defendant's motion to suppress evidence. The appeal was brought by the *Los Angeles Times* and one of its reporters, Gene Blake. The trial court could isolate or insulate prospective jurors but it should not close on the pretext that open proceedings put pressure on jurors without demonstrating that fact.[69] "[P]ublic scrutiny will encourage those who participate in the jury selection process to enhance the quality of the process and safeguard its integrity."[70] The decision against the district court was on the ground that it failed to make a proper inquiry and record to show that it had followed the procedures called for by Justice Blackmun in closing the voir dire and hearing.[71] The opinion also said Blake and the *Times* had not helped the trial court in that respect.[72]

Closed trials examined. Some seventy cases dealing with closure in 1981-1982 conform to the pattern described. The chief reason the appellate courts give for remanding orders to close is failure to follow procedural guidelines. In another category, closure to protect child witnesses who are victims of rape or sexual assault, courts will have to heed the Globe Newspaper decision discussed below. Closure or sealing cases in the group examined are listed in the notes.[73]

It fell to the Supreme Court of Washington state to decide two disputes over closure orders which threatened the continuance of the state's well-known bar, bench, and press council, a group of which the chief justice of the court is chairman. The council, up to this time, had been relied upon to conciliate conflicts over publication of evidence close to trials. Its services, however, were voluntary and the Gannett Company, the losing party in the DePasquale case, chose to renew the fight through its subsidiary, the *Bellingham Herald*. The editor explained later that he did not think the bar, bench, and press agreement was working.

In the first case, controversial ballistics information was to be offered and a hearing was scheduled on admissibility. The *Herald* twice reported this evidence before the hearing, according to the court, and a change in venue was ordered. A year later, in a second case, the trial court decided to leave the suppression hearing open but to limit attendance of reporters to those who agreed to abide by the guidelines. *Herald* reporters chose not to attend and the company sued to set aside the order excluding its reporters from the hearing, asserting that it constituted prior censorship in the Nebraska Press Association pattern. The state supreme court, with four justices dissenting, disagreed with the *Herald* and the Supreme Court of the United States declined to grant review.[74] The procedures of the trial court were faulty in the second case and had to be put to right in a third decision.[75]

California closure rule revised. In addition to reports on the progress of Washington state's bar, bench, and press council, several references have been made to California Penal Code section 868, the so-called Field Statute authorizing courts to close a preliminary hearing on a defendant's motion.[76] The statute was challenged several times in state courts and, after Gannett and Richmond Newspapers, was upheld again by the state supreme court.[77] The court said the two federal decisions created no media or public right to attend a pretrial suppression hearing and that no right of access arises under the federal or the state constitutions.

Three months later the legislature amended section 868 to declare preliminary hearings ''open and public'' and to lodge discretion to close in the court. In effect, closure requires a hearing and a formal finding that it is necessary to protect fair trial. The statute as revised continues to permit closure during the testimony of minors who are victims of a sex offense, or adults who can show a probability of psychological harm, and of witnesses who can persuade the court their lives are in danger if they testify openly. The statute suggests videotaped testimony and other options for keeping the court open and requires a transcript for the portion that may be closed.[78]

Rape victims and open court. For the most part, the press has omitted the names of rape victims; the laws of some states forbid publication but substantial dissent and frequent litigation persists. Five years before it got around to dealing with the problem directly, the United States Supreme Court absolved of blame a reporter who attended a closed hearing without knowing the rules and published what he heard. The journalist, an Atlanta television reporter, attended the trial of six high school boys who had inadvertently suffocated their seventeen-year-old gang rape victim. They pleaded guilty to rape. At the trial the reporter found the victim's name on the official complaint and broadcast it. The state law made the broadcast a misdemeanor and the victim's father sued for invasion of privacy. The station lost in state court but the U.S. Supreme Court said the name was obtained from public records in seemingly open court and, for that reason, the broadcast could not be made the basis of a civil liability.[79]

When the same basic issue was raised in the Supreme Court in 1981 by the *Boston Globe* it turned out that Supreme Court Justice Brennan was the author of the majority opinion.[80] The Massachusetts Supreme Judicial Court interpreted as mandatory a statute excluding the press and public from testimony of a minor victim in a sex offense trial. The United States Supreme Court held the statute, as construed, to violate the First Amendment. Justice Brennan said the trial record shows that closure did not accomplish the protection expected, and that the right of access to trials plays a particularly significant role "in the functioning of the judicial process and the government as a whole."[81] If the government wishes to close such a trial it must show a compelling government interest.[82]

The Massachusetts court had acted in good faith in an area of traditional sensitivity and it did not find Richmond Newspapers to be in conflict with its reasoning. But Justice Brennan wanted trial courts to "determine on a case-by-case basis whether closure is necessary to protect the welfare of a minor victim."[83]

Chief Justice Burger disagreed with the reversal and sought to restrict the impact of the decision narrowly. Justice Rehnquist joined the dissent. Justice Stevens dissented on another point: He did not think the Court should have accepted the case on appeal.

COMMENT

The courts have been embarrassed by isolated ad hoc efforts of judges to use censorship to protect rights of defendants to a fair trial. There is no longer any reason for such judicial tours de force because standards have been adopted nationwide. At the same time, a defendant in a criminal case, described by the Constitution as innocent until proved guilty, should not have to parade illegal evidence before potential jurors in order to get to trial. If the media will not interpret their needs so that the remedy of a motion to suppress such evidence can be pursued in public, without damaging publicity, then in that rare and critical time of necessity, the hearing will be in private. There has been no real doubt that the constitutional guarantee of open courts and open trial is not absolute. The Richmond Newspapers case, paired with Gannett v. DePasquale, however, makes clear the national commitment to justice and openness. In the constitutional showdown, no Supreme Court judge argued that hearings and trials, in circumstances of extreme risk, had to be kept open so a defendant thereby would lose his right to a fair trial.

Scores of state and federal cases have interpreted and applied the two major decisions. The trial courts, when they have suffered reversals, did so in substantial part because they had to learn to use the complex rules and instructions laid down by the higher courts for use in ruling on motions to close. The burden is on the moving party to prove a serious threat to fair trial. Openness is the rule; closure is the rare exception.

The Legislative Shield 5

The ideal working condition for journalists is political and economic independence, the ability to deal with all persons under a single standard based on accuracy and fairness. In order to achieve this ideal in a community of conflicting special interests, legal protection is needed for the journalists' watchdog role. They stand alert to report corruption, bribery, and flagrant misuse of political power. Corruption is always with us; one wave of crookedness follows another. In order to obtain publishable information about politics and crime, journalists often are reduced to taking a story under a pledge of confidence. They offer their credibility as justification of secrecy with respect to the source. At this point a conflict of interest arises between their duty as citizens and their obligations undertaken under the watchdog role. Prosecutors and those accused demand proof: names, dates, places, the facts. Reporters have sought to develop a legal privilege not to testify so they can protect their source's anonymity, but trial rules require judges to enforce a lawful demand for proof. A major dispute thus arises over fair trial and free press.

The landmark case based on this dispute, Branzburg v. Hayes, acknowledged that newsgathering is protected by the First Amendment but rejected the claimed privilege not to testify. Half of the states have sought to confer a limited privilege, but in case after case the courts limit the state shield laws. Where a reporter's evidence appears vital to the outcome of a case, courts order journalists to testify or go to jail. Leading prisoners have included William Farr, the Fresno, Calif., Four and Myron A. Farber of the *New*

York Times. More important, perhaps, are commonplace
routine instances of jeopardy which occur as journalists
throughout the country seek no more than the right to report
the day's news.

INDEPENDENT JOURNALISM

The contribution of journalism to self-government has received renewed public attention since the *Washington Post* brought about investigations by the Justice Department, the Senate, and the House of
the Watergate conspiracy and President Nixon's coverup of his part in
it. This was a spectacular and unusual example of the watchdog role
of the media. Yet this role is not new and it is not exclusively American.
It is confined by necessity to governments organized by political parties
and popular elections. It obviously cannot exist where the press is not
protected by the courts. The protection journalists prefer is public trust.
The shield law, conferring a legal privilege against forcing a reporter
to reveal in court his secret sources of information, implements that
trust. But what is the reporter's justification of the need for the shield?

The *Times* of London was one of the first major papers to assert
independence of political alliances and, at the same time, to be supported
by income from sales of copies and advertising. Hugh Chisholm, as
editor of *Encyclopaedia Britannica*, wrote in 1911: "The *Times* has
long stood in a class by itself among newspapers owing to its abundance
of trustworthy news, its high literary standard and its command of the
ablest writers, who, however, are generally anonymous in its columns.
It has always claimed to be a national rather than a party organ."[1] In
1840 the *Times* Paris correspondent obtained and printed details of a
conspiracy to deposit simultaneously several forged letters of credit on
a London bank to banks on the Continent. The story was credited with
thwarting massive fraud. The *Times* had to fight a libel suit over the
story, however, and was assessed court costs of £5000 even though the
jury awarded only one farthing in damages. A spontaneous public sub-
scription raised the expense money but the newspaper set it aside in a
fund for student scholarships.

The *Times* carried out many other investigative news ventures, including an 1843 campaign against stock frauds feeding on the rapid
growth of railroads. The paper recognized the importance of political

parties but it maintained the integrity of its news report and relative freedom of action to publish news against the interest of the party leaders it supported. This gave the paper prestige based on public confidence, a prestige which is the goal of the media today.[2]

In the United States, after the Civil War, some large newspapers inclined toward political muckraking and sensational reporting abandoned party affiliation and earned large incomes from the sale of copies and advertising. Joseph Pulitzer in St. Louis and New York and William Randolph Hearst, the chain newspaper owner, had sought influence through elective office. Pulitzer, in his early career, served stormily in the Missouri House of Representatives and Hearst ran unsuccessfully for governor of New York.[3]

The media carrying on the watchdog role rely on private informers and other secret sources for their information. When criminal acts are charged, the identity of the informers is at once sought by public prosecutors and grand juries as well as by private individuals who find themselves accused by faceless persons using the credibility and prestige of the media to influence the public.

Clarence K. Streit, while *New York Times* correspondent at the League of Nations in Geneva, explained in 1932 why the watchdog role and the use of secret sources must go together.

The journalist may get the truth on many things . . . only if his source is confident that the journalist, come what may, will not reveal the name of his source. It has therefore become the unwritten rule among reputable journalists never to tell who gave them their news, if by so doing they may injure their source.

This code of professional secrecy obviously tends to transfer from the source to the journalist the responsibility, as far as the public is concerned, for the news published through it. It exposes the journalist, moreover, to having his good faith imposed upon by the source, and unfortunately, this all too frequently occurs. . . . Naturally, the journalist much prefers his sources to take themselves the responsibility for what they give him. . . . But where it is necessary in order to report the news, the journalist will always remain willing to run the risks that his code of secrecy involves for him and to decide himself in each case how far it is safe for him to trust in the good faith of his informant and how much of what he thus learns he will take the responsibility of reporting.[4]

Crusading by journalists of whatever medium applies punishment by publicity, without due process of law, which is a form of political shellacking that, in the view of some victims, might be less desirable than a jury trial followed by a modest sentence to jail.

The Element of Risk

The *Washington Post*'s principal owner, Katherine Graham, risked her personal fortune and control of her newspaper and television properties on the judgment of her staff that President Nixon was one of the Watergate coverup conspirators. Subpoenas had been served on members of her staff in a $15 million libel suit by the Committee to Reelect the President when the corruption charges made by the *Post* were tried and proved in the courts.[5]

It was the work of the Congress and of the courts, as well as the work of journalists, that brought about the fall of the President.

Reporting Strategies

Journalistic moral precepts implicit in the watchdog role bring ends and means into conflict for the reasons that Clarence Streit mentioned. In order to get the news, the journalist is driven to assert an ethical position which is essentially contradictory. He asks the public to trust him but he cannot or will not offer proof. Since he is vulnerable to private reprisal and to official interrogation, he seeks cover under both his professional ethics and his testamentary privilege. His best procedure in the long run is to publish without favor the news of political rivalry which turns up. Such news is one of the means used by party rivals to force events of graft and special deals into the open. As carriers of the bad news, the media often are targets of legislative reprisal, such as higher taxes, tougher libel laws, loss of access to news. The First Amendment is the first line of defense against such tactics. Journalists can also wield influence on the local level near election time by their evaluation of the work of officials.

When the conflict is with the courts, which administer their own affairs and interpret the judiciary's constitutional powers, as in the use of gags or protective orders, journalists have sought and received the support of those judges who view open courts as necessary for the life of the system itself.

Journalists have made claims for protection in several important lawsuits. In them the press speaks for itself and a substantial segment of society when it asserts that a democratic people have a right to know of the acts of officials which affect them. Leaders should be alert, competent, and honest and the public should know when they are derelict in performance of duty. The traditional wages of political malfeasance is publicity—the loss of election, the rascals turned out.

Bureaucracy as the Enemy

There is a journalistic view which maintains that bureaucrats are personally selfish and are not to be trusted. Max Weber said that evils of personal influence and personal struggle for power exist under all systems of bureaucratic absolutism. Moreover, when they are maintained behind closed doors, they occur in exaggerated form and evade control.[6] This observation led Weber to add that "The degree of political maturity in a nation does not depend upon the more spectacular aspects of parliamentary government but upon the fact that the nation is kept informed of the manner in which public affairs are conducted."[7]

The level of democratic morality. The late Judge Learned Hand's view of public life, after forty years on the federal bench, was much the same as Weber's. In an exchange with members of a Senate subcommittee, he said:

I hope you will not think I am slack in my morals when I say that in judging public conduct we should always remember that it has to pass muster with the voters, or it will be an idle gesture. . . . I am personally disposed to lend a very large measure of forbearance toward much that I might not approve save for the end in view.

SENATOR FULBRIGHT: . . . Do you feel that our society is all that we can expect it to be or is there anything that can be done or should be attempted to be done about it?

JUDGE HAND: That is a dreadfully hard thing to answer. I do not suppose we have changed very much with time. These things [crime and corruption in high places] recur, you know. Take the government of the City of New York: there have been periodic arousals when the lid was opened and the people saw what had been happening, and then you had reform movements. . . . But then things slumped back as people got indifferent.

SENATOR DOUGLAS: Do you think it ever goes back to quite where it was before?

JUDGE HAND: Yes, I am afraid it does, Senator. . . . I do not want to say nothing can be done about it. I do not want to throw up the fight, if that is what you mean.[8]

By design, rather than by chance, the media of communication have been protected under the First Amendment as if our society views itself about as Judge Hand does and looks to the media to keep things from getting worse. Our culture leads us to prefer bad news to good, and news of disaster and conflict, throughout the West, receives top emphasis in the commercial press. However, news and comment upon government action are given the highest priority. The most coveted positions on the papers and networks are in government reporting in state and national capitals. The editors of editorial pages and their most prestigious writers are specialists in politics and government.

Can the press keep them honest? Chief Justice Hughes, for the Supreme Court, said in Near v. Minnesota that "charges of reprehensible conduct, and in particular of official malfeasance, unquestionably create a public scandal, but the theory of the constitutional guaranty [of freedom of the press] is that even a more serious public evil would be caused by authority to prevent publication."[9] Justice Black in Bridges v. California supported this view: "Since they punish utterances made during the pendency of a case, the judgments below [punishing a newspaper for contempt] therefore produced their restrictive results at the precise time when public interest in the matters discussed would naturally be at its height."[10]

The deference to the political role of the press, under the First Amendment, was rounded out by the Court in the *New York Times* libel case when it conferred on the press almost the same immunity to report and comment about public personalities as public officials had earlier received from the Court.[11]

Clearly the press, bolstered by the *New York Times* opinion, could lack no other incentive than courage to carry on continuous critical examination of the work of public officials. The ABA standards presumably leave the media free while restricting the police, prosecutors, and law enforcement staffs from communicating certain things to the press. The journalists do not see much practical difference and, on occasion, when one of these agencies stands to gain substantial advantage from publicity, leaks are available to the journalist under the promise that no source will be revealed.

Where trade competition still exists, one journalist may stand to gain commercially by obtaining such contraband information ahead of others. Where there is no competition, the question boils down essentially to considerations of public policy. If the watchdog assignment is to enable the public to see justice done, then the public cannot see unless the media can see. How much of the rectitude of the official actors in the pageant of justice depends on this visibility? How much honesty is lost when the law hides vital episodes in a pretrial hearing?

The press and the courts both assert fidelity to truth, and the search for truth endlessly requires a moral decision on the appropriate means to achieve the values under discussion. How much power must be given to trial courts to determine the appropriate definition of freedom of press in cases of conflict? When and to what extent must demands of the press be given priority over the demands of others in order to serve the community interest?

The need for independence. The courts and the press must decide conflicts over ends and means every time a case turns up which the media want to cover at will and the courts wish to restrict. Chief Justice Burger, speaking to the American Society of Newspaper Editors (ASNE) with this conflict in mind, said that the First Amendment and the independence of the judiciary epitomize two interrelated values that belong to everyone and that each supplies a kind of lateral support for the other. The relationship is clear: "Journalists keep their independence so long as there is an independent judiciary to give meaning to the words of the Constitution. A free press is imperative to assure that assaults on judicial independence are explored and answered."[12]

Who knows what news to print? Journalists say their experience teaches them that suppression of news, or giving in to pleas to withhold publication of news, are ordinarily one-party actions. Suppression, like publication, hurts some interests and helps others. Only time and tide can sort out wisdom and truth in a jumble of current events. The journalist who suppresses news, no matter for what high purpose, is making a decision without having an opportunity to know all the important facts involved. One of the assumed benefits of publication is that the news thus circulated will stir rejoinders from all persons who have information to share. If witnesses not on the record were present, they might give more good reasons for publication than for suppression. The only defensible course, according to the dictates of journalistic experience, is to get and print the news.

This view may hold for political controversy to be settled in Justice Holmes's famous marketplace of thought, but does it hold in a court governed by laws of evidence? Do these laws need to be renegotiated every time the press brings them under attack?

The Warren Commission report on the deaths of President Kennedy and Lee Harvey Oswald pointed out that the commissioners asked themselves how Oswald could have received a fair trial. The considerable frustration of judges and law enforcement officials with journalists, who always must be dealt with in investigating sensational cases, came to the surface in the commission's report. When the watchdog is prominent in the aftermath of an event, public attention will turn to the dog as well as to the event.

Later, when the Reardon Committee picked up the Warren Commission's cue it said that, largely in quest of popular support, state and municipal police, willing or unwilling, had become the gatherers and processors for the media of news of sensational crime. Many police administrators had been advised by counsel that the press, as a matter of right, was entitled to all information about cases.

Police forces in large cities maintain public relations sections, headed by a senior officer, whose job it is to provide the information the press wants. Free office space ordinarily is placed at the disposal of the press in police buildings. In some instances when desired information is not promptly given to the press, editorial criticism is sometimes focused on police for slowness and ineptitude in solving crimes. As a consequence of the assumed obligation to keep the public informed and of pressure by journalists, police officials and prosecuting attorneys, in sensational cases, usually provide details of the prosecution's case before trial.[13] Yet this cooperation violated a defendant's right to a fair trial and, in the view of the ABA and the courts, had to be regulated.

Protecting the investigator. Inevitably, the challenge of the investigative reporter is to work outside the law and the shield law is one of the tools fashioned by his legislative allies to encourage and protect him in doing so.

A Library of Congress study in August 1966 found twelve states which at that time granted to reporters the right to keep their sources of information secret when summoned as witnesses to courts or grand juries.[14] The publication was used by journalists in an effort to ask states and the Congress to provide shield laws. The movement has grown slowly, in part because the statutory privilege wanted by journalists has widened as a consequence of experience with early statutes. As of this writing, twenty-six states have some form of shield law: Alabama, Alaska, Arizona, Arkansas, California, Delaware, Illinois, Indiana, Kentucky, Louisiana, Maryland, Michigan, Minnesota, Montana, Nebraska, Nevada, New Jersey, New Mexico, New York, North Dakota, Ohio, Oklahoma, Oregon, Pennsylvania, Rhode Island, Tennessee.[15]

When public prosecutors, defense counsel, and grand juries read or hear revelations of criminal wrongdoing reported in the media which they cannot take to court for lack of proof, they often subpoena the reporter and, in effect, ask him or her to become a witness. At that point the journalist, sworn to silence, can lie or refuse to testify. If he is silent, he may go to jail under a court order for contempt. If he lies, he may eventually stand trial for perjury. In either case, he has been effectively removed for a time from newsgathering and his employer will have to pay heavily to get him out, or to keep him out, of jail. The court, which ordinarily protects his liberties, may now become his enemy.

Two examples, one of them simple, the other quite complex, explain and define shield laws. Arizona's statute, while up to date, is yet to be developed by appellate courts. It is chosen as representative of the first group. New Jersey's statute has been under heavy legislative pressure on several occasions and has developed in ways informative to other states. The Arizona statute will be copied without comment, but adequate description of the New Jersey law emerges most clearly from presentation of the cases which have made it.

The Arizona shield law reads as follows: "A person engaged in newspaper, radio, television or reportorial work, or connected with or employed by a newspaper, radio or television station, shall not be compelled to testify or disclose in a legal proceeding or trial or any proceeding whatever, or before a committee of the legislature, or elsewhere, the source of information procured or obtained by him for publication in a newspaper or for broadcasting over a radio or television station with which he was associated or by which he is employed."[16] The statute dates from 1937 and was amended in 1960 to include the language with respect to radio and television, a stipulation which other legislatures, including New York, got around to much later.

There is a variety of informed opinion on what shield laws ought to be which can be illustrated by the bills introduced in Congress by Senators James B. Pearson, Alan Cranston, Walter Mondale, and others.

The efforts differ mainly in the number of writing and editing activities covered and in the ease or difficulty with which they could be set aside by the court, in whole or in part. Senator Pearson's bill, for example, made the privilege unavailable to journalists being sued for libel and also provided exceptions for threats to human life, espionage, or foreign aggression. Senator Cranston sought to exclude all exceptions. Senator Mondale, observing that the Judiciary Committee was stalled by differences of opinion, drafted a compromise which introduced more exceptions but also brought in a three-point test for action on motions to divest the privilege.[17] None of these bills obtained committee approval.

The same proposals have been urged on the states and some of them have been adopted, as will become clear in this narrative.

Looked at as a working tool, journalists want a shield law to protect their information gathering and they do not want to be harassed in court to the point that they lose incentive to undertake tough investigative stories. The experience of Peter Bridge, a New Jersey journalist, illustrates the point. He published a story about attempted bribery of a public official and, under pressure, identified his source. Then he was jailed because he would not say where his source got the information. Statutes and court decisions in some states today would protect him.[18] Obviously, the question should have been addressed to the public official identified as the source.

A mixed lawyer-journalist task force of the Twentieth Century Fund, chaired by the former chief justice of Maine, Robert B. Williamson, backed a shield law in its 1971 report with much the same conditions proposed by Justice Stewart.[19] A study by Professor Vincent A. Blasi of the University of Michigan Law School for an all-journalism sponsor, the Reporter's Committee on Freedom of the Press, recommended an absolute privilege against subpoenas by grand juries, legislative and administrative bodies, and a qualified privilege in criminal and civil cases.[20]

Others who advocate protection preferred to leave development of the privilege to the courts on the pattern worked out by the U.S. Ninth Circuit Court in dealing with the case of Earl Caldwell of the *New York Times*, which is described later.

Sensitive information is part of the texture of politics and business as well as crime. Those in political life who bargain, as well as those who conspire, have to proceed to agreement by trade-offs, a search for consensus. Political parties and officials also bargain secretly for support. A witness to political bargaining may choose to talk in confidence to the press so he can affect the outcome of events. A journalist who uses such information essentially performs a political act, but he is almost certain to deny that news is partisan in nature. It is all in the public interest, he says, and it is—if it produces information valuable to self-government. Moreover, as one story triggers another, all of them together may add up to a truthful account.

A controversial claim to privilege made by journalists inevitably ends up in a court challenge. The journalistic privilege was sharply limited by the United States Supreme Court in Branzburg v. Hayes,[21] with which was joined the Caldwell case and that of Pappas.[22] This case will be explained fully below. Here it is noted only that the Caldwell case came up from the Ninth Circuit with a majority opinion that protected the desire of journalists to remain independent of law enforcement agencies, to be spared coercion which would make them legal informers. Under this opinion, if it had been approved by the Supreme Court, coercion could be used only when the desired information could not be obtained elsewhere. Justice Stewart, while a circuit judge, had written an opinion with a similar outlook. Journalists, however, disliked a conditional privilege, and that extreme position, not shared by all, should be explained.

Should the shield be absolute? Dan Paul, a Miami lawyer who often represents the *Miami Herald*, insists that a statute conferring absolute protection is required.[23] The case-by-case development in the courts— which some legislators support—even if favorable, Paul says, takes too long and costs too much. The cost would discourage editors and turn them away from controversial stories. Moreover, without absolute protection, reporters can be maneuvered, tricked, and eventually forced to testify.

Paul's rejoinder to those who criticize a statute as allowing the legislatures to tinker with constitutional freedoms is to include in his proposal a disclaimer that it limits or affects constitutional rights. Even so, that part of his statute would have to be construed. Paul agrees that an absolute privilege creates some miscarriages of justice but says the Fifth Amendment privilege has the same effect. The balancing of First Amendment rights against the state's need to find the truth is likewise rebuffed. Paul joins Justice Douglas in saying that "balancing has already been done in absolute terms by those who wrote the First Amendment."[24]

Writing as editor of the *Wall Street Journal* six months after Senator Mondale's compromise bill was introduced, Vermont Royster expressed reservations about "claims to special privilege from the obligations that rest on other citizens."[25] The right to confront an accuser is basic, Royster said. To give anonymity in every case "is to open a Pandora's box of evils. A dishonest reporter—and sadly there are some—could even pretend to sources he did not have."[26]

When the effort failed in Congress, Attorney General Elliot Richardson revised and reissued on October 20, 1973—four days before President Nixon fired him in order to get at special Watergate prosecutor Archibald Cox—a set of regulations designed to prevent harassment of reporters in the course of their work.[27] As in previous versions of the regulation, he required the consent of the attorney general when subpoenas or warrants for arrest of reporters were requested. His order gave effect to the concept of a free press stated by Judge Charles M. Merrill in his opinion for the Ninth Circuit in the Caldwell case. "The very concept of a free press requires that the news media be accorded a measure of autonomy; that they should be free to pursue their own investigations, to their own ends without fear of government interference, and that they should be able to protect their investigative processes. To convert newsgatherers into Department of Justice investigators is to invade the autonomy of the press by imposing a governmental function upon them. To do so where the result is to diminish their public capacity as newsgatherers is destructive of their public function."[28]

A summary of five years under Richardson's regulation showed that fifty-four subpoenas for 109 journalists had been approved by the attorney general and three others denied. In forty-two of the instances the reporters willingly supplied the information but asked to be subpoenaed first. In twenty-two cases, subpoenas were issued without asking the attorney general's approval. Reporters moved to quash subpoenas in ten cases in 1973 to 1975; one motion was granted, six denied, and three others either were denied or became moot. Few questions involved confidential sources of news.[29]

Duress for local writers. Behind the few cases which receive national attention are many more, in the course of a year, in which journalists seek to avoid testifying. Looking at a few of the cases suffices to show why journalists want the protection of a shield law. The incidents are disruptive; they tie up staff time and add to the cost of doing business— enough to discourage aggressive reporting. Many cases arise out of political feuds and lack a reasonable basis for appeal but they entail economic loss to the media if they accept the challenge to keep the public informed.

Graft, corruption, political infighting, and attempts to use the courts to personal and partisan advantage are common features of American life. Just handling the news that bubbles out in these incidents triggers subpoenas to testify as if informing the community justifies shifting attention from charges of crime to the reporter who got the news. A subpoena to a reporter is a substitute for investigative work by police and prosecutors.

Trouble arises when investigative reporters question witnesses, make voice records of conversations while in search of incriminating admissions, and insist at the same time upon immunity against subpoenas to testify. Reporters obtain secret reports of grand jury proceedings and sometimes identify witnesses who, in fear, ask for state protection. They accept and disseminate leaks from lawyers who, in a specific case, are under silence orders designed to protect petit juries. These events, contradictory in motive and consequence, are the heart of the court-press conflict, for the courts are required to exclude information not qualifying as evidence. The media, in effect, follow a law of their own: that the First Amendment gives them authority to tell the public everything. They argue that the public has a right to know about accusations and that it can judge whether prosecutions should follow. There is not much concern about apparent conflict between ethics and law.

Taken as a fact of journalistic life, local conflicts constitute a grinding weight of expense. Dan Paul complained about the heavy annual costs to newspapers and broadcasting stations of litigation if they protect a news source and resist subpoenas. The *Los Angeles Times* was reported to have spent $200,000 in a short time resisting thirty subpoenas and the threat of fifty more.[30]

Pressure put on Geraldine Oliver, a staff writer for the Delaware County, Pa., *Daily Times* is illustrative.[31] Her stories about the city election in which the mayor, Joseph F. Battle, was opposed by a policeman, William Riley, seemed based on Riley's personnel record. Riley was chagrined and sued to enjoin the city of Chester from using the record. Oliver refused in court to name her sources. The district court held her in contempt but the circuit court found that the information seemed to flow from Mayor Battle. It suggested that Riley direct his questions there and sent Oliver home free.[32]

In Tennessee, where even incumbents on the state supreme court seek party endorsement, a cry of money-for-votes arose as the state Democratic committee met. The charge was leaked to the media and the challenger of an incumbent judge was left, as a result of the publicity, to smoke in the political fires generated. He sued the state committee and subpoenaed the reporters. The latter were saved by the shield law and the lawsuit flushed out the person who spread the bribery charge.[33]

Charges were leaked that a sheriff running for re-election in Shelby County, Ala., had written bad checks in Las Vegas and had permitted prisoners to use drugs in jail. The day before the election, reporters went to get the sheriff's reaction to the charges. They were arrested by the sheriff on the charge that they were conspiring with a rival candidate to murder him. The rival also was arrested. The next day the sheriff was re-elected by 200 votes but he could not persuade the prosecutor to process the criminal charges. Civil lawsuits then began to fly. The pragmatic sheriff paid $5000 out of court to stop the lawsuits and retained his office.[34]

Two other routine examples will complete the sample. Tension between the public and the press arose in Indianapolis when two reporters looked into charges of police corruption. The stories said many police were involved but only five were indicted. The journalists then turned attention to the prosecutor, charging on the basis of interviews with seventy-eight former grand jurors that the proceedings had been manipulated. Dirty tricks began to appear and when the reporters were invited by a police informer to witness the bribery of an officer it was the reporters who were arrested and charged. The prosecutor soon had to run for re-election and the people and the media did him in, overwhelmingly.[35]

Lucy Ware Morgan published allegations in the *St. Petersburg Times* that apparently were taken verbatim from a secret grand jury report which charged county officials with corruption. She refused in court to name her sources, was found in contempt, and was sentenced to five months in jail. The grand jury again asked Morgan to cooperate and, when she refused, three months were added to her jail term. The Florida Supreme Court, which has been kinder to the press than the U.S. Supreme Court, balanced the grand jury's statutory authority against the public's need for information and held that unencumbered access to news is more important to the community.[36]

BRANZBURG V. HAYES: REJECTION OF THE SHIELD

The key constitutional decision in the privilege cases involved grand jury subpoenas of journalists, pitting an old and seldom criticized law enforcement institution against journalists seeking immunity against official interrogation. As a consequence of the confrontation, the law enforcement institutions came to look more carefully at the nature and function of the grand jury but the reform which occurred was limited. Grand juries are guided by a prosecutor, but are essentially composed of lay persons beyond coercion and unfettered by technical rules of gathering evidence.[37] They deal with evidence both legally and illegally obtained and with hearsay as well as with eyewitness reports. It is the quality of the mixture of fact and conjecture that determines the handling of a grand jury finding in court. Justice Douglas once praised the grand jury in its role of balance-maker in the criminal justice system by saying that it is intended "to make as sure as humanly possible that one after whom the mob and public passion are in full pursuit is treated fairly, that the grand jury stands between him and an aroused public." But a grand jury led by a militant and ambitious prosecutor, urged on by community pressures, can stray far from the ideal role assigned to it by Justice Douglas.[38]

The Branzburg case went to the Supreme Court at a time when journalists not only were resisting grand jury subpoenas, but were writing stories based on grand jury proceedings, that is official papers which, by law, could not be released until a judge had edited them for public use. In view of the grand jury's wide-ranging prerogative to make accusations and give vent to suspicions, journalists find the unedited reports a source of sensational news and one relatively free of risk of libel suits.

The cases of three journalists, Paul M. Branzburg[39] of the Louisville *Courier-Journal*, Earl Caldwell of the *New York Times*, and Paul Pappas of WTEV-TV, New Bedford, Mass., were consolidated into one by the U.S. Supreme Court. Although Branzburg's name is attached to the case report, he had the weakest defense because he sought immunity from grand jury questioning after asking permission on more than one occasion to witness and write about the making of illegal drugs, giving a promise not to identify the lawbreakers. Caldwell and Pappas were on similar errands: Caldwell was gathering news from the Black Panthers in California and Pappas was working at home on a single story, a meeting of Black Panthers from which the general public was barred. The Panthers, as a political and social action group, considered themselves under siege in an unfriendly society. They were ready to explain their mission and behavior to the press, but insisted that reporters not identify individuals or lead the police to them for purposes of harassment or prosecution.

Journalists then and now put forth sound reasons why they should be permitted to gather news from minority groups. Unless the press renders a useful and meaningful report about the antagonism between the Panthers and the police, the minority group may have little chance to gain public support. Journalists cannot blindly ally themselves with the police, particularly since the Panthers and other minority poor regarded police as storm troopers for a privileged majority. The grand juries that summoned Caldwell and Pappas were composed of well-fed and well-housed persons. The President's Commission on the Causes and Prevention of Violence had called attention to the misuse of police power on such national occasions as the convention of the Democratic Party in Chicago in 1968. The commission said 399 journalists were assigned to Chicago streets during the convention and 65 or more were "involved in incidents resulting in injury to themselves, damage to their equipment, or their arrest."[40] Although the public is helpless without faithful police protection, concern arises from stories of police corruption in the cities, for example those collected from Chicago, Detroit, Kansas City, and even Bristol, Conn., and Burlington, Vt., by John Lofton, former associate editor of the Pittsburgh *Post-Gazette*. The sentences of the criminal courts regularly discriminate against the black and the poor even though major court decisions and national reform efforts have markedly improved the situation in recent years.[41]

The Branzburg opinion by Justice Byron R. White for the Court was by a five to four vote. The Court held that reporters are obligated "to respond to grand jury subpoenas as other citizens do and to answer questions relevant to an investigation into the commission of a crime." Lower appellate and trial courts have interpreted this opinion on fairly narrow grounds, leaving room for the First Amendment right to gather news, as expressed by the majority, to develop in trial and circuit court opinions.[42] Justice White's opinion was exhaustive and thorough, but he could not suppress a waspish dig at the newspapers for past court cases in which publishers had put their First Amendment rights into an economic setting and asked the Court to protect them. In so doing he was blind to the fact that the persons who write the news do not have the same values as those who pay the bill.[43]

But Justice White made other points. The Court, he said, was being asked to give journalists a privilege that other citizens do not have. The press should seek a remedy in the legislatures, not in the courts. The First Amendment, of course, is burdened when grand juries require reporters to testify about crimes they have witnessed, but the "vast bulk of confidential relationships between reporters and their sources" is not affected. "There is little before us indicating that informants whose interest in avoiding exposure is that it may threaten job security, personal safety, or peace of mind, would in fact be in a worse position, or would think they would be, if they risked placing their trust in public officials as well as reporters."[44] "More important, it is obvious that agreements to conceal information relevant to commission of crime have very little to recommend them from the standpoint of public policy." There is no constitutional protection for informers and their identity cannot be hidden when the knowledge is critical to the case.[45]

Extra Workload Not Acceptable

The Court would not accept the administrative burden imposed by a qualified testimonial privilege. To do so, a trial court first must determine which categories of newsperson were entitled to protection. The First Amendment protects everybody, not just the journalist, "the lonely pamphleteer who uses carbon paper or a mimeograph just as much as the large metropolitan publisher who utilizes the latest photocomposition methods." When a reporter is subpoenaed, the court would have to decide whether proper grounds had been laid for requiring his appearance. "Is there probable cause to believe a crime has been committed? Could the grand jury obtain the information elsewhere? Is the public interest sufficient to outweigh the claimed privilege? Moreover, the Court stated, "the press has at its disposal powerful mechanisms of communication and is far from helpless to protect itself from harassment or substantial harm."[46]

Justice Stewart's Dissent

Justice Potter Stewart dissented from this decision. "The Court's crabbed view of the First Amendment reflects a disturbing insensitivity to the central role of an independent press in our society," he wrote, and Justices Brennan and Marshall joined him. Justice Douglas adhered to his customary position that the First Amendment protects a journalist in all his noncriminal activities and the Fifth Amendment gives him an absolute testimonial privilege when he is accused of criminal actions.[47]

Whether Justice White's opinion is crabbed or not may depend upon the reader's values. Both Justices White and Stewart obviously use their very considerable reasoning powers to support an emotional commitment. While the idea of a disciplined free press working to open and keep open the government thrills Justice Stewart, it rumbles through Justice White's mind, in this instance, as a plan to create a system of private informers unaccountable to the public.

Having the needs of Caldwell and Pappas in mind, Justice Stewart said the Court has steadily increased the opportunity for minority groups to avoid exposure for the sake of exposure and that closing them off from trusting contacts with the media confines them to a hapless public relations technique to state their grievances. He quotes Judge Merrill's opinion for the court of appeals with approval: "The need for an untrammeled press takes on special urgency in times of widespread protest and dissent. In such times the First Amendment protections exist to maintain communication with dissenting groups and to provide the public with a wide range of information about the nature of protest and heterodoxy."[48]

Justice White says grand juries, unlike congressional committees, do not go on wide-ranging fishing expeditions. Besides, their procedures are secret—a "further protection against the undue invasion of such right . . . and Grand juries are subject to judicial control and subpoenas [are subject] to motions to quash."[49]

Justice Stewart says the Court has not previously considered the extent to which the First Amendment limits the grand jury subpoena power. Nevertheless, he says, the Bill of Rights is "applicable to investigations as [it is] to all forms of governmental action." He continues: "Accordingly, when a reporter is asked to appear before a grand jury and reveal confidences, I would hold that the government must (1) show that there is probable cause to believe that the newsman has information which is clearly relevant to a specific probable violation of law; (2) demonstrate that the information sought cannot be obtained by alternative means less destructive of the First Amendment rights; and (3) demonstrate a compelling and overriding interest in the information.''[50]

Three dissenters thus support a qualified privilege and Justice Douglas said only an absolute privilege would do. Justices White, Blackmun, Rehnquist, and Chief Justice Burger rejected the privilege.

Justice Powell in the Middle

Justice Powell agrees with Justice White but differed in interpreting what the opinion of the Court means: "Certainly we do not hold, as suggested in [Justice Stewart's] dissenting opinion, that state and federal authorities are free to 'annex' the news media as 'an investigative arm of government.' " He says the Court will tolerate no harassment of newspeople. "The asserted claim to privilege should be judged on its facts by the striking of a proper balance between the freedom of the press and the obligation of all citizens to give relevant testimony with respect to criminal conduct. The balance of these vital constitutional and social interests on a case-by-case basis accords with the tried and traditional way of administering such questions." Justice Powell accepts the first of Justice Stewart's proposed limitations, a requirement that what a reporter is asked be directly relevant to the grand jury's inquiry, but his specific reference to the other two is vague and ambiguous. He prefers to balance the community need for testimony against its need for an untrammeled news report.[51]

The friends of the media, pursuing the goal which the Supreme Court consigned to the Congress in the Branzburg decision, as indicated, sought to obtain favorable legislation. The Court sent a new evidence code to the Congress for approval in 1972 which specifically excluded the privilege newspeople desired. The House Judiciary Committee replaced the Supreme Court text at that point with a restatement of existing law which had been interpreted as permitting federal courts, in trying state cases under the diversity of citizenship rule, to apply state newsmen's privilege statutes. The Senate Judiciary Committee disagreed with the change but it was approved in conference. The code became effective July 1, 1975.

WILLIAM FARR'S CELEBRATED CASE

William T. Farr is one of the best known of the journalists who took information from secret sources, published it, and then sought shelter under a state shield law. Farr originally was employed by the Los Angeles *Herald-Examiner*. He is regarded as hero and martyr by colleagues who support the shield law. To the trial judge he defied, he seemed to be a conspirator against the lawful rules of the court and deserved to stay in jail until he named his accomplices. The events in which Farr was caught up, the Charles Manson cult murders, seem a fantasy from a world in which the legislatures undertook to undermine the authority of the courts.

Manson and his codefendants, perpetrators of the crimes, had been widely publicized before they came to trial. Judge Charles H. Older, early in the case on December 10, 1969, issued an order that prohibited "any attorney, court, or employee, attaché or witness from releasing for public dissemination the content or nature of any testimony that might be given at trial or any evidence the admissibility of which might have to be determined by the court." This order is based on the American Bar Association standards.[52] Nearly eleven months later, as the case was about to be given to the jury and the jury was sequestered, a potential witness, Mrs. Virginia Graham, gave a written statement to a deputy prosecutor, Stephen R. Kay, which said that Susan Atkins, an executioner for the cult, had confessed the murders to her and had implicated Manson. Moreover, Atkins was reported as saying a cross-country bus trip was planned to murder other show people, including Elizabeth Taylor and Richard Burton. The court ordered that Graham's statement be edited to exclude matter inadmissible in evidence and that a copy be delivered to each attorney appearing for the defense and one to the trial court.

Farr as a reporter learned of the statement. He was aware of Judge Older's gag order with respect to publicity. Nevertheless, pledging secrecy, he solicited copies of the document and said he received three from persons bound by the court order, at least two of them attorneys in the case. Judge Older learned that Farr had a copy and asked him privately not to publish it. He also asked Farr who gave the statement to him. Farr declined to give that information.

William Farr published the story October 9, 1970. Graham testified the next day, but, according to the court, "much of the matter contained in the statement given by her to Kay and printed in the *Herald-Examiner* was not permitted in evidence.''

Why did Farr solicit attorneys to violate the order of the court and give him a copy of the statement? It was news. Moreover, the state shield law said reporters had immunity and could print or broadcast such stories.[53]

What did the lawyers stand to gain by releasing the statement? A mistrial? A claim for future favors from the press? Judge Older questioned the lawyers, yet all denied giving the statement to Farr. The prosecution blamed the defense staff and vice versa. All the lawyers publicly released Farr from his pledge of secrecy, but Farr said nothing more. He had told too much when, on advice of counsel, he said he got the transcript from lawyers bound by the court's order. This was held to be an effective waiver of the privilege and Judge Older pressed Farr at this point.

The Judge as Farr's Nemesis

In May 1971 the court opened an inquiry into the leak. Farr had left the *Herald-Examiner* that March to become a press secretary to the Los Angeles district attorney, the Manson trial prosecutor. This action, Judge Older said later, deprived Farr of protection under the shield law because he was no longer a journalist. Thus Farr came to be launched on a career as a defendant in many cases.

Judge Eric E. Younger has said that ''most contempt citations in restrictive order cases have, in fact, arisen out of good faith efforts to test the applicable First Amendment principles rather than any acrimonious ignoring of judicial power.'' Reporters, he said, ''will readily and willingly go to jail if a jail term is threatened. They can do so with the knowledge that the best counsel procurable in the United States promptly will line up and file petitions and briefs to justices of the United States Supreme Court before the sheriff has turned his key.''[54]

Farr's state and national colleagues rallied to his support and seven amicus briefs were filed. His newspaper employers, the *Herald-Examiner* and *Los Angeles Times*, and his other friends paid for his defense. Farr said the cost was more than $100,000. His attorney of record on the first appeal was Grant B. Cooper of Cooper & Nelson, Los Angeles, a former member of the ABA Legal Advisory Committee on Fair Trial and Free Press (Reardon Committee) and a past president of the American College of Trial Lawyers.

Anomalies of Law and Reason

Clearly the journalists are saying that the laws of evidence are wrong, that even in the name of fair trial nothing may be hidden or held back from the public or the jury. If hearsay, lies, coerced confessions, or irrelevant or controversial charges become available they should not be evaluated for publication by the court but by the press in terms of its interest and competence. The effect on the jury, on witnesses, and on the defendant is of less importance than the effect of legal restrictions on the media. On its face, the shield law modified the rules so that a journalist can print or broadcast irrelevant information which, upon investigation, may be found to compromise a trial. If so, mistrial and new trial must follow. The strict accountability of trial lawyers to the court is nullified if a journalist can be found who is willing to serve as a lawyer's mute agent in violating the judge's rules. The journalistic response is that, on the performance record, some judges show a tendency to close courts which only journalists can counter.

In Farr's case, the California Court of Appeal held that the shield statute was "an unconstitutional interference by the legislative branch with an inherent and vital power of the court to control its own proceedings and officers." While the legislature could reasonably restrict the court's inherent constitutional powers it could not "declare that certain acts shall not constitute . . . a contempt."[55] Farr went to jail for forty-five days. The California Supreme Court denied his appeal,[56] and the United States Supreme Court refused to grant certiorari.[57]

Farr then applied in U.S. district court for a writ of habeas corpus, which was denied. While his appeal was pending he asked Justice William O. Douglas in chambers for release on bond; this was granted on the ground that the issue presented was new in spite of denial of certiorari.[58] The U.S. circuit court, in due time, denied the appeal.[59]

The Complicated Line of Appeal

Meanwhile, a second appeal in state courts had been undertaken which asserted, among other things, that the indeterminate civil contempt sentence was cruel and unreasonable. The district court of appeal found the sentence part of an attempt to enforce a court order and therefore free of constitutional defect. However, the court suggested it was necessary to determine the point at which time in jail ceased to serve its coercive intent and became punitive. At that point, incarceration was limited to five days under the Code of Civil Procedure, Section 1218.[60] Farr asked for a determination on this critical point and the indeterminate sentence was suspended. Judge Older, still pursuing an answer, filed criminal contempt charges and sentenced Farr to five days in jail. Farr appealed and more than two years later the district court of appeal held the criminal citation void and forbade additional criminal contempt proceedings based on the same events.[61]

Two of the six attorneys in the case, Vincent Bugliosi and Daye Shinn, had been indicted for perjury by a state grand jury, tried, and acquitted. Farr was subpoenaed to testify but relied on the shield law and this time was excused. This action narrowed the group of suspects to four, few enough under the libel cases to provide a claim of identification and a basis for suit by any one of them.[62]

Two of the defense lawyers, Paul Fitzgerald and Irving Kanarek, sued Farr for $24 million in libel damages. Farr was questioned on deposition but did not name his Graham statement informant. Superior Court Judge Robert Weil then ordered him to respond. Weil said Farr had lost constitutional protection by narrowing his source down to six and that the state shield law did not apply in civil libel cases. The state court of appeal agreed. That court also said Farr could be held in default judgment for all legal fees, and the state supreme court declined to consider Farr's appeal. Judge Weil found difficulty in scheduling the case for trial and dismissed it two years later on the ground that the plaintiffs had not diligently pursued their suit.[63]

Four Journalists in Fresno Jail

Farr's case concerned publication of a statement by a prospective witness circulated only to attorneys and to the court. The case of the Fresno Four[64] had to do with a transcript of a secret grand jury hearing which the court had sealed only a day before it was to be made public.

Insofar as the journalistic attitude is concerned, the case shows that four journalists in a single incident will accept jail as readily as one rather than reveal their sources.[65] The law of the case was settled by Farr's appeal, but Judge Donald R. Franson's dissent on the Fresno appeal brings together the arguments for the journalists. In the case which precipitated the conflict, a city councilman, Marc Stefano, was indicted in November 1974 on a charge that he had accepted a $4000 bribe from a developer, Joseph Aluisi, who, in return received an $11,520 sewer fee rebate. Aluisi and a former city planning official, Norman Bains, also were indicted. The defendants wanted the transcript sealed until the trial was over although two of them had obtained a change of venue by the time the *Fresno Bee* published its story.

The charges against Bains had already been published several times, according to Justice Franson, and so

it was extremely doubtful that any material in the . . . news stories [based on the transcript] would have further prejudiced Bains in the eyes of prospective trial jurors in Fresno County. This is particularly so when we consider the fact that Bains, a former City of Fresno Planning Commissioner, previously [six months earlier] had been indicted and convicted in a widely publicized . . . jury trial of three counts of selling heroin and one count of possessing heroin. He was under a state prison sentence for these crimes when indicted by the grand jury. . . . Any concern for Bains' right to a fair trial in Fresno County should have been considered chimerical at best.[66]

The ABA standards, sections 8-3.1 through 8-3.6, are designed for a situation such as the trial judge, Denver C. Peckinpah, confronted. If Bains wanted a change of venue under the standard he could have had it for the asking. If on balance he found Fresno a forgiving and supportive location for his trial—as he apparently did—continuance was inadvisable. Fresno County, an urban center, offered a ready supply of jurors who could be carefully selected under voir dire.

Justice Franson added that "[t]here is something inherently wrong" in allowing a court to keep the public from reading sworn testimony about the misconduct of a sitting public official.[67]

The court had an additional complaint in the Fresno case: The testimony showed that one of the four had a master key to the courthouse obtained from a former bailiff, and this key could have opened at least one office where a copy of the transcript was kept in plain sight on top of a desk. The trial judge impulsively suggested that the Fifth Amendment, rather than the First, was now the appropriate shield for the journalists. He outdid the Farr judge in applying squeeze by asking each journalist a series of questions and treating each refusal to answer as a separate contempt. The district court of appeal, reviewing his rulings, approved citations of nineteen, seventeen, five, and fifteen separate contempts against members of the Four, respectively, and sent the case back to the judge to handle accordingly.[68]

Judge Peckinpah retired before the case was brought to an end. Chief Judge Hollis Best took over the effort to force the journalists to name their sources. After holding them in jail for fifteen days he listened to testimony from other journalists from whom he sought advice and released the Four, apparently persuaded that coercion—the justification for the contempt tactic—would not succeed.[69]

MILLION-DOLLAR DEFENSE OF MYRON FARBER

The *New York Times* experience with a state shield law in 1978 cost it more than a million dollars in fines, court costs, and lawyer's fees. Myron A. Farber, a seasoned and trusted investigative reporter, later assigned to the Paris bureau, decided to reopen a five-star whodunit case centered at Riverdell Hospital in Oradell, N.J. The central, and often pathetic, figure was an Argentine-born surgeon, Dr. Mario A. Jascalevich, who voluntarily surrendered his license as a result of the case and later returned to Argentina. He was accused by his hospital colleagues of causing the deaths of several patients with curare, a drug used by anesthesiologists to slow down breathing during thoracic surgery. He was indicted in three deaths, one of which was a four-year-old child. The motive advanced at trial, but not proved, was that he was jealous of a new colleague with whom he shared the hospital's surgical practice. Jascalevich had the drug in his locker, but he showed that he was using it in animal research and there was no direct evidence of guilt. No charges were filed at the time of the first investigation but more than nine years later, when new chemical tests for curare in human tissue came into use, Farber reviewed the evidence and asked new questions. Together with work by the prosecutor and consulting medical specialists, Farber's articles led to a murder indictment. During the trial, the surgeon's lawyer, Raymond A. Brown, showed that he was skilled in jury handling as well as in criminal law. He not only persuaded the jury but the spectators obviously were also his partisans. The trial lasted eight months and, at the end, Dr. Jascalevich won acquittal and some of his patients crowded around in a warm show of confidence and support. It was Farber's investigative work which made the difference between indictment and no prosecution.[70] Brown subpoenaed Farber's notes and papers, but Farber refused and went to jail. The *Times* was fined $100,000 down, so to speak, and $5000 a day until the records were produced in court, or until the trial ended.

Farber and the *Times* fought in every available court and the record shows where the million dollars went. As the trial began, Farber was in court as a reporter. He was at once subjected to the rule excluding witnesses from the proceedings. Since Farber was its expert on the case, the *Times* asked another New Jersey Superior Court judge for an exception to the rule. The judge would not grant it.

The pace of the action here can best be understood when each of the events is dated. The trial judge, William J. Arnold, on May 19, 1978, at Brown's request, signed a memorandum that Farber's notes and papers probably were important to the case. A New York court, by this time, had been asked to require Farber to come to New Jersey and had consented. The *Times* appealed and a month later the New York appellate division ordered Farber to comply.

By June 30 the *Times* had asked Judge Arnold to quash the subpoena. He refused. His action was appealed to the appellate division of the New Jersey courts, a hearing was held, and the petition was rejected. July 3 was Judge Arnold's deadline for Farber to submit his papers. The *Times* petitioned Justice Byron R. White of the U.S. Supreme Court to intervene; he refused and, in turn, so did Justice Marshall. Judge Arnold reset the hearing date for July 12 but Farber held out. He and the *Times* were convicted on July 24 of criminal and civil contempt.

U.S. District Judge Lacey set a hearing for August 8 on application for habeas corpus. Instead of helping, he launched an attack on Farber from the bench because Farber had contracted to publish a book on the case. Judge Lacey filed an opinion on August 14. Farber offered to surrender to Judge Arnold the draft copy of his book, unedited, in order to rebut Judge Lacey's charge that it contained the names of his confidential informants. Farber was pleading shield law protection. Arnold responded that the law did not protect the working papers of journalists. It was these that he wanted to see. This point was appealed to the New Jersey Supreme Court and Farber lost.[71] Judge Arnold received the book manuscript on August 18 and, with it, what the *Times* management said was all of its files relating to the contractual agreement with the book publishers.

In an effort to get Farber out of jail, the *Times* attorneys made another futile trip to the Supreme Court of the United States to petition individual justices and Farber stayed in jail until the trial ended October 24. He was then released. An appeal was prepared for the Supreme Court on broad First Amendment and shield law grounds. After all, the Branzburg opinion clearly approved of state shield laws. The Supreme Court, however, declined to grant review.

DEVELOPMENT OF THE SHIELD

Branzburg, the controlling case, came about in part because lawyers representing the media preferred to entrust development of the privilege to the courts rather than to legislatures. Hope for uniformity under the First and Fourteenth Amendments and for a more stable future lay in that direction. Left to the states, key newsgathering procedures are regulated in different styles which reflect, at least in part, local attitudes and crises. Some journalists, left to choose, would have preferred no shield law to such legislative hazards.

Branzburg had done more for the development of a First Amendment privilege than at first realized. The late Alexander Bickel, while a Yale Law School teacher acting as counsel for the *New York Times* and other major clients, suggested to the Court a qualified privilege for reporters much like that later developed by Justice Stewart from several sources, including the opinion of the Ninth Circuit Court in the Caldwell case. Stewart's test appears in the summary of his Branzburg dissent, mentioned earlier. Briefly, its three prongs require a showing (1) that the reporter has the information sought and that it is clearly relevant to a specific probable violation of law, (2) that the information cannot be obtained elsewhere, and (3) that there is a compelling and overriding interest in the information.

Justices Marshall and Brennan supported Stewart's requirement of the test but Justice Powell liked only the first point. He voted with Chief Justice Burger, thus maintaining a functional loyalty, but his opinion was couched so directly in First Amendment terms that the circuit courts used it to develop a qualified First Amendment privilege. Most of them have participated in this effort.[72] Powell recommended that the press ask that the state's interest in information be balanced against the values found in the secrecy of grand jury proceedings. He assured the working press that the Court would not let them suffer loss of legitimate First Amendment interests.[73]

Since that time, a few journalists have been held in contempt for refusal to testify but they were either eyewitnesses to crimes or caught up as actors in events which caused prosecution. An Oregon television crew, invited to film a police sting on the street, found its members subpoenaed by a person arrested, a person who said he was not trying to rob a police decoy lying in the street but to help a man desperately ill. The trial judge ordered them to come to court but the defendant did not show up and they were not needed.[74] Another example of common cases is when the Dallas school board fired its superintendent the day after a critical story appeared in a newspaper. Was the story part of the board's strategy in firing the official without a hearing? That was a legitimate question and the journalist who refused to answer was punished for contempt.[75]

In Boston, Edward R. Kopacz, Jr., went to trial for murder after a newspaper story reported that he had confessed to a reporter on the phone but sight unseen. The jury found Kopacz not guilty and the reporter, who relied on the shield, went to jail.[76] Obviously, he was the only source of information about the purported confession. Another Boston reporter, who based a murder story on an account of an eyewitness he would not identify, was tried, held in contempt, and fined. The court said there was no other way to get the name of the eyewitness.[77]

When the three-prong test is used, the court must actually hear evidence and decide whether there is an overriding need for the journalist's testimony. The finding must be in writing and become a part of the record.[78] When a reporter's papers are examined in camera, that is in private, the procedure forces even attorneys in the case to go without the information about sources until the court makes a finding. Since the procedure is somewhat new, however, a lawyer who fails to persuade a court in one trial may learn how to succeed in a similar case. Defendants who ask for too much information, a common fault, usually end up with nothing.[79]

Newspapers and broadcasting stations do not always respond in the same way to subpoenas, the broadcaster yielding and the print medium refusing. Compulsory due process of law is still under development in this narrow area and efforts to obtain forced testimony can take extra time, as CBS demonstrated in one of the suits based on its ''60 Minutes'' show.[80] The Tennessee statute gives original jurisdiction on motions to set aside the shield to the intermediate appellate courts, and some litigants go to the trial court, to their embarrassment, before discovering the rule. The procedural requirements of the three-prong test, if not carefully observed by the trial courts, may result in premature requests for a subpoena.[81] Regular revision of shield law statutes takes place as journalists seek additional protection. The New York courts, for example, are now in the process of deciding whether they should interpret the statute so as to require proof that the information being shielded was obtained upon a promise of confidence.[82] The Montana shield still protects even when a journalist publishes or broadcasts a portion of the privileged information, as William Farr did in California to his peril.[83]

The effort to make the shield law absolute, or close to it, took on added significance after the U.S. Supreme Court turned libel law development back to the states in 1974.[84] Donald M. Gillmor says that at least thirteen states (the count is now fourteen) cast their statutes in somewhat absolute terms, but judges do not always interpret them as the drafters intended.[85]

Revision of the New Jersey Statute

The media enjoyed a favorable balance in libel laws for a decade after the New York Times v. Sullivan decision in 1964.[86] When a shield difficult to penetrate stands in the way of libel plaintiffs who want a journalist to provide part of their evidence in court, the wide-ranging discovery process opened to libel plaintiffs by Gertz v. Robert Welch, Inc., in 1974 quickly loses its impact.[87] A plaintiff can hardly prove that a libel was written in malice, or in reckless disregard of whether or not it was true, unless the journalist can be required to testify as to his state of mind at the time of writing and editing.

The New Jersey supreme court interpreted the state's shield law, revised after Myron Farber's jail term, as conferring an absolute privilege and the U.S. Supreme Court declined to review the case. A bill in the state legislature to redress the balance was withdrawn after journalists turned out at a public hearing.[88] Shield laws, of course, invade the constitutional prerogative of courts to make and enforce their own rules. California's supreme court has demonstrated its treasured independence on several occasions when it adjusted shield statutes to conform to its rules. For that reason, voters were persuaded to put shield language into the state constitution, but the untested amendment at the moment expresses no more than a popular preference, and it awaits court interpretation. The federal courts apply state shield laws in diversity of citizenship cases as a result of action by the Congress.

The first New Jersey supreme court case of importance arising under the new statute, State v. Boiardo, assured journalists of a formal hearing, upon request, at the time they are about to be denied a testimonial privilege. Such a hearing was denied to Farber but now the three-prong test of Justice Stewart and the circuit courts is used. On this occasion the court said that neither the shield nor the Sixth Amendment impairs the right of an applicant to obtain evidence. However, compulsory process "has never been held to require the production of an item of evidence upon a defendant's mere unsubstantiated assertion that it would assist in his defense regardless of its availability through other sources."[89] The source shielded in the Boiardo case had given both oral and written statements for admission as evidence and was available for further questioning in court. The journalist was not needed.

The New Jersey finding of an absolute shield came in an opinion for the state court by Justice Morris Pashman, an ardent partisan of freedom of the press, who dissented with considerable feeling when the court sent Farber to jail. Pashman's opinion rejected a demand of a libel plaintiff that *New Jersey Monthly* reveal the sources it relied on to reach a conclusion that a veteran state senator, Joseph Maressa, deserved to be rated as among the worst performers in the senate. According to the court, the magazine said "Maressa's problem is not so much that he is evil as that he is sneaky, self-interested, and basically unprincipled."[90] This description, however unfair, is hardly exceptional in state politics and the senator, as a public official, had less to gain in money damages than by repairing his reputation—if, indeed, it had been impaired. The New Jersey court, however, unlike the U.S. Supreme Court in Herbert v. Lando, said the magazine editor could not be forced to disclose his reasoning. In states other than New Jersey, so far as the Lando rule applies, "the thoughts and editorial processes of the alleged defamer would be open to examination."[91]

The New Jersey amendments are the product of cooperation by journalists and sympathetic state legislators, including Senator Maressa. Judge Pashman's philosophy is about the same as that expressed by Justice Brennan in his plurality opinion for the U.S. Supreme Court in Rosenbloom v. Metromedia. Yet Justice Powell's later influence on the Court made it easier for some persons to maintain successful suits.[92] Recent decisions against large newspapers, and some not so large, have generated heavy damage awards. The Libel Defense Research Center said that in twenty-one cases the plaintiffs received $250,000 or more;

nine verdicts of more than one million dollars each were in this group. However, of forty-seven awards only seven were affirmed on appeal.[93]

CBS Fights Subpoenas

CBS, Inc.—along with other major media businesses—has had to fight a number of cases based on its "60 Minutes" show in addition to Herbert v. Lando. This libel suit required it, in the discovery stage, to explain why certain scenes were shown and others deleted. The Lando decision[94] precipitated premature panic among journalists because they thought "state of mind" questions violated their privacy. However, the U.S. Supreme Court held that the plaintiff, Colonel Anthony Herbert, was entitled to inquire into intent, to know why certain editing decisions were made, in an effort to prove his allegation of malicious error. This went no further than the Court in New York Times v. Sullivan, which journalists regarded at the time of decision as liberating.[95]

Listeners to and readers of investigative reporting might like to have chairside this quotation from Justice William J. Brennan in the New York Times v. Sullivan case: "Since there is no double-jeopardy limitation applicable to civil lawsuits, this is not the only judgment that may be awarded against petitioners for the same publication. Whether or not a newspaper can survive a succession of such judgments, the pall of fear and timidity imposed upon those who would give voice to public criticism is an atmosphere in which the First Amendment freedoms cannot survive."[96]

Unlike Lando, another CBS case is more representative of the bulk of those in this study than libel suits—and equally expensive. The CBS antagonist in this matter was Wild Bill's Family Restaurant franchise group, the subject of a Mike Wallace show. The firm was indicted on federal charges of fraud and conspiracy and, in preparation for trial, subpoenaed relevant CBS notes and filmed interviews both used on the air and those not used—"documents of any nature pertaining to preparation of the program 'From Burgers to Bankruptcy.' " CBS moved to quash the subpoena as too broad and pleaded a First Amendment privilege to gather and report news of Wild Bill's business activity. The trial judge ordered the government to provide CBS with a list of the trial witnesses and CBS was ordered to give the court, for in camera inspection before trial, all verbatim or substantially verbatim statements made by persons on the list. At that time the court had not made up its mind what, if anything, it would show to the defendants. The defense requested a second subpoena which expanded to 100 or more the verbatim statements CBS was expected to provide. The trial court did not enforce the second subpoena but added the persons named in it to the list of those whose statements would be examined in camera. CBS declined to comply with the amended order and was held in civil contempt. On appeal, the Third Circuit Court held that the defendants could not examine the materials in the hands of the trial court in time, under the rules, to use it for impeachment of witnesses. They had no knowledge of any exculpatory information it might contain; they merely had hopes.[97]

As to the claim of First Amendment privilege, that required balancing against the fair trial needs of the defendants. On this occasion, which was the first of two appeals to the circuit court, the balancing was up to the trial court. With the additional materials now in hand,[98] the trial court had trouble deciding between CBS and the defendants and, according to the circuit court on the second appeal, chose the wrong party.[99] The second appeal arose because the trial court decided to give some of the CBS interviews with government witnesses to the defendants. CBS objected that the court order did not meet the standards of Rule 17(c) of the Federal Rules of Criminal Procedure because it did not show CBS to be the only source of the desired information. Nor did the material qualify as exculpatory under the rule, as interpreted. Rule 17(c) deals only with the admissible evidence to be obtained by subpoena and the trial court had not correctly determined what was admissible. The defendants made no showing that they had tried to get the information from others, that only the CBS reporters had it, and that their knowledge was sufficiently important to the defendants to overcome the First Amendment privilege.[100]

Chief Judge Seitz, concurring in the judgment, said that under United States v. Augurs,[101] neither CBS nor the government was under legal obligation to provide nonevidentiary material merely helpful to the defense. Obligation was attached only if the material appeared to lead to admissible evidence.[102]

The New Jersey Statute

The New Jersey shield law was singled out early in the chapter for comparison with the Arizona law to show the pattern expected to result from litigation and heavy use. The text of the statute is appended to the chapter notes and it will suffice here to point to the features which have accumulated in use. A shield law is designed to protect journalists against conceivable hazards and this intention, alone, adds detail. The art of the lawyer is directed at creating rulings favorable to a client and much work goes into definitions of persons and things to be protected, the tribunals whose powers are to be limited, the myriad ways in which protected information moves in the process of newsgathering and dissemination, and extensive description of the media of communication eligible for protection. The use of the privilege has to be confined to criminal cases, mostly at the pretrial stage, and an obligation is placed upon those who would extract information or use the privilege to demonstrate their right to the benefits claimed. The authority of the courts to hold hearings on the subject of the privilege is defined. Otherwise there is inadequate basis in law for either side to appeal a trial court ruling. When all its detail is read, journalists can see what happens when they use the courts for the purpose of administering what seemed a simple matter like protecting a source of information.

Examination of their work leaves no doubt that the New Jersey courts and the legislature are deeply concerned about the protection of the newsgathering process insofar as it serves a public purpose. The statute and the court cases clarify the hazards of newsgathering and provide effective guides to protection of a journalist's work product against misuse.

GRAND JURY SECRECY

Ground Rules

Grand jury proceedings are traditionally secret because the jurors are not bound by the strict rules of evidence and have somewhat the same freedom as journalists to ask questions. Far too often a jury report damages individual reputations without laying a proper factual basis for doing so. That is why the juries report to the court and why the court feels compelled to edit the reports before release. It is the editing to which journalists object and which motivates them to get the original documents if possible. In so doing, they assert that the grand jury is under attack for departures from its statutory purpose. The political charges which some grand juries make ought not to be kept secret. Yet, when a journalist obtains a transcript illegally he faces the risk of going to jail, as in the case of the Fresno Four.

The Reporter's Committee for Freedom of the Press argues that political manipulation has made the grand jury one of the most controversial agencies in government.[103] Political manipulation sometimes causes individuals to be brought before a grand jury without adequate notice of the subject of inquiry, not so much with the intent of getting evidence about crimes, but in order to leak critical stories based on noncriminal conduct.

It is commonly known that President Nixon was designated an "unindicted co-conspirator" by the grand jury reporting to Judge John W. Sirica and that the grand jury report was sent to the House Committee on the Judiciary then considering articles of impeachment. Was Judge Sirica acting against tradition? He said the jury's report was factual, a "straight-forward compilation of information," and that President Nixon did not object to its release.[104] The report cited the case against Attorney General Mitchell, who was then on trial, but Judge Sirica said mention was indirect and that Mitchell would have ample opportunity to defend his reputation during trial.[105] There are, then, obvious exceptions to the rules of secrecy. The complaints against freewheeling grand juries that depart from the law and instructions to issue sweeping political pronouncements are well documented.[106] While prosecutors can be required to assist grand juries in drafting indictments and reports with which they may not agree, they cannot be required to sign them. The authority of the judge to suppress or disclose a grand jury report is unquestioned, but power and wisdom are separate matters.[107] For example, a grand jury dealing with the Kent State University antiwar demonstrations made sweeping political charges, with the judge's consent, that had little to do with a show of military force and the untimely deaths of students.[108] But in its intended role, the grand jury can stand between a prosecutor seeking an indictment and a defendant; if the jurors have courage, their hands cannot be forced.[109]

Political Communication

However noble in purpose, the grand jury can be used and is used to express political judgments both by law enforcement officials and journalists. By reporting leaked testimony, journalists sometimes put witnesses in an unfavorable, even criminal, light. The rules of secrecy, designed to prevent this result, are evaded and persons caught in publicity traps sometimes complain to the court, which already is humiliated by the breach of its protocol. Courts have held, however, that no defendant is entitled to have "an indictment dismissed because it was obtained by means of illegally obtained evidence." Efforts to throw out indictments on the ground that prejudicial publicity influenced the jury have not been successful.[110] Indictment stands even though based on hearsay alone.[111]

COMMENT

The shield law controversy shows that journalists have struggled to investigate criminal behavior and noncriminal political events by claiming a reporter's privilege to operate outside the law but under ethical constraints. They have been aided in their objectives by the community's clear need to monitor individuals in government, and in other positions of trust and power, so that the electorate can make its decisions in a wise and timely manner. This is not to say that journalism, any more than other high callings, is always able to serve as well as the community expects or deserves. The traditional safeguard when individuals and institutions are permitted to operate with little regulation is limited self-regulation, that is, use of a private system of law based on ethics, or public utility status in which private managers are bound by government-imposed regulations. Moreover, journalism is not the only significant monitor. The tripartite form of government distributes powers so that legislators, administrators, and judges are, in effect, responsible to each other as well as to the community. To the extent that ethical values become internalized, each individual is responsible for monitoring behavior. But the individual and government alike require the assistance of agencies of mass communication to focus public attention on events in the day's news that deserve public indignation.

This chapter has recounted the efforts of journalists to obtain as much elbow room under law as they could and has noted the consequences. The major episode was a decision of the United States Supreme Court (Branzburg v. Hayes) placing rather clear limits on the scope of special testamentary privilege. It became clear, under that reasoning, that while journalists had much freedom to gather and write news, they also were subject to regulation in the public interest—not as public utilities, but as the carriers of information and opinion upon which society must depend for the formulation of policy.

Moreover, once the major policy decision was made, the U.S. circuit court majorities facilitated rather than impaired journalism's watchdog role. Regrettably, from journalism's viewpoint, this kind of facilitation limits the absolutist version of freedom of speech and press, and it requires the individual writer and editor to confront his own motives and to respect his professional work standards in order to avoid retribution defined by law. This risk of retribution is imbedded in two lines of cases, one shielding the journalist against revealing his or her sources of information when asked to testify in court, and the other subjecting him, under court rules that define the limits of privilege, to intensive interrogation about his standards of work and the motives which energized his treatment of the subject. While the pilgrimage to today's definitions of freedom has not been completed without journalistic martyrs, and a treasure in litigation costs, the facts reviewed do not show major shifts in freedom of the press.

***

We turn now to another area of press and court tension of long standing: use of cameras in the courtroom. Like the events in this chapter, the result is a set of working rules which gives journalists an opportunity to expand their photographic news coverage but also requires respect for the courts and the principles of fair trial.

The Camera's All-Seeing Eye   6

HOW THE TV BAN WAS PROVOKED

The camera is well on its way to becoming as sensitive and as silent as the human eye, but its reputation in court was made, over the years, by far less sophisticated equipment. This leads to a kind of social lag because more people say they get news from television now than any other medium. Inadequate lenses and lighting forced photographers for years to be close to their subjects and, of course, they still wish to be. In court, standing close sometimes means walking back and forth near the counsel table and jury box to take pictures that will reproduce on newsprint, or popping flash bulbs in the hallway to photograph a shy witness. The flash bulb, itself, is relatively new and the flash powder which it succeeded was a disaster in any company. Telephoto lenses on contemporary silent cameras can pick a lawyer's notes right off his yellow pad and microphones can relay his whisper to a client to the audience.

The consequences, distracting or upsetting as they are to the participants in a trial and to the judge on the bench, are not the whole reason for the camera's exile from the courtroom for a generation. That exile came because insensitive manners, on the one hand, and competition, on the other hand, reduced photographers in some instances to the level of rule breakers and hooligans.

In the trial of Bruno Richard Hauptmann, for the kidnap-murder of Charles A. Lindbergh, Jr., the great and the near-great of journalism thronged to the town of Hopewell, N.J., and its small courthouse, built for the light traffic of felonies and torts, contract disputes, and replevins of a gentle society.[1] So great was the demand for pictures and copy that the swollen press herd trampled its way into history, and into a flat ban on cameras in the courtroom which is still as tight as a hangman's noose in federal courts and is being relaxed only slowly, and fearfully, in state courts.[2]

The courtroom disorder occasioned by the bustle of reporters and photographers was repeated, perhaps in a smaller frame, in the Sam Sheppard trial which is described by the Court in its opinion.

Newsreel cameramen at Hopewell persuaded the trial judge to let them install a camera in a balcony overlooking the jury stand and witness box, promising to use it only when the court was in recess. The judge learned the level of their honesty when films of the trial sessions appeared in newsreel theaters.

The Jack Ruby Trial

Judge Joe E. Brown, sitting in Dallas at the trial of Jack Ruby, the person who shot Lee Harvey Oswald to death on network television, was importuned to let TV cameras into court. He demurred, but he was in an elective office and the desire to please the press is an impulse not unknown to the heart. When it was time for the jury's verdict, he agreed with the TV crews that a pool camera, just one, could enter the courtroom to photograph the return of the verdict. As the courtroom door opened and the pool camera trundled in the other cameras followed in stampede style. They were able to provide a national audience for Melvin Belli, the disappointed defense attorney, as he criticized the people of Dallas for setting up a climate in which his client was found guilty.

Afterward, outside the courthouse to meet the press, as he had agreed, Judge Brown wore a frown and complained that the "boys" had broken their promise. The boys had had no practice in joint use of a pool camera and no conventions governing such a new idea. They trundled into court, got their story, and turned away to other news events. Competition had won the day.

It is already known that at least two First Amendments exist, one laid down by the courts, and one that lives in ideal form in journalistic discourse. Individual journalists, responding to this ideal, breach the rules of court often enough to keep fresh the unhappy aspects of their reputation. A Dallas television reporter, shortly after the United States Supreme Court had chased television out of the courts in the Billie Sol Estes case, which is mentioned below, personally ignored an order of federal Judge Sarah T. Hughes banning cameras in the courthouse. He was arrested, fined, and released not exactly a hero.[3]

What Makes a Good Picture?

Organized journalism has had difficulty fighting its way back from Hopewell, N.J., because violence ranks high in the criteria of what makes a picture interesting. The "two persons and a piece of paper" pose curdles the journalistic mind. Photographers know that writers have scored their greatest triumphs trolling in the stream of human emotion. When press photographers hang their work in galleries, tragedy and triumph, joy and despair, violent death and happy birth, clash. The workmanlike prints try to answer the question "How do you feel?" Unfortunately for man, and for photography, more news is made by feeling bad than by feeling good. To pass along the bad news the photographer seeks the utmost simplicity of language. With pictures, aided by parsimony in words, he etches emotions shared by all mankind. The photographer who can catch tragedy, surprise, horror, laughter in the human face or form has painted his masterpiece for the day and must set out to do as well tomorrow.

The face of the mother called by the police who lifts the cover from the body of her daughter, drowned or murdered, and cries out in recognition and despair, will flow out of the television and onto newsprint all over town, and she will not forget that the media showed her agony. Great work, journalists say, photographs the soul as emotion opens its windows.

Journalists are realists. They wish to report things as they are, not as shaped and tinted by the masks of convention. They may intrude on privacy, but the popular demand for mass communication arises because such images are for sale. Like the child in the pornography shop, we are driven to look but ashamed to see. Since every person, not only journalists and judges, defines freedom of the press for himself or herself the guarantee has to be renegotiated with citizens every time their sense of privacy comes into conflict either with the physical intrusion of a journalist or the stunning results of his work.

When feelings are hurt, in the rush to get news and pictures, the complaining party must appeal to the journalist in terms of his values for correction and redress, and the appeal ordinarily is heard no more widely than the journalist himself chooses to permit.

Judges, however, do have recourse. They make the rules for the conduct of trials and can enforce them no matter how much the media complain of mistreatment. The National Opinion Research Center study by Fred Siebert in 1968, described in Chapter 2, showed that only 9.7 percent of the judges felt photographs should be permitted.[4] This is the area of tension so far unresolved, but great progress has been made and today journalists, for the first time since Bruno Hauptmann's trial, stand a chance to demonstrate the extent of the socialization they have undergone. They stand on the verge of accomplishment, however, not because of their ability to show the anguish people feel but because judges want the people to see justice done in open courts.

THE EFFORT TO GET BACK IN COURT

The effort to recover from the Hauptmann trial defeat has proceeded in two waves. The first was characterized by use of lawyer's techniques in which, through years of fruitless hearings, the journalists sought to wear down the resistance of the bench and bar. One bright passage in this phase was conversion of the Supreme Court of Colorado to the use of still and television cameras in the courtroom, but this success was broken off for a time by the anger and fear of the U.S. Supreme Court as it reacted to television's use in the Billy Sol Estes case. The second could be termed "socialization" of the photographers. Both are historical phases in American journalism and deserve attention.[5]

The ABA Ban: Canon 35

After the Hauptmann trial in 1934 the American Bar Association formed a special inquiry committee on criminal trials, which was chaired by Justice Oscar Hallam of the Minnesota Supreme Court. The report reflected the emotional resentment of the bench and bar.[6] In succession, another committee was chosen to represent both the bar and the press, but it was soon handicapped by the death of its distinguished chairman, Newton D. Baker, and another ABA council, Professional Ethics and Grievances, invaded its jurisdiction and secured the adoption of Canon 35 to exclude cameras. The canon, Sec. 3A(7) Code of Judicial Conduct, read: "Proceedings in court shall be conducted with fitting dignity and decorum. The taking of photographs in the courtroom, during sessions of the court or recesses between sessions, and the broadcasting of court proceedings are calculated to detract from the essential dignity of the proceedings, distract the witness in giving his testimony, degrade the court, and create misconceptions with respect thereto in the minds of the public and should not be permitted.''

The special committee lingered on for a few months and, in 1941, asked that it be dissolved. It was reestablished in 1954 after television stations began to exert pressure for reconsideration of the canon. Four years later, the ABA House of Delegates recommended a broad new study. This was to be headed by a leading opponent of cameras in court, Whitney North Seymour of New York. It was understood that outside money was needed to do its work and none was raised. It was Seymour who, with Richmond C. Coburn of St. Louis and John H. Yauch, Sr., of Newark, N.J., later provided the amicus brief of the ABA opposing cameras in the Billie Sol Estes appeal. Their brief argued that a defendant ''should not be put to the burden of proving in every instance 'what no amount of research can ever adequately measure.' . . . The burden of showing the subtleties of adverse effects on judges, jurors, witnesses, lawyers, and parties, many of whom would shy away from admitting any such effects, would ordinarily be greater than the burden of showing the adverse consequences of the absence of counsel.''[7]

The broadcasters, using local persuasion, were particularly successful in Colorado and Texas where the trial and appellate courts not only were sensitive to political conditions but had considerable experience with cameras. In Colorado, with the help of the National Association of Broadcasters, television was used under the guidance of trial judges. The Colorado high court ruled that a defendant's objection to the presence of cameras was not conclusive; this was also the position of American Newspaper Publishers Association attorneys. Photographers were commonplace in the state courts until Estes v. Texas restored the veto power of the defense. The Texas State Bar favored cameras and their use was left to the discretion of trial judges. Courts in Indiana, Oklahoma, North Carolina, and Ohio adopted similar rules.

The press petitions ABA. While the ABA study proposed in 1958 was not completed, the committee was impelled by the pressure of controversy to continue its work. It could have no intimation of the Estes case decision to be handed down in a few years. It received a substantial body of evidence in 1962 when Yauch was chairman. The committee saw portions of a film of the John Gilbert Graham murder trial in Colorado in which the defendant was convicted of placing a time bomb in an airplane that took forty-five lives, including Graham's mother's. The committee noted that filming of the trial had been permitted, under the rules, over the objection of the defendant.

Respected voices inside as well as outside journalism circles, including John H. Colburn, head of an American Society of Newspaper Editors committee, continued to urge the media to do a more effective job of policing themselves.[8]

Representatives of the National Press Photographers Association (NPPA), the National Association of Broadcasters, the Radio and Television News Directors Association, and National Editorial Association conferred with the ABA committee. Chief Justice Day of the Colorado Supreme Court said that cameras had been present at ninety-five trials between February 27, 1956, and his appearance in 1962, nearly all of them criminal cases. He explained that the Graham trial, which lasted twenty-one days, was recorded in full but stations gave only about one hour of broadcast time to it each day. The camera was concealed in a booth in the courtroom to make it as inconspicuous and least distracting as possible. Sometimes, Justice Day said, cameramen came in only to get the testimony of certain witnesses.

Television crews had not previously been active in Colorado courts, but newspaper photographers used the privilege extensively. Justice Day said newspapers dealt with trials in a more intelligent and objective manner in the courtroom than when they tried to photograph people in the streets. He thought use of cameras had improved the public's conception of courts.[9]

Opposition to cameras. Superior Court Judge Henry S. Stevens of Phoenix, Ariz., told the ABA committee, "Woe be unto that judge who has sufficient courage to exclude photography in a celebrated case. I venture to say he will not be dealt with in a kindly manner by the press. I know from bitter experience that disfavor with the press can be a pretty rough ordeal." He said he found it too burdensome to police photographers in court. Letters from bar associations and bar leaders also were quoted to the committee. For example, Thomas K. Younge of Grand Junction, Colo., former president of the state bar association, said the state supreme court judges were influenced by the need for publicity at election time when they agreed to receive cameras. He not only wanted cameras excluded, but he wanted a nonelective system of selection for state judges.[10]

The Judicial Conference of the United States adopted a resolution condemning cameras in court while the ABA committee was writing its report. The federal judges, through the chief justice, said constant pressure on them to negate the rule excluding cameras "prompted the reaffirmation and extension of it by the conference."[11]

Second Effort by the Media

In spite of opposition, and the barrier of the Estes decision, the media continued to seek permission for the use of cameras in state and federal courts. The effort was coordinated by the Radio-Television News Directors Association through its members in key cities. Unlike their previous efforts, the journalists now studied the reactions of the judges and came up with standards of their own for courtroom behavior. Professor Bill Seymour of West Virginia University, chairman of the Freedom of Information Committee of the National Press Photographers Association, prepared guidelines which aided the Florida Supreme Court, and other courts, in drafting its own rules. In addition, he demonstrated for courts and journalists how to use cameras unobtrusively in court.[12] The guidelines emphasize decorum, understanding of the rules and needs of courts, and they counsel avoidance of intrusion in dealing with jurors and witnesses.[13]

In this second phase of the effort to gain acceptance, Colorado in 1970 was the first state to return cameras to court. After the Estes decision it had required the consent of the parties to photograph a trial and, if any witness objected, television was excluded. The earlier experience of attorneys and clients with cameras reduced the opposition in Colorado.[14] Other states were slow to move, but—as an example— the Supreme Court of Washington state issued guidelines and admitted television in 1977. A committee representing the courts, the law enforcement administration, and print and electronic journalists drew up rules which were adopted by the court. A murder trial was filmed in Prosser, Wash., and was shown to judges in other states by the proponents of the admission of cameras.

The turning point in phase two came when Florida Post-Newsweek stations petitioned the state supreme court to permit cameras in court, and the Prosser, Wash., videotape was part of the supporting exhibits. Despite serious opposition from lawyers and judges, the court ordered a one-year experiment. The rules adopted at first required consent of the parties for use of cameras but, when this proved obstructive, the rule was changed to place discretion on the trial judge. Objections to cameras are now heard prior to trial and journalists, as well as the parties, may appear. If the judge agrees with the defendant objector, he is required to set out reasons for excluding cameras and the same rule applies if he closes any portion of the trial.[15]

The Florida experiment received national publicity when cameras were admitted in 1978 to the Ronald A. Zamora trial. Zamora, fifteen years of age, was accused of the murder of an eighty-three-year-old neighbor and his defense was, in part, that he had watched so much crime on television his judgment was impaired. At the end of the year's experiment, the court admitted cameras regularly under its rules.[16]

THE SUPREME COURT ESTES CASE

Even though the event now seems anticlimactic, the Estes v. Texas[17] case must be reviewed. It is a 1965 case in which a Texas swindler eventually was convicted. During a pretrial hearing, cameras moved into an unprepared courtroom and worked under conditions which the judge could not control. The Estes lawyers, having few facts with which to defend their client, claimed he was deprived of "due process by the televising and broadcasting of his trial"—a notorious, heavily publicized, and highly sensational criminal trial. These adjectives, even though borrowed from court descriptions, hardly fit the case. The only thing sensational about the facts was the flair which Estes had for swindling his friends and neighbors. The Supreme Court agreed with the Estes lawyers, but a majority of the Court did not bar television from all courts as a matter of law. The ban, as it turned out, applied only to highly publicized cases where the defendant had not given his consent, but it took the community a long time to figure out the meaning of the several opinions of the justices. Justice Tom C. Clark wrote the opinion for the Court.

There is little moderation in Justice Clark's opinion or in the concurring opinion of Chief Justice Earl Warren. Even that beloved absolutist adherent to the First Amendment, William O. Douglas, voted against cameras, as did Justice Arthur J. Goldberg, a liberal most of the time.[18]

It was Justice John M. Harlan, at times a formidable opponent of extending the First Amendment, who cast the deciding vote, but he limited the ban on cameras to highly publicized, sensational cases. His reservation, debatable in meaning, took hold because views of the majority were mixed. Chief Justice Warren, whose feelings were strong, had written an opinion banning television forever under the Sixth and Fourteenth Amendments. When he failed to get the votes he needed, Justice Clark took up the task of writing a majority opinion. With hardly a citation to fact in it, but in indignation and fear, he found cameras a threat. His opinion was not factually proved, but awesomely conjectural. The chief justice did not rewrite his opinion to conform to the changed situation and it stands to witness his agitation. Even the members of the minority did not want to admit television immediately but only after photographers proved they would accept authority and work without distracting the court.

The fears arise because the culture of the camera and of the court conflict. Intrusion and distraction divert the attention of judge and jury from the defendant's case to the photographer. Even momentary distraction may keep the jury from hearing a critical word or phrase. A journalist who resists discipline can cause trouble for a court not only during a trial but when he carries his complaint to everyone in town.

Justice Clark described operation of cameras as probably prejudicial to a case. Telecasts seen by a juror may affect his vote and it is difficult to go home at night without watching television or reading a newspaper. The probable effect on witnesses is of major concern. Some of them, confronting a camera in court, may be embarrassed, or demoralized, by the unaccustomed role of television actor and witness. After their faces are telecast, they no longer are private persons and may be harassed by strangers who offer advice or make threats.

Supervision of photographers places a major extra burden on a trial judge, Justice Clark says. His personal sensibilities, his dignity, and his ability to concentrate on the business of the court, rather than on distractions of the press, are at stake. A defendant is "entitled to his day in court and should not be forced into a stadium for trial."[19] Television in court is foreign to our system. Without intending to, a television cameraman can destroy an accused and his case. Not all lawyers want to work under the presence of a television camera and thus, through distractionn or pressure, they may fail to protect their client.

Justice Stewart, in dissent, said he thought the media, under the protection of the First Amendment, could not be required to prove that cameras would not affect a case. He was unwilling to hold that the Constitution "absolutely bars television cameras from every criminal courtroom, even if they have no impact on a jury, no effect upon any witness, and no influence on the conduct of the judge.''[20]

The Florida rule clearly was inspired by Justice Stewart's opinion. With Justices Clark, Goldberg, Douglas, Harlan, and Chief Justice Warren gone, the Supreme Court approved the Florida plan for admission of cameras eight to zero in Chandler v. Florida.[21] The Court's opinion cleared the way for other states to admit cameras to court and it also prompted the ABA House of Delegates to repeal its ban on cameras even though only a short time ago it had rejected the same proposal by Judge Alfred T. Goodwin's Legal Advisory Committee on Fair Trial and Free Press.[22]

The Court observed that the Florida court grounded its rule in its supervisory powers, not in the First Amendment. The rule, therefore, had to be judged by the state's constitution, not by that of the United States. The burden of Chief Justice Warren's opposition, but not his anxiety, was at last lifted, but photographers still had to conciliate, every day, opponents in bar associations and judges of state courts. Chief Justice Burger, who wrote the Chandler opinion, did not retract his promise to keep cameras out of federal courts during his lifetime.

The facts of the Chandler case are run-of-the-mill: Policemen were caught using radio equipment to coordinate an act of common housebreaking. They were overheard by a ham radio operator and arrested. At their trial, television news showed interest only in the state's chief witness and in the closing arguments. The whole trial got less than three minutes of air time.

Dealing with the Chandler case, the Supreme Court went at once to limit the Estes opinion. There could be no lawful place for cameras unless it did so. This task was complicated by the fact that Justices White and Stewart, writing separately, said Estes laid down a per se rule that the mere presence of cameras in court violated a defendant's due process rights under the Fourteenth Amendment. They had dissented on that holding in Estes and now wanted the decision overruled. But Chief Justice Burger, for himself and five other judges (Justice Stevens took no part), said Estes turned on a much narrower point chosen by Justice Harlan for his concurring opinion. Burger said Harlan did not approve the per se rule. The decision meant only that Estes was deprived of his fundamental rights by a notorious, sensational, and widely publicized trial. In the circumstances, television news coverage was not itself unconstitutional but the way in which it was used deprived Estes of his due process rights.[23]

The Court said risk of juror prejudice is present in media handling of any trial, but the appropriate safeguard is that a defendant can show the coverage compromised the jury's ability to adjudicate fairly.

FLORIDA'S RULES FOR CAMERAS

Preparation for Trial

It was less than twelve years after the 1965 Estes decision that state courts began to experiment again with television and still cameras. Three years later the Supreme Court had approved their efforts. By this time cameras were quieter than in 1965, they were using videotape, and very high speed film was available if needed. Photographers often wanted more light than judges would permit, but the substitution of high-intensity bulbs in existing fixtures served well. The Florida policy led the way and has approval of the Supreme Court. For that reason it was of particular interest to other states developing their own procedures. The Zamora trial tested the Florida policy and the presiding judge, Paul Baker, took care to report fully to the state supreme court. Judge Baker said he appointed a coordinator to deal with the photographers on his behalf. This person had the assistance of attorneys for the *Miami News*, the *Miami Herald*, and WCKT-TV. All journalists were briefed so that they understood the rules of the supreme court and could comply with them. Judge Baker said attendance at the briefing should be mandatory.[24] The coordinator, although accepting Judge Baker's authority, was an executive of a television station. Instructions relayed through him were obeyed and Judge Baker commented that such assistance should be provided at all times.

The journalists were told at the outset that only one portable color camera would be in court and that all members of the camera pool would depend upon it. Photographers using one black and white and one color 35 mm still cameras were assigned seats in the courtroom. The National Press Photographers' standard, which calls for two television cameras, presumably could be accepted in other states.

The Florida rule specified by brand name the camera equipment admitted to court. This provision came about after trial and error. The shutter of one brand popular with the media clicked so loudly that it was banned in the original rules. A photographer at the Zamora trial who broke this rule was asked to leave the courtroom and the remaining still photographer used two cameras. Judge Baker said that, the state supreme court rules notwithstanding, the trial judge alone should determine the location of cameramen in the room.

Seating and storage space. Specific courtroom seating for journalists was allocated in order to stop the public from competing with them for seats. Radio broadcasters used the audio pickup on the pool television camera.[25] The operator of the television camera was instructed not to use his directional microphone to pick up conferences at the bench, between attorneys, or between lawyer and client; when conferences took place at the bench, the microphone had to be turned off.

One problem the court encountered on the first day of the trial was to clear away camera equipment in the courthouse corridors. This was done by assigning a room for storage of equipment. Acceptance of a pool arrangement obviously could not require sixty camera crews to leave their equipment at home. Also, because Judge Baker found that the visitors interfered with normal business by using courthouse telephones, he recommended that the media install their own telephone in assigned space.

Broadcast reporters and cameramen without equipment in court sat in the reserved area. There was no in-and-out movement during the proceedings. Yet because the presence of the cameras made unfettered dissemination of information possible, Judge Baker sequestered the jury at once. He asked the journalists to be discreet, as indicated by his restrictions on picking up attorney-client and bench conferences. The inherent powers of the court, interacting with the conscience of the media personnel, had to be relied upon to avoid conflicts.

Judge Baker said he could not accept electronic or photographic coverage of a sexual assault case or, for that matter, any case involving a child. He also would protect police undercover agents or informants and, in order to avoid conflict, he suggested that the media agree to such limitations in advance. The code of conduct imposed on lawyers and judges was the pattern he had in mind, he said.

Distractions avoided. The jurors in the case naturally wanted to see themselves on television but the sets were taken out of their hotel rooms. They asked for a set without sound but that also was denied. They did not have newspapers, magazines, or radio and were carefully supervised so they could not talk about the case before the deliberations began.

The court rules forbade taking pictures of the jury leaving or entering the courthouse or courtroom and were enforced against some of the foreign journalists present. The court wanted no cameras or lights, nor interviews, in the corridors, ruling that the courtroom arrangements had to suffice.

The court also required that the bulb in the ruby lamp of the television camera be removed. Justice Clark had criticized the "telltale red light" in the Estes opinion, and print media journalists who enjoyed the criticism helped publicize the objection.[26]

Justice Clark had said witnesses would watch televised trials and, in this way, violate the strict rule against listening to testimony in advance of their own appearance. But Judge Baker's response was that such witnesses are the same ones who, without television, would avidly read newspapers about the trial. "Compliance with the rule is a matter of integrity on the part of the witness and if he violates the court's instructions there are sufficient sanctions available to the trial judge to admonish him.[27] Regarding his own actions being televised, he explains, "The public has a right to know whether a judge is decisive or indecisive, attentive or inattentive, courteous or rude, whether or not he can maintain control over the trial proceedings and if he appears learned or confused. To this extent it makes little difference whether the judge is observed by spectators in the courtroom or by spectators viewing television."[28]

Judge Baker wants viewers to remember that, unless they see the whole of the trial, they lack insight into some of the issues. He also fears that some attorneys might play to the "theater audience" at the expense of their clients. This risk is real, he said, and the remedy is postconviction relief. "In addition, such conduct on the part of an attorney would be so deplorable as to merit disciplinary proceedings by the bar and the [state] Supreme Court." Any judge or attorney who solicits television coverage of a trial should be disciplined, he feels.[29]

The jurors were interviewed after the trial and explained to Judge Baker that the cameras distracted them but did not break their concentration. They were uneasy about the impact of the broadcast on the defendant and his family.

The Florida Supreme Court used rules for photographers comparable in form to those governing civil and criminal procedures. If the media accept the custom of rulemaking and participate in enforcement, as the cooperating trade associations recommend, they should ask for a journalist-coordinator between them and the trial judge to help smooth the way. The provision for a coordinator, however, takes money and the media must consider how it can be provided. If the position is not funded privately the job may be assigned to a court official. Acceptance of the standards may put cameras into court as a commonplace of the television age but the evidence indicates that much missionary work remains to be done.

EXPERIENCE IN OTHER COURTS

Florida judges presiding over televised trials included Judge Thomas E. Sholtz of Palm Beach County. His report to the state high court said "it is not only possible but highly probable [that television] will have a direct bearing on a juror's vote." The telecast forced him to sequester the jury, Sholtz said, and the media ought to absorb the expense.[30] The Florida Conference of Circuit Judges voted against extension of the television experiment, saying through the chairman that "the brief segments presented to the public did not warrant the continuous tension and recurring delays and disruptions." Yet a survey of court personnel, jurors, and judges in Florida showed 76.6 percent of the circuit judges felt that television caused no serious disruptions and 68.1 percent thought witnesses were not affected. Thirty-five percent of the jurors questioned found the cameras distracting.[31]

The Conference of State Chief Justices voted forty-four to one in 1978 in favor of admission of cameras under guidelines. The conference took an influential part in persuading the ABA to change its rule on photography.

ROLL CALL IN THE STATES

Twenty-eight states had permanent rules regulating photographers when the ABA House of Delegates voted approval of cameras on August 11, 1982. The rules approved by the ABA, and by the states following the ABA pattern, contain several restrictions on cameras, including requirements for notice and consent for the use of cameras. The rules bar cameras in certain types of judicial proceedings, notably with respect to selection of jurors, divorce, and child custody hearings.

An annual compilation of state regulations by Ernest J. Schultz, Jr., executive vice president of the Radio and Television News Directors Association, as interpreted by Lyle Denniston of the *Baltimore Sun*, shows that reservation and dissent continue to limit picture taking in state courts.[32] Both houses of the Maryland legislature, for example, voted to drop an experiment on the use of cameras which had been approved by the state's highest court.[33] Denniston's analysis shows that, as of the summer of 1982, at least thirteen of twenty-four states permitting cameras in criminal trials also permit a veto by participants. New York and eleven other states permit television coverage without establishing veto rights.

The Florida pattern thus has been adopted in only ten other states: California, Iowa, Kentucky, Massachusetts, Montana, Nevada, New Hampshire, New Jersey, Ohio, and West Virginia. Utah permits still camera use only. Sixteen states permit no television coverage in criminal trial courts at all. Restrictions persist as well in civil courts.

The chief complaint voiced is that cameras in court make no effort to tell a complete trial story and thus distort the cases presented.

Beyond Fair Trial, Hope   7

JOURNALISTS AND JUDGES AS UNEQUALS

The Basis of Confusion

In summary we realize that a well-rounded fair trial policy has been accepted by the courts and is in use.[1] The area of fair trial litigation is much reduced by court decisions and the media have less productive opportunity to raise objections to procedure. The issue, however, is based on emotions as much as on reason and more cases are likely.

The winding down of conflict could be an end or a beginning of improved relationships between the media and the courts. In this concluding chapter the material is chosen to emphasize the opportunities of the journalist and to advance the thesis that there is significant hope for new beginnings.

Dogged pursuit of victory in the fair trial cases demonstrates the fortitude, even stubbornness, of media leaders. However, these leaders also are either realists or masochists because they customarily seek out the bad news of their own standing with the public as one means of preparing themselves to do a better job. In a national study done especially for them, George Gallup, Jr., said people told him "newspapers sometimes publish information that is not in the best interests of the nation and should be kept confidential."[2] Gallup also reported that the public thinks journalists "distort and exaggerate the news in the interest of making headlines and selling newspapers, and rush into print without first making sure all facts are correct." President Reagan, as we shall see, has similar opinions.

The assertions reported by Gallup, in a manner of speaking, are all true. The public demands that the news be interesting as well as important. But perception is selective and value lies in the eye of the beholder. It is just as true to say of the courts that they deny petitions of right, that they keep people in crowded jails for trial, and that they send persons to ignoble conditions in prison. Such truth is relative and misleading. Both the courts and the press work with trained personnel who operate under well-tested and proved conditions. The news unfolds from day to day and journalists, in reporting it, expect readers to do their part by following it carefully in order to get the whole story. In Gallup's context, if there is fault in the media and in the courts, it is partly due to incomplete perception by readers and viewers. They may even be misled on occasion by persons who stand to gain by criticizing the media or the courts.

Gallup says the worst news uncovered in his survey is that the people are "increasingly indifferent—and to some extent hostile—to the cause of a free press in America." They lean "2 to 1 to the view that present curbs on the press are 'not strict enough' rather than 'too strict.' " Gallup's study calls for "(1) greater efforts to give journalists and others on the media a renewed sense of the need for professional standards, and (2) raising the level of consciousness of the American public regarding their basic freedoms."

The American Bar Association made several important gestures to the media, in an institutional sense, after it began to study and write the standards in 1966. The first, symbolized by the invitation to leaders to present their arguments formally at the 1967 ABA convention in Hawaii, was to recognize the media as an institution organized with a representative leadership qualified to bargain for the whole. The record of contacts over the years shows that law and journalism met in good order on their differences and that constructive negotiation resulted. But the two parties were not equal. The ABA talked to the judicial establishment, where the power lies, and got its program accepted. The press took its arguments to the legislatures and to the public, but Gallup's survey indicates that a lack of credibility affected the public's reception of the message.

Court Discipline, Media Style

Meaning arises on at least two levels from the cases in which the media have been pitted against the courts. The first level, obviously, has to do with issues of trial: who wins, who loses, and why. On the second level are the establishments representing journalism and the courts. One is a loose confederation of volunteers working on topics outside their expertise; the other, a diversified, professional association that appears willing to accept limited objectives and is patient enough to wait out delays. The ABA has used its bureaucratic structure, the experience of federal and state judges, and resources of the federal and state legal departments to sequester information and keep the media from getting and using some sensitive news of crime.

The courts, through their rulemaking powers, defined the objectives, tested the rules, and parceled out constitutional rights between the press, the courts, and the criminal case litigants. Even when Congress and legislatures used statutory powers to intervene, the courts shaped the result so that it conformed reasonably well to their needs. If the court system had been monolithic, if there had been no publicity, if a single idea had characterized planning and action, the nation would be an autocracy and the free press would be extinct. But a judicial act, which is an exercise of discretion or judgment, differs from the work of writing and editing news mainly in that the principles upon which judgment is based have been developed as a discipline of language and form over long periods of time. The principles of news editing may be the same in Erie and Peoria but, if so, it is by chance or choice rather than from discipline.

Because there is ample room for individual choice, editors say they are free. Because the exercise of legal form and judgment leaves room for discretion, the country has political freedom—the chance to select or reject values entering into law and the common mind. The judicial system, as noted, took fifteen years to determine the limits of key portions of the ABA standards of fair trial and free press. An autocratic system would not have discussed standards for the press outside of courtrooms, and journalists would have been there as defendants, not as persons of recognized interest.

Justice Brennan's Analysis

The dispute between the media and the courts has been over methods of operations, or functions. The courts wish to try cases according to their own sense of what is proper. They add great weight to their fair trial rules by assigning them to the Sixth Amendment. The media desire freedom to pursue information and to print it as news without restraint. In order to persuade the community to support them, they make claims under the First Amendment. Since, in contrast to the courts, they are undisciplined, they come to believe, quite unconsciously, that more and more of their functional activities are protected by the authority of the First Amendment.

Shortly before the First Amendment Congress in 1980, Justice William J. Brennan helped dedicate a new Law Center at Rutgers University which was built by a gift from the late Samuel I. Newhouse, the publisher and broadcaster.[3] Justice Brennan's audience represented the professional community but his words were meant for journalists in New York City, Erie, Peoria, and elsewhere in the country. He sought particularly to explain to them that all the functional conveniences desired by the press are not guaranteed by the First Amendment.

Six months previously, the Court had decided that journalists defending libel suits had to explain their state of mind at the time they produced the article or broadcast in litigation. That is, they had to explain in court, under cross-examination, their thoughts and acts while producing the story on which the lawsuit was based. The basic libel law is contained in New York Times v. Sullivan, an opinion which Justice Brennan wrote for the Court. Journalists say they like it because it keeps public office holders and public persons from collecting damages unless the journalist can be shown to have produced a story that he knew to be false or had put together so carelessly and recklessly that he clearly did not care whether it was false or not. When a CBS News producer was ordered by the Supreme Court to explain to a libel plaintiff how and why he designed a film story used in "60 Minutes," the media had objected stridently, or as Justice Brennan put it in his Rutgers address, "with particular bitterness."

Why? It was because the journalists were confused by the Court's frame of reference. They were reacting as if their basic free press rights were under attack. Not so, said Justice Brennan. No interference with freedom of the press was involved. Reporters were simply being asked, as other citizens are, to answer questions considered routine by the courts. The newsgathering process is protected by the First Amendment, of course, but in this litigation the society's interest in enforcing the law must be balanced against a journalist's right to "perform a protected function," that is, to publish, to broadcast.

"This inquiry is impersonal, almost sociological in nature," Justice Brennan explained at the Newhouse Center. But it does not fit comfortably with the absolute rhetoric associated with the model of the individual speaker. The right of the press to gather and publish infor-

mation is not being abridged. "If a journalist knew that he was publishing defamatory falsehood, however, the First Amendment would
offer him no protection," Justice Brennan explained.

Apparently without journalists being aware of it, their outcry was an
effort to stop the libel plaintiff from applying to them the rules of
discovery, "one of the most common procedures in the law."[4] "It
would scarcely be fair to say that a plaintiff can only recover if he
established intentional falsehood [on the part of the media] and at the
same time to say that he cannot inquire into [the journalist's] inten-
tions," said Justice Brennan. He added that "In my view reporters will
not cease to publish because they are later asked about their state of
mind."[5]

Justice Brennan's comment on the indignant criticism—"unjustified
violence" he termed it—names some great newspapers: *Washington
Post, Birmingham News, Portland Oregonian, St. Louis Post-Dispatch,
New Orleans Times-Picayune, Atlanta Constitution, Miami Herald, Los
Angeles Times, New York Times.* He also named important journalists:
Marquis Childs; Tom Wicker; William Leonard of CBS News; and Jack
Landau, director of the Reporter's Committee for Freedom of the Press.
The mistakes in press comment were not for want of wit; the response
of journalists to other important case decisions showed they are intel-
ligent and perceptive. Justice Brennan, who had made an outstanding
intellectual contribution to the First Amendment, now pleaded with
journalists—partners of the Court, he termed them—to turn off their
scorn and to turn on their reason.

Growth of the First Amendment

Perhaps Justice Brennan's comment points the way toward an improved relationship, but the First Amendment ideas with which the
journalists wanted to hide their thoughts from libel plaintiffs are indeed
powerful—even if misunderstood once in a while. Since the Near v.
Minnesota decision in 1931, the First Amendment, in the hands of the
Court, has been a growing and liberating force in our society. The
recorded courtroom events have mentioned the First Amendment many
times and, in so doing, have contributed to that growth. A defeat for
the media in one case can be turned into victory tomorrow if energy,
money, and scholarship are made available for that purpose. Moreover,
the ideas established so far are a powerful source of inspiration and

motivation for both journalists and lawyers who want to advance political freedom.

Justice Oliver Wendell Holmes, Jr., helped set the contemporary standard by which controversial political speech is liberated and encouraged. He said, "The question in every case is whether the words used [by speakers] are used in such circumstances and are of such a nature as to create a clear and present danger that they will bring about the substantive evils that Congress has a right to prevent. It is a question of proximity and degree."[6] The framework for judging speakers regarded by some persons as politically dangerous was stated in 1919.

When President Nixon was struggling to keep the Watergate conspiracy from breaking into the open he had reason to resent the way news and comment added to his difficulties. He told the country in a radio address on March 9, 1974, that a federal libel law was needed. There had been no such law since Jefferson's election to the presidency. The private reputations of public men must be saved from press abuse, President Nixon said. Otherwise, competent persons will not run for office and serve their government. He and his advisers had approved a draft statute, he explained, that would redefine the terms "public figure" and "public man" in New York Times Co. v. Sullivan,[7] that is, in effect, impose on the media strict liability for error. If the stories about Watergate constituted a danger to the nation, the reasoning of Justice Holmes and the Court was available for deciding whether censorship was available to help President Nixon with his political problems. But the President did not want a free speech confrontation. Instead, he wanted a federal libel law which could be used legally for purposes of political harassment. The country he sought to save was his own administration.

Similar perturbations arise every time a powerful person is frustrated by events. President Reagan, in his time, confessed his aggravation with the media more than once. When he tried to implement a controversial military and political policy in El Salvador, and the press reported conflicting and contradictory information, he complained that his ideas were wrongly portrayed in terms of a "Vietnam syndrome." He wished, he said, that reporters would "trust us and put themselves in our hands." He continued, "I could say to the press, 'Look, I will trust you by telling you what we're trying to accomplish. If you use that story, it will result in harm to our nation, and probably make it impossible to do what we're trying to do.' " Then he added, sadly, "But they just go with the story." In rebuttal, a television network officer said his job was to give "extensive attention to all sides."[8]

In this day of the no-party, no quarter-press, no leader—Nixon, Carter, Reagan, or anyone else—can expect a sympathetic bias to the flow of news, even when staying in office seems to require it. What is more, the development of the First Amendment means that the states cannot do the work of coercing the press either. Justice Edward T. Sanford, appointed by that frustrated son of Ohio politics, Warren G. Harding, wrote for the Court in 1925 that the fundamental personal rights and liberties protected by the First Amendment are also to be enforced against the states by the due process clause of the Fourteenth Amendment.[9]

Inspiration by Justice Brandeis. If journalists and lawyers need further inspiration to continue the work of building fundamental rights and liberties they can find it in a 1927 opinion of the Court and in a concurring opinion by Justice Louis D. Brandeis which ranks as great First Amendment literature:

Those who won our independence believed that the final end of the state was to make men free to develop their faculties, and that in its government the deliberative forces should prevail over the arbitrary. They valued liberty both as an end and as a means. They believed liberty to be the secret of happiness and courage to be the secret of liberty. They believed that freedom to think as you will and to speak as you think are means indispensable to the discovery and spread of political truth; that without free speech and assembly discussion would be futile; that with them, discussion affords ordinarily adequate protection against the dissemination of noxious doctrine; that the greatest menace to freedom is an inert people; that political discussion is a political duty; and that this should be a fundamental principle of the American government. They recognized the risks to which all human institutions are subject. But they knew that order cannot be secured merely through fear of punishment for its infractions; that it is hazardous to discourage thought, hope and imagination; that fear breeds repression; that repression breeds hate; that hate menaces stable government; that the path of safety lies in the opportunity to discuss freely supposed grievances and proposed remedies; and that the fitting remedy for evil counsels is good ones. . . . If there be time to expose through discussion the falsehoods and fallacies, to avert the evil by the processes of education, the remedy to be applied is more speech, not enforced silence.[10]

Forty-two years later, in 1969, a troubled and divided Court extended the benefits of Justice Brandeis's thought to high school students: "It can hardly be argued that either students or teachers shed their constitutional rights to freedom of speech or expression at the schoolhouse gate,'' Justice Abe Fortas wrote. Justice Black on that occasion could not agree, but in spite of his doubts the First Amendment kept on growing.

Limited government. Perhaps Justice Brennan gave new strength to the Brandeis thesis when, during the days of Martin Luther King, Alabama officials tried to chase the *New York Times* out of the state with what amounted to a suit for criminal libel: ''[There is] a profound national commitment to the principle that debate on public issues should be uninhibited, robust and wide open, and that it may well include vehement, caustic and sometimes unpleasantly sharp attacks on government and public officials.''

Brennan's thought gains force from a subsequent case, a unanimous opinion of the Court written by Chief Justice Burger in 1974: ''The choice of material to go into a newspaper, and the decisions made as to limitations on the size of the paper, and content, and treatment of public issues and public officials—whether fair or unfair—constitutes the exercise of editorial control and judgment. It has yet to be demonstrated how governmental regulation of this crucial process can be exercised consistent with the First Amendment guarantees of a free press as they have evolved to this time.''[11]

First Amendment limits. As the First Amendment kept on growing the individual speaker became more and more dependent upon the mass media to carry thoughts and to stir dialogue. The cases on First Amendment guarantees, therefore, shifted to institutions and less attention was given to individual episodes. Institutions are supplanting individuals in the social process and more and more are demanding the civil rights conceived of originally for the protection and development of individual persons alone. This is the kind of switch from the ''speech model'' to the ''structural model'' developed by Justice Brennan at the Newhouse Center. He was referring in part to Branzburg v. Hayes, a case seven years earlier, which denied to journalists the testimonial immunity they dearly wanted. What the Court majority meant, according to Justice Brennan, was that the First Amendment assures the individual's right to speak but it does not guarantee secrecy either to one who confides in a journalist or a right to testimonial silence to the journalist. Protection against self-incrimination, if it comes to that, is a matter for the Fifth Amendment, not the First. Only Justice Douglas, on that occasion, thought a journalist should be immune to questioning in his newsgathering role under either.[12]

The limits of privilege. The Branzburg decision limited the high drive of investigative reporting, a drive which inevitably challenges persons and institutions of power great enough to checkmate the press. The solid investigative idealism conflicts both with the state prosecution function and the need of defendants. Journalist and prosecutor want the same information but must meet quite different standards to use it. Journalism's need is to protect against libel and loss of news sources. The prosecution and defense need to satisfy due process and to persuade a jury; both are supervised by the court. The journalist answers mainly to his coworkers and readers, if to anyone. This fact makes journalists outsiders in dealing with the Court because, unlike members of the bar, they have no professional system of responsibility to handle charges against individual journalists for unethical conduct—using the privilege to hide a criminal or criminal conduct, for example. The need for professional organization to stand between individuals and the court is illustrated by the case of Earl Caldwell joined in Branzburg. Caldwell, as earlier mentioned, was the *New York Times* reporter who had built up a working relationship with the Black Panthers, particularly in California, and was writing about their program and policies for his newspaper. The relationship was ended by a subpoena to testify to a grand jury about rumored criminal activities of the Panthers. Caldwell believed it would destroy the confidence of the Black Panthers in him if he testified in secret outside of their hearing. Therefore, he presented the Court with a question he felt to be of First Amendment quality: Which is most important to the community, to have continuing news access to an important dissident group that, otherwise, would remain hated and outcast, or to force Caldwell to end the relationship and answer the grand jury's questions?

The grand jury and the prosecutor asserted that the constitutional question arose in the Sixth Amendment where availability of evidence is more important. Dissenting justices tried to save the information-gathering priority by suggesting limits to be used by the courts in administering the claimed privilege, but important leaders in journalism treated this proposal as abridgement of the First Amendment. They wanted an absolute privilege and were willing to accept no substitute. Two other dissenters spoke through Justice Stewart, who argued, as the Court had done previously, that the press has been a "mighty catalyst in awakening public interest in governmental affairs, exposing corruption among public officers and employees and generally informing the citizenry of public events and occurrences." He continued "there is obviously a continuing need for an independent press to disseminate a robust variety of information and opinion through reportage, investigation and criticism, if we are to preserve our constitutional tradition of maximizing freedom of choice by encouraging diversity of expression.[13]

The dissenters argued that a right to gather news implies the necessity of a confidential relationship between a reporter and his sources. "The uncertainty arises," they said, because the judiciary has traditionally given the grand jury its head. In a showdown with the press, the grand jury is likely to win, but as the price of forced testimony Stewart wanted the grand jury to demonstrate convincingly that questions to Caldwell are substantially related to the information sought and that "an overriding and compelling state interest is at stake." The government should be required to show that Caldwell had information clearly relevant to a specific probable violation of law which cannot be obtained by alternate means less destructive of First Amendment rights.[14]

It must be made clear that some journalists are uneasy about the demand for absolute privilege. David S. Broder, one of the leaders in the Washington press corps, said, "There is a further problem when we rely on the press as a public grand jury. And that is that the power of the press undisciplined by professional standards can also be made subject to great abuse."[15]

Efforts at Reconciliation

These developments have been summarized not only for their focus on the question of responsibility but to ask what journalists can do with them in educational terms to win rules more advantageous to newsgathering. Several methods have been attempted, such as federal legislation; state shield laws; bar, bench, and press councils; and moral issue seminars designed to focus on the consequences of traditional newsroom practice. State shield laws and proposed federal legislation alike conflict with individual responsibility by taking it out of consideration even to the extent proposed by Justice Stewart and his codissenters in the Branzburg decision. The cutting line there is that when a court has made every reasonable effort to favor the information-gathering function, and a defendant's liberty or life hangs on the reporter's testimony, the privilege can give way to the extent necessary to provide fair trial. Journalists can keep Justice Stewart's recommendations alive by bringing them forward as alternatives when news and testimonial privilege conflicts arise. The conditions represent a revision of the absolutist objective, but a more reasonable position is needed. The original definitions of freedom of press in state constitutions clearly associated freedom and responsibility.[16] In fact, responsibility as a joint tenant with freedom survives to this day. The present preference for freedom dates from the Near v. Minnesota opinion in 1931. Journalists who reify their business to the status of absolute power and absolute truth invite incredulity in the political community. There is danger that some future Court will rewrite Near v. Minnesota and other preferences for freedom in First Amendment law. At present the Court position is that the state, not the speaker, should be restrained.

Councils deserved support. As to the bar, bench, and press councils, these experimental dialogue builders and stress management centers deserved more support than they got. One of the reasons may have been the decision to close the proceedings of these councils to publicity. This decision not only deprived them of power but of public support. But the twin afflictions of tension and apathy attend efforts of this kind. The council members who are willing to consult and to take special trial circumstances into consideration have to maintain control. They also have to maintain a high level of energy and concern to keep a council from becoming moribund. The councils were set up originally to reinforce areas where legal controls were inadequate. ABA standards provided that the courts would take over council functions as soon as the rules could be made effective. At the same time rule changes designed to acknowledge journalists as parties at interest in the formal information-control process developed. The ability of journalists to argue against closure and sealing orders on a timely basis made the councils less important. When the Supreme Court approved closure of pretrial hearings the councils, some of which had arbitrated this kind of dispute, lost their most valuable function. Now the discussion is confined to legal justification for closing, a matter for lawyers, not journalists, to handle.

Using the council situation in Washington state as an example, trial judges after Gannett v. DePasquale had to work without an effective council. They quickly dropped the cooperative attitude of 1971, when the council, not the court, was expected to deal with conflicts. In the major pre-Gannett case, the Washington state supreme court did its part as one of the council sponsors by keeping judges in line while telling the media to respect the trial guidelines or suffer restraint.[17] After Gannett, because a newspaper published a controversial ballistics report in advance of a suppression hearing, the court excluded the press and public.[18] In hearing arguments for closure, the trial court asked the accused person to make some showing that a fair trial was in jeopardy, as Justice Lewis Powell had suggested, but when the newspaper proposed alternatives to closing, the court put the burden on the paper to show that its proposals would result in a fair trial. The newspaper, under the voluntary guidelines, had the option of using the council or of publishing ballistics evidence and taking the consequences. The consequences were the closing of the hearing and an expensive and unproductive lawsuit.

Even the dissenting opinion had the flavor of bitterness: Let the court step out from between the accused and the newspaper, Justice James M. Dolliver argued, taking his idea from Justice Hans Linde of the Oregon Supreme Court. In his view, the defendant has no right to expect the trial court to close the hearing and the state supreme court, as far as he could see, lacked constitutional powers to do so. With the court to one side, the resulting publicity, if it violates the accused's rights, can be the subject of an appeal to the community. The public has the power to amend the constitution. Perhaps the prospect of having the public pass judgment on press behavior will persuade the newspaper to let pretrial hearings proceed in the open without publicity that endangers fair trial.[19]

The next flareup in Washington state was even worse because the trial court treated the voluntary bar, bench, and press guidelines as established policy and excluded journalists from a pretrial hearing who would not promise to abide by them.[20] When the voluntary guidelines were restated as orders of the court in Nebraska,[21] some journalists abandoned support of them. Now a Washington judge was ordering the court closed to dissenters to the guidelines and open only to those who had "seen the light." The word "voluntary" had disappeared. What is more, this court seemingly treated the hearing as "open" and, according to the high court, took inadequate steps to justify the motion for closure. Federated Publications, the journalists' employer, argued that the partial closure and exclusion of its reporters amounted to prior censorship. But what writing was suppressed, the high court majority asked? "As we view this measure," the state supreme court said, "it was a good faith attempt to accommodate the interests of both defendant and the press which, hopefully, would prove both practical and effective as an alternative to closure." The trial court issued no orders prohibiting publication and it did not threaten sanctions if the reporters attending the hearing violated the guidelines.

The judge who dissented at length in the previous case, Justice Dolliver, dissented again. He said the condition imposed on attendance at the hearing was prior restraint. "Before prior restraint can be invoked by a court, there is, as the majority correctly notes, a heavy burden on the trial court of showing justification for the restraint. . . . [T]here is no factual basis for the trial judge's ruling." The United States Supreme Court declined to rule on the exclusion of the nonsigners but another state decision, this one unanimous, may have modified or overruled the second decision. In the third case the trial judge closed not only the pretrial hearing but also the argument on the motion to close; then he sealed the record for the duration of the trial and, he said, perhaps permanently. The state supreme court, through Chief Justice Robert F. Brachtenbach, held that the judge was in error in closing the hearing without determining, on the record, the likelihood of jeopardy to the defendant's fair trial and without showing a serious and imminent threat to the "other interests." The other interests, it was hinted, had to do with the possibility that a witness in the closed hearing was in danger in some unexplained way. The supreme court said perhaps closure of the hearing and sealing of the record was justified, but the trial court would have to put the reasons in the public record.[22] The bench, bar, and press council had no opportunity to conciliate the cases in advance and the council's machinery apparently is not now being used. Perhaps the council will be reorganized.

The Socratic dialogues. The third effort at promotion of court and press understanding, the ethical dialogues, as explained, was in substantial part a project of the Ford Foundation. In the short run, these seminars helped by bringing the parties together to consider philosophical and moral conflicts implicit in assumptions about the work processes, mostly, it seems, of journalism. The seminars had to be open at both ends, like a wind tunnel, and unless an individual was shaken up by the turbulence no ethical changes took place. If the seminars could have been linked to bench, bar, and press councils, the changes generated by dialogue might have had effect in the work of the councils. However, the desire of some journalists to be absolutely free caused them to reject councils and other cooperative ventures. One of the consequences of the restructuring of media into chains and large associated companies is that management is able to improve commercial efficiency through interoffice communication. If central management were to reduce abrasive relations with the courts in favor of council-type cooperation, the process of learning about due process in criminal law might improve.

First Amendment rights of lawyers. Since some trial lawyers desire more freedom under the First Amendment, in order to communicate with the public and with the bar on behalf of clients, an opportunity for an informal alliance with journalists exists which would benefit both parties. The nature of this opportunity has been set out in summaries of Chicago Council of Lawyers v. Bauer, Hirschkop v. Snead, and other cases. In its efforts to improve legal practice, the bar has promulgated canons of professional responsibility which are administered, usually, by committees or boards which report serious violations to the court. In addition, the trial lawyer is made subject to rules of court administered by trial judges. The relationship to the trial court is either cozy or tight, depending upon one's interpretation, but the eloquent argument of Judge Luther M. Swygert for the Seventh Circuit Court— even though the U.S. Judicial Council chose to reject it—is a plea for the liberty of lawyers which journalists can share and understand. Judge Swygert argued that extra judicial comment by counsel should be evaluated by a test of serious and imminent danger to the fairness of trial. The Judicial Council opted for a test which in Judge Swygert's view is vague and overbroad. Yet that may be the reason why the Judicial Council likes it, for the nature of the test puts an attorney at serious disadvantage and increases his degree of hazard if he speaks for a client, no matter how discreetly, outside of judicial channels. The choice of test, or yardstick, with respect to the effect of speech, as Justice Black and the Court demonstrated in limiting liability for constructive contempt of court, is decisive. Use of the serious and imminent danger test, in any of its forms, puts the burden on the complainant to show specific serious and imminent probable consequences of speech protected by the First Amendment. Judge Swygert's analysis,[23] and its criticism by the Fourth Circuit Court,[24] show that judges, like politicians, struggle to establish a particular point of view. The selection of

Judicial Council committee members, and particularly the chair, has visible influence on the direction chosen in deciding such policy matters. Trial lawyers have less freedom than journalists to keep the political issue alive. Journalists should recognize this and accept a special responsibility to support the lawyers who work to maintain elbow room and a reasonable opportunity to explain their clients to the public. Lawyers need professional freedom in order to be effective in influencing administration of the law. But journalists need a more serious and informed insight into basic judicial politics than they demonstrate now. If the First Amendment is to continue its healthy growth in the future, a cadre of lawyers with journalistic understanding (or journalists trained and qualified to practice law) must be available to develop choices such as the one discussed. The First Amendment was developed by lawyers and judges, not by journalists, and the most likely way it will continue to grow is from inside the legal profession. The self-interest of journalists, demonstrated in their trade hyperbole applied to the First Amendment, a document conceived with all the people in mind, makes it imperative that they rely on others to plead their case in court. There are a number of strong judges like Luther M. Swygert and Alfred T. Goodwin of the Ninth Circuit, who, as an ABA committee chairman, took some of the restrictive spirit out of the Standards of Fair Trial and Free Press in 1978. Goodwin's attitude in 1978 was apparent in his work in 1965-1966. His usefulness to the American Bar Association in this matter came about because the general opinion in the association turned more to the Goodwin point of view than away from it. Obviously, the ABA demonstrated its resilience and responsiveness by making the revisions possible.

Opportunities for publicity. The opportunity to influence some fair trial rules is lost for the time being but journalists could well spend more effort learning from the judicial friends of open courts and less trying for absolute victories. So much is awry in the court system that could be helped by the press through perceptive study and constructive publicity. Only the barest summary has been put together in this book, but clearly the public needs a more realistic understanding of the court system. Intense differences exist over degrees of openness for pretrial hearings; yet the trial system is so structured that plea bargaining, in deep secrecy, handles the great bulk of criminal cases. What community treats the election or appointment of its prosecutors with the realization that, when they get into office, they will perform a task of this magnitude? Why do judges, who handle only a relative handful of the cases, outrank prosecutors in prestige? Should the community discuss the negotiated plea system as a matter of public policy?

Journalists tend to give the weight of publicity to the rare and unusual case. The pursuit of an occasional unethical judge is, of course, a matter of importance, but pursuit of changes in a cumbersome and inefficient judicial system seems to be left to legislators, who have far less time and fewer facilities for it than journalists, and to the judges, whose limited legislative powers are wholly inadequate to the task. Journalism's priceless, indispensable contribution to the community is to promote justice, fair trial for everyone—not just for the affluent—and to preserve institutions that protect and serve individual liberties. Political activity to that end is the true conservator of the First Amendment. How many publishers and broadcasters rank this value high when making their editorial decisions at election time?

Journalism's Absolutists

How has the professional character of the press developed in its interaction with the ABA? Have its attitudes toward professional values and even toward professional structure changed in a significant way?

Journalists have undoubtedly drawn closer together. The most important change, perhaps, is extensive recruitment and use of counsel to represent the media in dealing with the courts and the ABA on a day-to-day basis. The media now have widespread representation for the first time in courts, bar associations, and councils. There has been extended interaction between the press and bar in meetings. Important organizations, notably the American Society of Newspaper Editors, have cleansed official communication of the words of hatred, distrust, and fear which still characterize the patois of some journalists with respect to troubles with the bar and bench. Not only is there less paranoia on both sides but more genuine respect and cooperation.

This new relationship with the bar, if journalism chooses to see itself as a mature institution with constitutional standing—no more and no less—can develop beyond rivalry to an identity of constitutional interests. The American Bar Association is a quasi-democratic, professional assembly which is open alike to qualified practitioners specializing in journalism and in other branches of law. It is an institution for professional association, mutual education, research, discussion, and joint action. It abounds in diversity of views and in groups to espouse some of these views.

It is necessary for journalism to have its idealists. Only from such a breed can inspiration and new work arise. The idealists, when well-prepared and informed, provide a marvelous energy and drive which keep the media worthy of a place in the Constitution. At the same time, journalists now have everything required for professional status except a willingness to accept public responsibility for professional standards. They have demonstrated respect for the principles of fair trial, within the limits shown, and their work is seldom irresponsible. Their failure to have coherent organization is knowing and deliberate. They do not wish to take on the burden of professional self-government, even though it is clear that the society grants absolute freedom to no individual and no institution. The way to maximize freedom, as journalists well know, is to organize for its development and protection. But the ideal of journalism, as yet, is not freedom under law but freedom.

The space between freedom under law and freedom, while shifting and illusory, appears to the journalist to be the creative living space of his craft or profession. Every time journalists get less than they ask for from the courts, a cry goes up that freedom of the press is being taken away. The loss the journalist feels is in the living space between law and his dream of absolute freedom. In reality, it sometimes takes years, as in the complex Sheppard fair trial decision, for reliable conclusions to be drawn on the impact of the case. Yet journalism's cry of pain is instantaneous and short-lived.

The coercion of self-government is as objectionable to journalists as any other kind. This position, while described as one of freedom, is also one of irresponsibility. It means that the values of individual journeymen, not those of the community, apply in the reserved areas.

In addition to ideological objection, there are two practical obstacles to professional organization. First, the owners have to put up the money. They have shown interest in improved hired help but almost no interest in professional organization. Second, journalism's idealists have more tactical room to take action through their loose confederation than they would have with a formal structure. In recent years, some editors have been increasingly activist—in the same sense that the Warren Court was activist—seeking not only to report events but to influence their outcomes. They say that intuition, rather than formal reason, must guide them in a complex and fast-breaking news situation. To subject action in this framework to the second-guessing of a professional committee is to inhibit if not to frustrate investigative reporting.

The task of developing an institutional position, of teaching it to others, and of persuading them to respect it, is regarded as too burdensome. Yet this is the heart of professional obligation and function. Without accepting this obligation, no profession can have the tools of destiny in its own hands.

Freedom, in order to be expressed in law and protected according to law, must be defined. If it never gets beyond the emotional level it cannot take the form of statute and constitutional decision. It can have neither positive nor negative enforcement in court. Individuals who cannot codify their needs may be doomed to feel frustrated rather than to write constitutions. The journalist, nevertheless, senses that the act of defining freedom means limiting it and that impels him to stick with emotion and to avoid codes.

The outlook is that, as far as reporting of crime news is concerned, the Supreme Court will set the standards, as it has done since 1966, not the professional press. This is not necessarily undesirable but it does confine journalism to an underdog role in determining its own freedom. The Court has demonstrated from time to time that it understands the need for free communication and, up to a point, supports it. Acceptance of the Court's role enables us to see the future: In Judge Medina's phrase, journalists must continue to fight like tigers for their point of view. Let us hope the fight can be carried on with understanding and appreciation of law as well as of journalistic idealism.

The Court protected its own existence when Chief Justice Marshall asserted the primacy of the Constitution and the logic of judicial review of legislative action. A Court strong enough to construe acts of Congress is not weak enough to fall to the power of the press. The Court has been a strong protector; it could prove to be even stronger if the press and the people give it a bit more help.

Notes

CHAPTER 1: INTRODUCTION

1. American Bar Association Project on Minimum Standards for Criminal Justice, *Fair Trial and Free Press—Tentative Draft of Standards* (New York: Office of Criminal Justice Project, Institute of Judicial Administration, 1966). This is cited as the Reardon Report. The draft approved by the ABA House of Delegates is dated 1968. The committee is ongoing and has had several chairmen whose names are associated with revisions subsequent to Justice Reardon's term. The standards quoted here, unless otherwise indicated, come from the text as revised by the committee under Judge Alfred T. Goodwin, dated 1978. The draft approved by ABA in 1979 deleted Standard 8-3.6(a) with respect to cameras in the courtroom but this action was reversed August 11, 1982. The committee's title was changed in 1980 to the Adjunct Committee on Fair Trial and Free Press of the Standing Committee on Association Communication. The standards are Chapter 8 of the *Standards for Criminal Justice* (Boston: Little, Brown, 1980).

2. *New York Times*, February 3, 1980, p. 1. See also Nick Kotz, "ABSCAM'S Loose Cannons," *New Republic*, March 29, 1980, p. 21.

3. U.S. Attorney Peter Vaira of the Eastern District of Pennsylvania was reprimanded for talking to Jan Schaffer of the *Philadelphia Inquirer*. "Abscam Agents and Attorneys are Disciplined," *News Media & the Law*, June-July 1981, p. 17. Schaffer was cited for contempt when, on advice of counsel, she declined to testify, but was released without going to jail. "U.S. Judge Lifts Contempt Order in Schaffer Case," ibid.

4. Edward L. Barrett, Jr., "Criminal Justice: The Problems of Mass Production," in *The Courts, the Public and the Law Explosion*, ed. Harry W. Jones (Englewood Clitfs, N.J.: Prentice-Hall, 1965), pp. 109-12.

5. Hubert L. Will, "Free Press v. Fair Trial," *De Paul L. R.*, Spring-Summer 1963, pp. 197-98.

6. J. Skelly Wright, "Fair Trial-Free Press," Federal Rules Decisions 38:435 (1966). Federal Rules Decisions is hereafter cited as F.R.D.

7. See "Save the FOI Act," *News Media & the Law*, June-July 1981, p. 3; "Opposition Derails Model State FOI Act," ibid., p. 5. Generally, as reflecting the substance of these paragraphs in the text, see any edition of this publication, which is produced primarily for journalists.

8. James Bryce, "United States: Constitution and Government," *Encyclopaedia Britannica*, 11th ed., vol. 27 (1910-11), pp. 646-61, 649.

9. Arthur T. Vanderbilt, *Men and Measures in the Law* (New York: Alfred A. Knopf, 1949), p. 115; Klopfer v. North Carolina, 386 U.S. 213 (1967).

10. John W. Poulos and Jerry P. Coleman, "Speedy Trial, Slow Implementation: The ABA Standard in Search of a Statehouse," *Hastings L.J.* 38:357 (November 1976).

11. The President's Commission on Law Enforcement and Administration of Justice, *The Challenge of Crime in a Free Society* (Washington, D.C.: U.S. Government Printing Office, 1967), p. 14.

12. *ABA Journal* 62:1455 (November 1976).

13. Caleb Foote, professor of law and criminology, University of California, Berkeley, in *Minneapolis Star*, November 21, 1977, p. 9A.

14. For general background, see Andrew M. Schatz, "Gagging the Press in Criminal Trials," *Harvard Civil Rights-Civil Liberties L.R.* 10:608 (1975); Wright, "Fair Trial-Free Press"; John E. Stanga, Jr., "Judicial Protection of the Criminal Defendant Against Adverse Press Coverage," *William and Mary L.R.* 13:1 (1971); Justice Hans A. Linde, Oregon Supreme Court, "Advice to the Press," *Center Magazine*, January-February 1979, p. 2.

15. William J. Campbell, "Delays in Criminal Cases," F.R.D. 55:229 (1972). For a more general criticism, see Leon Jaworski and John M. Price, "A Criticism and a Defense of the American Criminal Justice System," *New York State Bar Journal* 47:548 (November 1975).

16. Campbell, "Delays in Criminal Cases," p. 235.

17. Peyton v. Rowe, 391 U.S. 54 (1968).

18. Campbell, "Delays in Criminal Cases," pp. 236-37. See supporting evidence for his argument in William H. Levit and Dorothy W. Nelson, "Expediting Voir Dire: An Empirical Study," *Southern Cal. L.R.* 44:916-17 (1971).

19. Alfred Friendly and Ronald Goldfarb, *Crime and Publicity* (New York: Twentieth Century Fund, 1967), p. 35 n.

20. Bill Green, "Janet's World—The Story of a Child Who Never Existed— How and Why It Came to Be Published," *Washington Post*, April 19, 1981, p. 1.

21. Howard Simons and Joseph A. Califano, Jr., eds., *The Media and the Law* (New York: Praeger, 1976), p. 2.

22. Ibid., p. 5.

23. Ibid., p. 19.

24. Ibid., p. 37.

25. See David S. Broder, "Politicians and Biased Political Information," in *Politics and the Press*, ed. Richard W. Lee (Washington, D.C.: Acropolis Books, 1974), pp. 60, 61-66. Leon V. Sigal, *Reporters and Officials* (Lexington, Mass.: D.C. Heath, 1973). For the views of the country's premier editor on the press-court conflict see A. M. Rosenthal, "The Press Under Attack," *Bar Leader*, March-April 1982, p. 25. This summarizes his Lovejoy address on freedom of the press at Colby College, Waterville, Me.

CHAPTER 2: CONFLICT AND BARGAINING

1. Bridges v. California, 314 U.S. 252 (1941).

2. Sheppard v. Maxwell, 384 U.S. 333 (1966); 231 F. Supp. 37 (S.D. Ohio 1964); 346 F. 2d 707 (1965). The Ohio Supreme Court affirmed the 1954 conviction at 165 Ohio 293 (1956).

3. Ibid., 384 U.S. 333 (1966), p. 339.

4. Ibid., pp. 338, 341.

5. The newspaper's story is told by Louis B. Seltzer, *The Years Were Good* (Cleveland: World Publishing Company, 1956).

6. Voir dire is the process by which persons summoned for jury duty are examined for fitness. In federal courts, the judge usually asks the questions, with advice of counsel. In state courts the attorneys, under tolerant court supervision, sometimes select jurors deemed most likely to be favorable to their client.

7. "Clark Explains Sheppard Ruling," *New York Times*, August 8, 1966, p. 11.

8. Phoenix Newspapers Inc. v. Superior Ct., 101 Ariz. 257, 418 P. 2d 594 (Supreme Ct. Ariz. 1966). Gilbert Geis, "Preliminary Hearings and the Press," *UCLA L.R.* 1961, pp. 396, 409-13.

9. People v. Eliot, 54 Cal. 2d 498, 354 P. 2d 225 (Supreme Ct. Cal. 1960); *Editor & Publisher*, March 31, 1979, p. 12; San Jose Mercury-News v. Municipal Ct., 30 Cal. 3d 498, 179 Cal. Rptr. 772 (Supreme Ct. Cal. 1982). The legislature conformed the statute to U.S. Supreme Court precedents in March 1982. "News Notes," 8 Med. L. Rptr. March 30, 1982, back cover.

10. American Bar Association Project on Minimum Standards for Criminal Justice, *Fair Trial and Free Press: Tentative Draft of Standards*. (New York: Office of Criminal Justice Project, Institute of Judicial Administration, 1966), p. 29. Also, "Criminal Justice Act, 1967, Chapter 80" in *The Public General Acts and Church Assembly Measures 1967*. Part I, Criminal Procedure, Etc. Sections 1-10. London: Her Majesty's Stationery Office, 1967, p. 1625.

11. *Editor & Publisher,* April 29, 1967, p. 9.

12. American Society of Newspaper Editors, *Bulletin*, November 1966, p. 14.

13. F.R.D. 45:391, 400-403 (1969).

14. The President's Commission on Law Enforcement and Administration of Justice, *Task Force Report: The Courts* (Washington, D.C.: U.S. Government Printing Office, 1967), p. 9.

15. *Editor & Publisher,* April 24, 1965, p. 18.

16. Home Office Circular No. 31/1964, "The Judge's Rules and Administrative Directions to the Police," *Criminal Law Review,* March 1964, pp. 165, 173.

17. Alfred W. Blumrosen, "Contempt of Court and Unlawful Police Action," *Rutgers L.R.* 11:526, 531, 545 (1956-1957).

18. Albert M. Pearson, *Memorandum* as reporter for the Legal Advisory Committee on Fair Trial and Free Press, July 29, 1977 (Chicago: American Bar Association, 1977), Part I, p. 2.

19. Working papers of W. Theodore Pierson, Radio and Television News Directors Association, pp. 6-7; Arthur B. Hanson, American Newspaper Publishers Association; J.Edward Murray, American Society of Newspaper Editors; Elmer W. Lower, ABC News; Paul Conrad and Walter Potter, National Newspaper Association. Also, Gerald B. Healey, "Press Asks for Revisions in ABA's Fair Trial Rules," *Editor & Publisher,* August 12, 1967, p. 11. Murray's text was published in American Society of Newspaper Editors, *Bulletin,* November 1, 1966, p. 1.

20. Dennis v. United States, 341 U.S. 494 (1951).

21. Harold R. Medina, *Freedom of the Press and Fair Trial* (New York: Columbia University Press, 1967), p. 11-13.

22. Ibid., pp. 12-13.

23. "Fight Like Tigers on Gag Orders—Judge Medina," *Quill,* January 1976, p. 7.

24. Medina, *Freedom of the Press and Fair Trial,* p. 25.

25. Ibid., p. 28.

26. Ibid., p. 29, 30-31, 33-34, 67-68.

27. New Jersey v. Joyce, 4 Med. L. Rptr., 1419 (Superior Ct. N.J. 1978).

28. State v. Allen, 373 A. 2d 377 (Supreme Ct. N.J. 1977).

29. American Bar Association Standards Relating to the Administration of Criminal Justice, Chapter 8, *Fair Trial and Free Press,* 2d ed. (Chicago: American Bar Association, 1978), p. 2. This edition was approved August 9, 1978, except for Standard 8-3.4(a); approved text dated 1979.

30. Ibid., p. 4.

31. Bridges v. California, p. 252.

32. Craig v. Harney, 331 U.S. 364 (1947).

33. Wood v. Georgia, 370 U.S. 373 (1962).

34. The Court said in Bridges that silence orders stopped public discussion at the precise time when interest is highest and the most important topics are under consideration.

35. United States v. Tijerina, 407 F. 2d 349 (10th Cir. 1969); 412 F. 2d 661,

663-65 (10th Cir. 1969), cert. denied, 396 U.S. 990 (1969). The first case dealt with pretrial publicity, the second with a contempt charge for refusing to obey a gag order.

36. Chicago Council of Lawyers v. Bauer, 522 F. 2d 242 (7th Cir. 1975), cert. denied, 427 U.S. 912 (1976).

37. Hirschkop v. Snead, 594 F. 2d 356 (4th Cir. 1979); also, Hirschkop v. Virginia State Bar, 421 F. Supp. 1137 (D. Va. 1976).

38. "Free Press-Fair Trial Proposed Revised Guidelines of the Judicial Conference of the United States—1980: A Recommendation Relating to Information by Attorneys in Criminal Cases." The text was approved September 15, 1980. The preliminary text title in this source, 6 Med. L. Rptr. 190 (1980), differs from the approved text in that "civil contempt" was removed. See also, "Rules of Criminal Procedure," Rule 43, 91 F.R.D. 289, 365 (1981) and "News Notes," Med. L. Rptr., December 7, 1982, front cover, p. 3; Garden State Bar Assn. v. Middlesex County Ethics Committee, 643 F. 2d 119 (3d Cir. 1981).

39. *American Bar Association Standards Relating to the Administration of Criminal Justice, Fair Trial and Free Press* (Washington, D.C.: American Bar Association, 1978). Approved Draft. See "Commentary," pp. 2-5.

40. Ibid., pp. 20-23.

41. Ibid.

42. Gannett Co. Inc. v. DePasquale, 443 U.S. 368 (1979).

43. ABA Standards, pp. 20-23.

44. Grant B. Cooper, "The Rationale for ABA Recommendations," *Notre Dame Lawyer* 42:857 (1967).

45. The principal sources relied upon in the description of the operations of the Washington bar, bench, and press council include the text of addresses by Judge Alfred T. Goodwin, Justice Charles F. Stafford of the Supreme Court of Washington, and Paul Conrad of the Washington Allied Daily Newspapers, at the convention of the Association for Education in Journalism, Seattle, August 13, 1978; Robert C. Finley, "Free Press and Fair Trial: A Commonsense Accommodation," *New York State Bar Journal* 41:9 (1969); manuscript copies of addresses by Hu Blonk, Justice Finley, Paul Conrad, Judge Eugene Wright, Dan Riviera, and Judge Stafford at the American Bar Association convention in Hawaii, August 3, 1967, and a letter from Blonk dated February 1, 1978. For an account of councils in California and New York, see "National News Council Report," *Columbia Journalism Review*, March-April 1980, p. 75. See also Thomas W. Gerber, "In New Hampshire: Almost Hearts and Flowers," American Society of Newspaper Editors, *Bulletin*, December-January 1980, p. 22.

46. State ex. rel. Superior Ct. v. Sperry, 79 Wash. 2d 69, 483 P. 2d 608 (Supreme Ct. Wash. 1971).

47. Charles F. Stafford, "The Washington Story," a paper read at the ABA convention in Hawaii, August 3, 1967, pp. 2-3. Remarks by Paul Conrad, a member of the Washington council, to the Association for Education in Journalism, Seattle, August 13, 1978 (voice tape.)

48. Robert C. Finley, address to ABA convention in Hawaii, August 3, 1967, pp. 2-3.

49. Stafford, Hawaii address, pp. 3-6.

50. Blonk, Hawaii address, p. 1.

51. Cox Broadcasting Corp. v. Cohn, 420 U.S. 469 (1975); Oklahoma Publishing Co. v. District Ct., 430 U.S. 308 (1977).

52. Blonk, letter, pp. 1-2.

53. Blonk, letter, p. 1.

54. Stafford, Hawaii address, pp. 3-5.

55. Conrad, Hawaii address, p. 4.

56. American Bar Association, *Fair Trial/Free Press Voluntary Agreements* (Chicago: ABA, 1974), p. 6. This handbook is useful for the purpose of organizing and operating councils.

57. Blonk, letter, p. 2.

58. Jack C. Landau, "Fair Trial and Free Press, A Due Process Proposal: The Challenge of the Communications Media." *ABA Journal*, January 1976, p. 55. Paul H. Roney, "The Bar Answers the Challenge," ibid., p. 60.

59. "Talk of the Town: Media and the Law," *New Yorker*, July 12, 1976, p. 26. The italics are in the original.

60. Howard Simons and Joseph A. Califano, Jr., eds. *The Media and the Law* (New York: Praeger, 1976). Washington Post conference. The Nesson and Miller discourses on national security, privacy, and confidential sources for the press are in this volume. *The Media and the Law, Conference Handbook* (New York: The Ford Foundation, undated). Foreword by Fred W. Friendly. John Foley, Robert C. Lobdell, and Robert Trounson, eds., *The Media and the Law* (Los Angeles: Times Mirror Press, 1977). Southern California conference. Miller and Nesson were joined by Professor John Kaplan, Stanford Law School. The dialogues in this seminar program, according to Fred Friendly, have been replaced by a series in similar format dealing with moral issues arising out of the impact of the media on society.

61. Terrence P. Goggin and George M. Hanover, "Fair Trial and Free Press: The Psychological Effect of Pretrial Publicity on the Juror's Ability to Be Impartial: A Plea for Reform," *Southern Cal. L.R.*, Summer 1965, p. 672. Seymour Pollock, M.D., assisted in the preparation of this article.

62. American Society of Newspaper Editors, *Bulletin*, Nov. 1, 1966, pp. 1, 10-12.

63. American Bar Association, *Fair Trial and Free Press.* (Washington: Standing Committee on Association Standards for Criminal Justice, 1978), p. 14.

64. Ibid., p. 20.

65. Alice M. Padawar-Singer and Allen H. Barton, "The Impact of Pretrial Publicity on Juror's Verdicts," in *The Jury System in America*, ed. Rita James Simon (Beverly Hills: Sage Publications, 1975), pp. 131, 134.

66. F. Gerald Kline and Paul H. Jess, "Prejudicial Publicity: Its Effect on Law School Mock Juries," *Journalism Quarterly*, Spring 1966, p. 13; Maxwell McCombs, "Experimental Analysis of 'Trial by Newspaper,' " a paper read at Association for Education in Journalism, Iowa City, August 1966; Mary Dee Tans and Steven H. Chaffee, "Pretrial Publicity and Juror Prejudice," *Journalism Quarterly*, Winter 1966, p. 647; Rita James Simon, "Murder, Juries and the Press," *Transaction*, May-June 1966, p. 40.

67. Fred S. Siebert, Walter Wilcox, and George Hough III, *Free Press and Fair Trial—Some Dimensions of the Problem*, ed. Chilton R. Bush (Athens: University of Georgia Press, 1970), pp. 1, 7, 9, 11. The research was supported by the American Newspaper Publishers Association Foundation on a grant of funds from the Chicago Tribune. The interviews reported were conducted in 1968.

68. Walter Wilcox, "The Press, the Jury and the Behavioral Sciences," ibid., p. 100.

CHAPTER 3: TRIAL STANDARDS IN USE

1. Fred Graham, "A Newspaperman's View," in "Symposium on Free Press and a Fair Trial," Donald W. Dowd, ed. *Villanova L.R.*, vol. 11 (1966), pp. 677, 680.

2. William B. Monroe, "A Radio and Television Newsman's View," ibid., pp. 677, 687.

3. Nebraska Press Assn. v. Stuart, 427 U.S. 539, 570 (1976). See Justice Brennan's concurrence, pp. 572, 595, 598-604, 607-11.

4. "Bold Press Needed, Says Jaworski," *Editor and Publisher*, April 23, 1977, p. 116.

5. Leon Jaworski, *The Right and the Power* (New York: Pocket Books, 1977), p. 6.

6. Frank G. Raichle in "Symposium—Fair Trial-Free Press," *Criminal Law Bulletin*, April 1966, pp. 3, 9-16.

7. *United States Code, Annotated*, Title 18 (St. Paul: West, 1975), p. 43 (Rule 21) and p. 109 (Rule 24).

8. Irvin v. Dowd, 366 U.S. 717 (1961).

9. Ibid., pp. 722-23.

10. Rideau v. Louisiana, 373 U.S. 723 (1963).

11. Corona v. Superior Court, 24 Cal. App. 3d 872, 876; App. 101 Cal. Rptr. 411 (Ct. of App. 3d D. 1972).

192   Notes

12. Ibid., pp. 876-77.
13. Ibid., p. 878.
14. Ibid.
15. Ibid., pp. 874, 884.
16. Lenora Williamson, "Pretrial News Effects on Jury, Judges, Studied," *Editor & Publisher,* June 6, 1976, p. 11; *Minneapolis Tribune,* May 9, 1978, p. 3A.
17. *Minneapolis Star and Tribune,* Dec. 16, 1982, p. 9A.
18. David Robertson, reporter, *Reports of the Trial of Colonel Aaron Burr for Treason and for a Misdemeanor* (Philadelphia: Hopkins and Earle, 1808), vol. 1, pp. 43-385, 368.
19. Ibid., pp. 369-70.
20. Ibid., p. 415.
21. Ibid., pp. 414-22.
22. Spies v. Illinois, 123 U.S. 131 (1887).
23. Allen v. United States, 4 F. 2d 688 (1924); cert. denied, 267 U.S. 597 (1924).
24. Murphy v. Florida, 363 F. Supp. 1224 (S.D. Fla. 1973); 421 U.S. 794, 798-804 (1975).
25. Murphy v. Florida, 421 U.S. 794, 798-804 (1975).
26. Ibid., pp. 804-5.
27. The Sheppard opinion says the press and the public did not have the right to be "contemporaneously informed by the police or prosecuting authorities of the details of the evidence being accumulated against [Sheppard]." Sheppard v. Maxwell, 384 U.S. 333, 361 (1966).
28. Ibid. The suggestions are found on pp. 360-63. A directive, rather than a suggestion, tells the trial courts to instruct news people not to disturb the judicial calm and serenity in the courtroom to which a defendant is entitled. Pp. 357-58.
29. Nebraska Press Assn. v. Stuart, 427 U.S. 539, 551 (1976).
30. Eric E. Younger, "The Sheppard Mandate Today: A Trial Judge's Perspective," *Nebraska L.R.* 56:1 (1977).
31. Claude R. Sowle, "Press-Created Prejudice in Criminal Trials—A Mirage?" *Nieman Reports,* September 1964, p. 16.
32. J. Skelly Wright, "Fair Trial-Free Press," F.R.D. 38:435 (1966).
33. Clifton Daniel, "Free Press and Fair Trial," an address to the National District Attorneys Association, Houston, Tex., March 17, 1965, p. 8, manuscript copy.
34. Reardon Report (American Bar Association Project on Minimum Standards for Criminal Justice, *Fair Trial and Free Press*—Tentative Draft of Standards [New York: Office of Criminal Justice Project, Institute of Judicial Administration, 1966]), pp. 42-45.

35. Evelle J. Younger, "Fair Trial, Free Press and the Man in the Middle," *ABA Journal* 56:127 (1970).

36. William H. Levit et al., "Expediting Voir Dire: An Empirical Study." *Southern Cal. L.R.* 44:916, 917, 923, 940-45 (1971).

37. Paul C. Reardon, "The Fair Trial-Free Press Controversy—Where We Have Been and Where We Should Be Going," *San Diego L.R.* 4:255, 264 (1967).

38. Younger, "The Sheppard Mandate Today," pp. 1, 9.

39. United States ex rel. Stukes v. Shovlin, 464 F. 2d 1211 (3d Cir. 1972).

40. John E. Stanga, Jr., "Judicial Protection of Criminal Defendants against Adverse Press Coverage," *William and Mary L.R.* 13:1, 16 (1971).

41. Younger, "The Sheppard Mandate Today," pp. 1, 10.

42. D. R. Wright, "Fair Trial and Free Press, Practical Ways to Have Both," *Judicature* 54:377 (April 1971).

43. Standard 8-3.5(b) provides that

Both the degree of exposure and the prospective juror's testimony as to state of mind are relevant to the determination of acceptability. A prospective juror testifying to an inability to overcome preconceptions shall be subject to challenge for cause no matter how slight the exposure. If the prospective juror remembers information that will be developed in the course of the trial, or that may be inadmissible but does not create a substantial risk of impairing judgment, that person's acceptability shall turn on the credibility of testimony as to impartiality. If the formation of an opinion is admitted, the prospective juror shall be subject to challenge for cause unless the examination shows unequivocally the capacity to be impartial. A prospective juror who has been exposed to and remembers reports of highly significant information such as the existence or contents of a confession, or other incriminating matters that may be inadmissible in evidence, or substantial amounts of inflammatory material, shall be subject to challenge for cause without regard to the prospective juror's testimony as to state of mind. [Approved text, 1979].

44. Beck v. Washington, 369 U.S. 541 (1962).

45. Delaney v. United States, 199 F. 2d 107 (1st Cir. 1952).

46. Dale v. Broeder, "Voir Dire Examinations: An Empirical Study," *Southern Cal. L.R.* 1965:503-8, 521-23.

47. Margoles v. United States, 407 F. 2d 727, 729-30 (7th Cir. 1969).

48. Ibid., pp. 729-30.

49. Ibid., p. 730.

50. United States v. Hearst, 412 F. Supp. 873, 875 (N.D. Cal. 1976).

51. Ibid., p. 876.

52. Ibid., pp. 866-67.

53. Calley v. Callaway, 382 F. Supp. 650, 657, 685-86 (D. Ga. 1974); 519 F. 2d 184, 205-10 (5th Cir. 1975).

54. Jaworski, *The Right and the Power*, p. 335.

55. Ibid., pp. 278-79.
56. Ibid., pp. 285-87, 291.
57. United States v. Mitchell, 397 F. Supp. 166, 179 (D. D.C. 1974).
58. This same plea has been rejected in a variety of cases. United States v. Archer, 355 F. Supp. 981 (S.D. N.Y. 1972).
59. The *Times* applied for and received a writ holding the protective order invalid. The order was judicial overkill, said the court of appeals. See Younger v. Smith, 30 Cal. App. 3d 138, 106 Cal. Rptr. 225 (Ct. of App. 2d. D. Cal. 1973), rehearing denied, hearing denied (1973). ABA Standard 8-2.1(c) provides,

From the commencement of the investigation of a criminal matter until completion of trial or disposition without trial, a law enforcement officer [attorney, in the case of Rule 7-107] within this agency shall not release or authorize the release of any extrajudicial statement, for dissemination by any means of public communication, if such statement poses a clear and present danger to the fairness of the trial. In no event, however, shall a law enforcement officer make an extrajudicial statement concerning . . . (ii) . . . (A) the prior criminal record (including arrests, indictments, or other charges of crime), the character or reputation of the accused, or any opinion as to the accused's guilt or innocence or as to the merits of the case or the evidence in the case.

See Hirschkop v. Virginia State Bar, 421 F. Supp. 1137 (D. Va. 1976).
60. People v. Sirhan, 102 Cal. Rptr. 385, 396-98, 497 P. 2d 1121 (Supreme Ct. Cal. 1972).
61. Abby Propis Simms, "Sequestration: A Possible Solution to the Free Press-Fair Trial Dilemma," *American University L.R.* 29:923, notes 140, 141 (1974).
62. United States v. Pfingst, 477 F. 2d 177 (1973).
63. Ibid., p. 187.
64. United States v. Howard, 506 F. 2d 865, 866-69 (5th Cir. 1975).
65. United States v. Titsworth, 422 F. Supp. 587, 588-591 (D. Neb. 1976).
66. Turner v. Louisiana, 379 U.S. 466, 472-73 (1965).
67. For example, United States v. Polizzi, 500 F. 2d 856, 881-887 (9th Cir. 1974).
68. Standard 8-3.6(b), Sequestration of Jury, reads,

Sequestration shall be ordered only if it is determined that the case is of such notoriety or the issues are of such a nature that, in the absence of sequestration, there is a substantial likelihood that highly prejudicial matters will come to the attention of jurors. Either party may move for sequestration of the jury at the beginning of the trial or at any time during the course of the trial, and, in appropriate circumstances, the court may order sequestration on its own motion. Whenever sequestration is ordered, the court, in advising the jury of the decision, shall not disclose which party requested it. As an alternative to sequestration in cases where there is a significant threat of juror intimidation during or after the trial, the court may consider an order withholding public disclosure of jurors' names and addresses as long as that information is not otherwise required by law to be a matter of public record.

A related standard provides for sequestration of witnesses, before their appearance, "when it appears likely that in the absence of sequestration they will be exposed to extrajudicial reports that may influence their testimony."

CHAPTER 4: GAG RULE BY THE COURTS

1. Marbury v. Madison, 1 Cranch 137 (1803).

2. Eric E. Younger, "The Sheppard Mandate Today: A Trial Judge's Perspective," *Nebraska L.R.*, 56:1, 13-14 (1977).

3. American Society of Newspaper Editors, *Bulletin*, November 1, 1966, p. 12.

4. Oliver v. Postel, 327 N.Y.S. 2d 444, 457 (Sup. Ct. App. Div. N.Y. 1971).

5. Bridges v. California, 314 U.S. 252 (1941); Pennekamp v. Florida, 328 U.S. 331 (1946); Craig v. Harney, 331 U.S. 364 (1942); Maryland v. Baltimore Radio Show, 338 U.S. 912 (1950); Wood v. Georgia, 370 U.S. 375 (1962). Contrast Branzburg v. Hayes, 408 U.S. 665 (1972) and United States v. Dickinson, 465 F. 2d 496 (5th Cir. 1972).

6. Eric E. Younger, "The Sheppard Mandate Today," p. 14.

7. An account which captures the atmosphere of the community is by Fred W. Friendly, "Aftershock," *New York Times Magazine,* March 21, 1976, p. 16.

8. United States v. Schiavo, 504 F. 2d 1, 3 (3d Cir. 1974).

9. Pennekamp v. Florida, p. 331.

10. United States v Schiavo, pp. 1, 22.

11. Ibid.

12. State ex rel. Superior Ct. v. Sperry, 79 Wash. 2d 69, 483 P. 2d 608, 614-19 (Supreme Ct., Wash. 1971).

13. Ibid., p. 614.

14. New York Times Co. v. Starkey, 380 N.Y.S. Supp. 2d 239, 247 (Supreme Ct. App. Div. N.Y. 1976).

15. United States v. Dickinson, p. 496. See also Stewart v. Dameron, 321 F. Supp. 886 (D. La. 1971).

16. Sheppard v. Maxwell, 384 U.S. 333, 362-63 (1966).

17. Ibid.

18. United States v. Dickinson, pp. 496, 514-15.

19. United States v. Dickinson, 349 F. Supp. 227 (M.D. La. 1972).

20. United States v. Dickinson, 476 F. 2d 373 (5th Cir. 1973).

21. Nebraska Press Assn. v. Stuart, 427 U.S. 539 (1976).

22. State v. Simants, 194 Neb. 783, 236 N.W. 2d 794 (Supreme Ct. Neb. 1975).
23. [Thomas G. Abbey], "Note, Constitutional Law—Judicial Restraint of the Press—Nebraska Press Assn. v. Stuart," *Creighton L.R.* 9:693, 695 (1976).
24. Transcript of Oral Argument in Supreme Court, *Editor & Publisher,* May 1, 1976, p. 46D.
25. Abbey, "Constitutional Law," pp. 693, 694-96.
26. Freedman v. Maryland, 380 U.S. 51 (1965).
27. State v. Simants, pp. 794, 798-99.
28. Nebraska Press Assn. v. Stuart, pp. 539, 548, 554-55.
29. Ibid., p. 559.
30. Ibid., p. 561.
31. Ibid., pp. 564-65.
32. Ibid., p. 567.
33. Ibid., p. 568.
34. Arnold S. Trebach, *The Rationing of Justice* (New Brunswick, N.J.: Rutgers University Press, 1964), pp. 15-18, 55.
35. Walter V. Schaefer, "Federalism and State Criminal Procedure," *Harvard L.R.* 70:26 (November 1956).
36. In re Oliver, 333 U.S. 257 (1948).
37. Nebraska Press Assn. v. Stuart, pp. 539, 546-47.
38. Times-Picayune Publishing Corp. v. Schulenkamp, 419 U.S. 1301 (1975).
39. Irving R. Kaufman and the Committee on the Operation of the Jury System on the Free Press-Fair Trial Issue (the Kaufman Report) F.R.D. 45:391, 403 (1969).
40. Ibid.
41. King v. Jones, 319 F. Supp. 653 (N.D. Ohio 1970), Hammond v. Brown 323 F. Supp. 326 (N.D. Ohio 1971), affmd. 450 F. 2d 480 (6th Cir. 1971); CBS, Inc. v. Young, 522 F. 2d 234 (6th Cir. 1975).
42. CBS, Inc. v. Young, p. 234.
43. Hamilton v. Municipal Court, 270 Cal. App. 2d 797, 76 Cal. Rptr. 168 (Ct. of App. Cal. 1969); cert. denied, 396 U.S. 985 (1969).
44. "*Inquirer* Withdraws Appeal of Gag in Criminal Trial of State Judge," *Press Censorship Newsletter,* vol. 10 (1976), p. 30.
45. United States v. Cianfrani, 573 F. 2d 835 (3d Cir. 1978).
46. Ibid., pp. 848-49.
47. Oliver v. Postel, 30 N.Y. 2d 171, 282 N.E. 2d 306 (Ct. of App. N.Y. 1973).
48. Gannett Co., Inc. v. DePasquale, 443 U.S. 368, 99 S. Ct. 2898 (1979).
49. Richmond Newspapers, Inc. v. Virginia, 448 U.S. 555, 100 S. Ct. 2814 (1980).

50. Gannett Co., Inc. v. DePasquale, 443 U.S. 368; 99 S. Ct. 2898, 2906 (n. 9), 2907 (n. 11), 2909, 2916 (text and n. 23), 2919 (n. 25).
51. Gannett Co., Inc. v. DePasquale, 401 N.Y. Supp. 2d 756 (1977).
52. Laurence H. Tribe, attorney for the newspapers, responding on oral argument to a question from Justice White.
53. Gannett v. DePasquale, 443 U.S. 368, 99 S. Ct. 2898.
54. Ibid., 99 S. Ct. 2930-31.
55. United States v. Cianfrani, p. 835.
56. Gannett v. DePasquale, 443 U.S. 368, 99 S. Ct. 2898, 2932-34.
57. Harold L. Cross, *The People's Right to Know* (New York: Columbia University Press, 1953).
58. Richmond Newspapers, Inc. v. Virginia, 448 U.S. 555, 100 S. Ct. 2814, 2825.
59. 100 S. Ct. 2814, 2823-24.
60. Ibid., 2832.
61. Ibid., 2839.
62. Ibid., p. 2841.
63. Gannett v. DePasquale, 443 U.S. 368, 99 S. Ct. 2898, 2936.
64. Ibid., p. 2937.
65. United States v. Criden, 675 F. 2d 550 (3d Cir. 1982).
66. Ibid., p. 554.
67. United States v. Brooklier, 8 Med. L. Rptr. 2177, 2179 (9th Cir. 1982).
68. United States v. Powers, 622 F. 2d 317; (8th Cir. 1980). See also this court's opinion in In re United States ex rel. Pulitzer Publishing Co., 635 F. 2d 676 (8th Cir. 1980).
69. United States v. Brooklier, pp. 2177, 2181.
70. Ibid., p. 2179.
71. Ibid., 2180.
72. See also Philadelphia Newspapers, Inc. v. Jerome, 98 S. Ct. 546 (1978).
73. Some of the cases in which the courts ordered closure or sealing of documents are the following: Sacramento Bee v. United States District Ct., 656 F. 2d 477 (9th Cir. 1981), the trial court's conclusion that defendant's case would be prejudiced by press attendance at two evidentiary hearings was well-founded even though alternatives preferable to closure existed, jury sequestration not feasible on short notice; State v. Blake, 53 Oregon App. 906, 633 P. 2d 831 (Ct. of App. Ore. 1981), defendant moves to open that part of pretrial hearing devoted to plaintiff's sexual history, denied (more than half of the states permit closure for such testimony); State v. Burney, 276 S.E. 2d 693 (Supreme Ct. N.C. 1981), no error in closing courtroom during testimony of twelve-year-old child, no First Amendment issue; People v. Jones, 7 Med. L. Rptr. 2096 (Supreme Ct. App. Div. N.Y. 1981), adult witness demonstrates that she is

psychologically unable to describe in public explicit details of a violent sexual assault, her testimony is closed; Sherman Publishing v. Goldberg, 8 Med. L. Rptr. 1489 (Supreme Ct. R.I. 1982), by informal agreement, journalists were admitted to family court and were barred from future attendance when name of a juvenile defendant, obtained elsewhere, was published—exclusion order held too broad, is prior restraint; the high court does not recognize informal agreements—closure of hearing approved; Kansas City Star v. Fossey, 7 Med. L. Rptr. 2250 (Supreme Ct. Kan. 1981), closure approved because tests were met, serious extent of publicity noted; Capital Newspapers v. Clyne, 7 Med. L. Rptr. 1536 (Supreme Ct. App. Div. N.Y. 1981), brief in camera conference with judge on impact of prior convictions if defendant testifies is not an evidence hearing; In re San Juan Star Company, 7 Med. L. Rptr. 2144 (1st Cir. 1981), order banning circulation of discovery material to press is upheld; United States v. Edwards, 8 Med. L. Rptr. 1145 (7th Cir. 1982), court finds that access to wiretap evidence for broadcast during trial would prejudice defendant even though newspaper had already printed verbatim excerpts; Abell Co. v. United States, 5 Med. L. Rptr. 1506 (4th Cir. 1979), transcript of in camera hearing is subject to same access conditions as original hearing; State v. Couture, 37 Conn. Sup. 705, 435 A. 2d 369 (Superior Ct. App. Sess., Conn. 1981), closure granted on assertion that important parts of the evidence were taken illegally and determination by court that alternatives to closure were not adequate; Commonwealth v. Stetson, 7 Med. L. Rptr. 2342 (Supreme Judicial Ct. Mass. 1981), court closed brief portions of voir dire and trial itself after testimony that family of witness might be in grave danger; Patuxent Publishing Corp. v. State, 48 Md. App. 689, 429 A. 2d 554 (Court of Special App. Md. 1981), closure order requested is too sweeping, brief bench conferences will suffice.

The Reporter's Committee, in *News Media and the Law,* June-July 1981, p. 53, counted 217 closure motions since Gannett which had been upheld on appeal and thirty-two reversals; 159 other motions had been refused or withdrawn.

74. The cases are Federated Publications v. Kurtz, 94 Wash. 2d 51, 615 P. 2d 440 (Supreme Ct. Wash. 1980), the "first case" and Federated Publications v. Swedberg, 633 P. 2d 74 (Supreme Ct. Wash. 1981). The denial of certiorari is at 102 S. Ct. 2257, 1982). Only Justice Brennan and Justice Marshall voted to grant review.

75. Seattle Times v. Ishikawa, 640 P. 2d 716, 8 Med. L. Rptr. 1041 (Supreme Ct. Wash. 1982).

76. People v. Eliot, 54 Cal. 2d 498, 354 P. 2d 225 (Supreme Ct. Cal. 1960).

77. San Jose Mercury-News v. Municipal Ct., 30 Cal. 3d 498, 638 P. 2d 655 (Supreme Ct. Cal. 1982).

78. "News Notes—Decisions Summary," 8 Med. L. Rptr., March 30, 1982, back cover.

79. Cox Broadcasting Corp. v. Cohn, 420 U.S. 469 (1975); see also Oklahoma Publishing Co. v. District Ct., 430 U.S. 308 (1977).
80. Globe Newspaper Co. v. Superior Ct., 102 S. Ct. 2613 (1981).
81. Ibid., p. 2680.
82. Ibid., pp. 2621, 2622.
83. Ibid., p. 2621.

CHAPTER 5: THE LEGISLATIVE SHIELD

1. Hugh Chisholm, "Newspapers," *Encyclopaedia Britannica*, 11th ed. vol. 19 (1911) pp. 544, 558.
2. Ibid.
3. Edwin Emery and Michael C. Emery, *The Press and America* (Englewood Cliffs, N.J.: Prentice-Hall, 1978), pp. 219-26, 243-57.
4. Clarence K. Streit, in *Cooperation of the Press in the Organization of Peace (False News)*. League of Nations Publication Conf. D. 143, Nov. 1, 1932 (Geneva: League of Nations, 1932).
5. Leon Jaworski, *The Right and the Power* (New York: Pocket Books, 1977), p. 335.
6. Reinhard Bendix, *Max Weber, An Intellectual Portrait* (Garden City: Doubleday, 1960), p. 445.
7. Ibid., p. 448.
8. From "Morals in Public Life [1951]" in hearings of a subcommittee of the Senate Committee on Labor and Public Welfare, quoted in Irving Dilliard, ed., *The Spirit of Liberty: Papers and Addresses of Learned Hand* (New York: Alfred A. Knopf, 1952), pp. 227, 231, 233.
9. Near v. Minnesota, 283 U.S. 697 (1931).
10. Bridges v. California, 314 U.S. 252, 303-4 (1941).
11. New York Times Co. v. Sullivan, 376 U.S. 254 (1964); Barr v. Matteo, 360 U.S. 564 (1959).
12. "Chief Justice Says Press Must Obey Invalid Censorship Orders until They Are Later Reversed," *Censorship Newsletter*, vol. 8 (1975), pp. 44, 45.
13. These statements with respect to police practice are based on questionnaires returned to the author by twenty-seven chiefs of police in large cities and twenty-two sheriffs in adjacent metropolitan counties where more than 60 percent of all criminal cases arise. Gerald O. Williams, "Crime News and Its Relation to Police-Press Problems," *Police*, May-June 1964, p. 60, July-August 1964, p. 63; September-October, 1964, p. 57, explains the police view on public relations activity.
14. Freeman W. Sharp, *The Newsman's Privilege*, for Senator Edward V.

Long's Subcommittee of the Senate Committee on the Judiciary (Washington, D.C.: U.S. Government Printing Office, 1966).

15. Donald M. Gillmor and Jerome A. Barron, *Mass Communication Law*, 3d ed. (St. Paul: West, 1979). See note 87 below.

16. *Arizona Revised Statutes Annotated*, Title 12, section 2236, "Courts and Civil Proceedings," Vol. 4A (1982).

17. *Hearing (Freedom of the Press)* before the Subcommittee on Constitutional Rights of the Committee on the Judiciary, United States Senate, 92d Congress, First and Second Sessions, September 28-30, October 12-14, 19-20 (1971) and February 1-2, 8, 16-17 (1972), p. 999.

18. In re Bridge, 295 A. 2d 3 (Supreme Ct. N.J. 1972), cert. denied, 410 U.S. 991 (1973).

19. Task Force on the Government and the Press, Twentieth Century Fund, *Press Freedoms Under Pressure* (New York: Twentieth Century Fund, 1972), pp. 11-13, 61-84.

20. Vincent A. Blasi, "The Newsman's Privilege: An Empirical Study," *Michigan L.R.* 70:229 (1971).

21. Branzburg v. Hayes, 408 U.S. 665 (1972); United States v. Caldwell, 434 F. 2d 1081 (9th Cir. 1970); In re Pappas, 408 U.S. 665 (1972).

22. United States v. Caldwell; In re Pappas.

23. Dan Paul, "Why a Shield Law?" in "Media Law Conference," *University of Miami L.R.* 29:459 (1975).

24. Ibid., pp. 460-461.

25. "Thinking Things Over," *Wall Street Journal*, February 28, 1973.

26. Ibid.

27. Code of Federal Regulations Vol. 28 sec. 50:10, p. 416. This administrative rule first took effect August 10, 1970.

28. United States v. Caldwell, 434 F. 2d 1081, 1086 (9th Cir. 1970).

29. "Justice Department Issues 76 Subpoenas to Press in Past Two Years: 29 Percent of Subpoenas Violate Guidelines," *Press Censorship Newsletter*, vol. 8 (1975) p. 35.

30. Jack R. Hart, "The Case of Jay Shelledy and His Controversial Claim to Newsman's Privilege," *Quill*, February 1978, p. 24.

31. Riley v. Chester, 612 F. 2d 708 (3d Cir. 1979).

32. See also United States v. Cuthbertson, 651 F. 2d 189 (3d Cir. 1981), cert. denied, 101 S. Ct. 945 (1981).

33. "*Nashville Banner* Reporters and Sources Testify in Libel Suit," *Press Censorship Newsletter*, vol. 10 (1976), pp. 43-44.

34. Ibid., vol. 7 (1975), p. 6.

35. Ibid., pp. 15, 28-29.

36. Morgan v. State, Fla. 337 So. 2d 951 (Supreme Ct. Fla. 1976).

37. Costello v. United States, 350 U.S. 359, 364 (1956).

38. Justice Douglas, dissenting, in Beck v. Washington, 369 U.S. 541, 587 (1962).

39. Branzburg v. Hayes.

40. The National Commission on the Causes and Prevention of Violence, *Rights in Conflict*, p. 255.

41. See John Lofton's *Justice and the Press* (Boston: Beacon, 1966), pp. 212-15, 227-32, 240, 253, 263-65, 337-41, 350-52. The cases referred to are, among others, Gideon v. Wainwright, 372 U.S. 335 (1963), appointive counsel for indigents accused of felony offenses; Mapp v. Ohio, 367 U.S. 643 (1961), exclusion of evidence illegally taken; Miranda v. Arizona, 384 U.S. 436 (1966), the privilege against self-incrimination is extended to persons in police custody, access to counsel required during police interrogation for prisoners who request it; United States v. Wade, 381 U.S. 218 (1967) and Gilbert v. California, 388 U.S. 263 (1967), the right to have counsel present at certain pretrial lineups.

42. Branzburg v. Hayes, p. 681.

43. American Newspaper Publishers Association, *Convention Bulletin*, pt. 4, no. 4 (1944), p. 174.

44. Branzburg v. Hayes, pp. 665, 695.

45. Ibid., pp. 695-96.

46. Ibid., pp. 697-98, 706.

47. Ibid., p. 711.

48. Ibid., p. 729 (n. 5), quoting Caldwell v. United States, 434 F. 2d 1081, 1084-85 (9th Cir. 1970).

49. Branzburg v. Hayes, p. 729.

50. Ibid., p. 743 (footnotes omitted).

51. Ibid., pp. 665, 709-10.

52. Farr v. Superior Ct., 22 Cal. App. 3d 60, 64, App. 99 Cal. Rptr. 342 (Ct. of App. Cal., 1972).

53. Ibid., p. 65.

54. Eric E. Younger, "The Sheppard Mandate Today: A Trial Judge's Perspective," *Nebraska L.R.* 56:1, 5 (1977).

55. Farr v. Superior Ct. pp. 60, 69. Proposition 5, incorporating an absolute shield law, as defined, into the constitution, was adopted by California voters in June 1980 without significant opposition from the bar. However, the provision is subject to interpretation by the courts.

56. In re William T. Farr, 64 Cal. App. 3d 605, 611 (Ct. of App 1976).

57. Farr v. Superior Ct., 409 U.S. 1011 (1972).

58. Farr v. Pitchess, 409 U.S. 1243 (1973).

59. Farr v. Pitchess, 522 F. 2d 464, 469 (9th Cir. 1975).

60. In re William T. Farr, on habeas corpus, 36 Cal. App. 3d 577, App. 111 Cal. Rptr. 649 (Ct. App. 1974).

61. In re William Farr, on habeas corpus, 64 Cal. App. 3d p. 605; App. 134

Cal. Rptr. 595 (Ct. of App. Cal. 1976). See this opinion for a list of the Farr cases.

62. Neiman Marcus v. Lait, F.R.D. 13:311 (D. N.Y. 1952).

63. "Farr Case Finish," *Quill*, January 1977, p. 6; February 1977, p. 6; *Minneapolis Tribune*, April 10, 1979, p. 2A.

64. Joe Rosato and William K. Patterson, reporters; George F. Gruner, managing editor; and Jim Bort, city editor, of the *Fresno Bee*.

65. Rosato v. Superior Court, 51 Cal. App. 3d 190, App. 124 Cal. Rptr. 427 (Ct. of App. Cal. 1975). See Maurice Van Gerpen, *Privileged Communication and the Press* (Westport, Conn.: Greenwood Press, 1979), pp. 24-26.

66. Rosato v. Superior Ct., pp. 238-40.

67. Ibid., p. 241. The House of Delegates of the California Bar Association agreed with Justice Franson that the journalists should not have been sent to jail. See Albert G. Pickerell, "Protective/Restrictive Orders and Judicial Review," a paper read at the Association for Education in Journalism, Law Division, University of Washington, Seattle, August 1978, p. 20.

68. Rosato v. Superior Court.

69. Van Gerpen, *Privileged Communication and the Press*, p. 26.

70. See Myron Farber, the *New York Times*, "Evidence of Curare Sought in 9 Deaths," January 7, 1976, p. 1; and "Testimony by Dr. X in 1966 About Curare a Key Factor of New Inquiry into Deaths," January 8, 1976, p. 1; Matthew L. Lifflander, *Final Treatment: The File on Dr. X* (New York: W. W. Norton, 1979), pp. 36-37. Farber's own book appeared three years later, *Somebody Is Lying: The Story of Dr. X* (New York: Doubleday, 1982).

71. In the Matter of Farber, 394 A. 2d 330 (Supreme Ct. N.J. 1978). Governor Brendan Byrne pardoned the *Times* as he was leaving office January 19, 1982. The state remitted the fines. Farber also was pardoned but already had served his term in jail. *Minneapolis Tribune*, January 19, 1982, p. 8B.

72. Donald M. Gillmor, "Journalist's Privilege and the Constitution," *Journal of Media Law and Practice*, September 1981, p. 115, 122; Branzburg v. Hayes, pp. 681, 707-8.

73. Branzburg v. Hayes, p. 710.

74. Oregon v. Knorr, 8 Med. L. Rptr. 2067 (Circuit Ct., 4th Div., Ore. 1982).

75. Trautman v. Dallas School Dist., 8 Med. L. Rptr. 1088 (N.D. Tex. 1982).

76. Commonwealth v. Corsetti, 8 Med. L. Rptr. 2113 (Supreme Judicial Ct. Mass. 1982).

77. Commonwealth v. McDonald, 6 Med. L. Rptr. 2230 (Superior Ct. Suffolk County, Mass. 1980).

78. New Hampshire v. Siel, 7 Med. L. Rptr. 1904 (Superior Ct. N.H. 1981). A March 1982 decision by the same court upheld the qualified privilege.

79. Ohio v. Geis, 7 Med. L. Rptr. 1675 (Ct. of App. Franklin County, Ohio 1981).

80. Washington v. Texas, 388 U.S. 14 (1967); Austin v. Memphis Publishing Co., 7 Med. L. Rptr. 1986 (Ct. of App. Tenn. 1981).

81. United States v. Blanton, 8 Med. L. Rptr. 1107 (S. D. Fla. 1982).

82. People v. Innaccone, 112 Misc. 2d 1057, 447 N.Y. Supp. 2d 996 (Supreme Ct. N.Y. County 1982). See also In re Dack, 5 Med. L. Rptr. 1886 (Supreme Ct. Monroe County, N.Y. 1979); Gagnon v. Fremont District Ct., 7 Med. L. Rptr. 1755 (Supreme Ct. Colo. 1981); Taylor v. Miskovsky, 7 Med. L. Rptr. 2408 (Supreme Ct. Okla. 1981).

83. State v. Louquet, 7 Med. L. Rptr. 1410 (Dist. Ct. Mont. 1981).

84. Gertz v. Robert Welch, Inc., 418 U.S. 323 (1974).

85. Gillmor, "Journalist's Privilege and the Constitution," pp. 115, 124.

86. New York Times Co. v. Sullivan, 376 U.S. 254 (1964).

87. Gertz v. Robert Welch, Inc.

88. Maressa v. New Jersey Monthly, 89 N.J. 176, 445 A. 2d 376 (Supreme Ct. N.J. 1982); "News Notes," 8 Med. L. Rptr., March 30, 1982. Cert. denied 51 U.S.L.W. 3287 (1983). For 1981 changes in the New York statute, see Art. 7, "Miscellaneous Rights and Immunities," sec. 79-h, and accompanying notes, *McKinney's Consolidated Laws of New York Annotated*, Book 8, Civil Rights Law (St. Paul: West, 1982).

89. State v. Boiardo, 416 A. 2d 793 (Supreme Ct. N.J. 1980).

90. Maressa v. New Jersey Monthly.

91. Herbert v. Lando, 441 U.S. 153, 161 (1979).

92. For Brennan's opinion, see Rosenbloom v. Metromedia, 403 U.S. 29 (1971). Powell wrote for the Court in Gertz v. Robert Welch, Inc.

93. "LRDC Study Shows Trend Toward Large Damage Awards," in "News Notes," 8 Med. L. Rptr., August 31, 1982, inside front cover.

94. Herbert v. Lando.

95. Herbert v. Lando; New York Times Co., v. Sullivan.

96. New York Times Co. v. Sullivan, p. 279.

97. United States v. Cuthbertson, 630 F. 2d 139 (3d Cir. 1980).

98. United States v. Cuthbertson, on remand, 7 Med. L. Rptr. 1172 (D. N.J. 1981).

99. United States v. Cuthbertson, 651 F. 2nd 189 (3d Cir. 1981).

100. Ibid., 7 Med. L. Rptr. 1377, 1381-82.

101. United States v. Augurs, 427 U.S. 97 (1976).

102. United States v. Cuthbertson, 651 F. 2d 189 (3d Circ 1981), 7 Med. L. Rptr. 1377, 1382-85.

103. Austin Wehrwein, in "Grand Jury Secrecy Goes Under Attack," *Minneapolis Star,* June 22, 1977, p. 14A.

104. In re Report and Recommendation of June 5, 1972, Grand Jury Concerning Transmission of Evidence to the House of Representatives, 370 F. Supp. 1219 (D. D.C. 1974).

105. Ibid., 1230.
106. United States v. Briggs, 514 F. 2d 794, 801-4 (5th Cir. 1975).
107. In re Report and Recommendation of June 5, 1972, Grand Jury, pp. 1222, 1226.
108. Hammond v. Brown, 323 F. Supp. 326 (N.D. Ohio, 1971), affmd. 450 F. 2d 480 (6th Cir. 1971).
109. Chief Justice Warren in Wood v. Georgia, 370 U.S. 375, 390 (1962).
110. United States v. Anzelmo, 319 F. Supp. 1106 (D. La. 1970).
111. Costello v. United States, 350 U.S. 359 (1956).

The New Jersey Shield Law

(Summarized in Part)

2A:84A-21, Rules of Evidence, Newspaperman's Privilege. Rule 27
Subject to Rule 37, a person engaged on, engaged in, connected with, or employed by news media for the purpose of gathering, procuring, transmitting, compiling, editing or disseminating news for the general public or on whose behalf news is so gathered, procured, transmitted, compiled, edited or disseminated has a privilege to refuse to disclose, in any legal or quasi-legal proceeding or before any investigative body, including but not limited to, any court, grand jury, petit jury, administrative agency, the Legislature or legislative committee, or elsewhere

a. The source, author, means, agency or person from or through whom any information was procured, obtained, supplied, furnished, gathered, transmitted, compiled, edited, disseminated, or delivered; and

b. Any news or information obtained in the course of pursuing his professional activities whether or not it is disseminated.

The provisions of this rule insofar as it relates to radio or television stations shall not apply unless the radio or television station maintains and keeps open for inspection, for a period of at least 1 year from the date of an actual broadcast or telecast, an exact recording, transcription, kinescopic film or certified written transcript of the actual broadcast or telecast.

This portion of the statute is accompanied by 317 words of definition of the terms news media, news, newspapers, magazines, news agency, press association, wire service, and the clause "in the course of his professional activities."

The statute is limited to resolution of conflicts between a newsperson and a criminal defendant primarily at the pretrial stage. It places the burden on both parties to prove that they are entitled to coverage of the act, and attempts to cure the defect under which Myron Farber, for example, was denied a hearing on his rights under the First Amendment and the state shield statute.

The authority of a court to order production of materials for in camera inspection is defined. The parties have full opportunity to be heard. Findings of fact and conclusions of law must be in writing or set out in the record. If an interlocutory appeal occurs, the court is instructed to seal material in dispute and return it to the claimant of the privilege at the close of the proceedings.

Documentary materials used in newsgatherings are protected from search and seizure but exceptions are made in the event of allegations of criminal conduct, threat to life, or imminent loss of vital evidence. Search can be authorized by a court order or subpoena subject to appellate review. The statute authorizes civil action for damages against the state and against employees accused of violating the rights of persons under the statute and the attorney general is authorized to settle claims.

CHAPTER 6: THE CAMERA'S ALL-SEEING EYE

1. Hauptmann v. New Jersey, 115 N.J. Law 412, cert. denied, 296 U.S. 649 (1935).

2. William L. Prosser, "The Lindbergh Case Revisited," a review of George Weller's *Kidnap*, in *Minnesota L.R.* 46:383-91 (1961). The trial, Prosser said, was nothing less than an orgy.

3. Dallas *Times-Herald*, March 11, 1966, p. 1.

4. Fred S. Siebert, "Free Press and Fair Trial: Some Dimensions of the Problem," in *Free Press and Fair Trial,* ed. Chilton R. Bush (Athens: University of Georgia Press, 1970), p. 110. These figures are outdated by a decade of technical progress in photography.

5. An ABA ban on artists' sketches in the courtroom never was supported in the states. It was dropped when the canons were reissued as the *Code of Judicial Conduct*. The turning point was the decision in United States v. Columbia Broadcasting System, Inc., 497 F. 2d 107 (5th Cir. 1974). The court held that Judge Winston E. Arnow, who had cited a sketch artist in his court for contempt, should have disqualified himself and transferred the complaint to another judge. Sketching thereafter was accepted in federal courts also.

6. Oscar Hallam, "Some Object Lessons on Publicity in Criminal Trials," *Minnesota L.R.,* March 1940, p. 453.

7. Supreme Court of the United States, Billie Sol Estes v. The State of Texas, *Brief of the American Bar Association as Amicus Curiae.* For the American Bar Association, Whitney North Seymour, Richmond C. Coburn, John H. Yauch, Sr., p. 22.

8. American Bar Association, Special Committee on Proposed Revision of Judicial Canon 35, Interim Report and Recommendations, July 23, 1962, p. 14.

9. Ibid., pp. 19-20.

10. Ibid., pp. 46-47.

11. Ibid., p. 99.

12. Lenora Williamson, "Courtroom Camera Guidelines Formulated," *Editor & Publisher*, July 22, 1978, p. 16. Drafts of guidelines by Professor Seymour were submitted to supreme courts in Nebraska (October 1, 1982), West Virginia (May 12, 1981), and North Carolina (October 18, 1982).

13. For the New Jersey guidelines, adopted after a two-year experiment ending in 1981, see "N.J. Supreme Court Sets Courtroom Camera Guides," *Editor & Publisher*, July 11, 1981, p. 28.

14. James L. Hoyt, "Cameras in the Courtroom: Another Chance," *Public Telecommunications Review*, May-June 1978, p. 29.

15. Bannister v. State, Fla. App. 358 So. 2d 1182 (Dist. Ct. of App. Fla. 1978) and Green v. Florida, 7 Med. L. Rptr. 1025 (Supreme Ct. Fla. 1981) went further. It required a full evidentiary hearing by a trial court when a defendant asserts such an adverse psychological impact from cameras as to render her incompetent to stand trial. On the facts in the Green case, the Florida Supreme Court held that when a defendant now competent shows that the presence of cameras alone renders her "incoherent and incompetent," that is reason to exclude the electronic media and cameras. In State v. Palm Beach Newspapers, 395 So. 2d 544 (Supreme Ct., Fla. 1981)] the state high court added other details to this test and defined the "evidentiary hearing" required.

16. In re Petition of Post-Newsweek Stations, 347 So. 2d 404 (Supreme Court, Fla. 1977); 370 So. 2d 764 (Supreme Ct. Fla. 1979). See also 358 So. 2d 1360 (Supreme Ct. Fla. 1978).

17. Estes v. Texas, 381 U.S 532 (1965).

18. The views of Justice Douglas are in "The Public Trial and the Free Press," *ABA Journal*, August 1960, p. 840.

19. Estes v. Texas, pp. 532, 536.

20. Ibid., p. 615.

21. Chandler v. Florida, 449 U.S. 560 (1981). See also Chandler v. State, 376 So. 2d 1157 (Supreme Ct. Fla. 1979).

22. American Bar Association Standards, *Fair Trial and Free Press* (2d ed. tentative draft) (Washington, D.C.: ABA, 1978). *The Rights of Fair Trial and Free Press: The American Bar Association Standards* Chicago: ABA, 1981, p. 37. The House of Delegates action adopting a new canon 3(A)(7) is summarized in "News Notes," 8 Med. L. Rptr., August 24, 1982, inside front cover. The vote was 162 to 112.

23. Chandler v. Florida. For Chief Justice Burger's attitude toward television, see *News Media & the Law*, April 1978, p. 22. See also 4 Med. L. Rptr., inside front cover, August 22, 1978.

24. "Florida Judge Evaluates Camera Coverage of Trial," *Editor & Publisher*, January 7, 1978, pp. 22, 26.

25. Ibid., p. 27.

26. Ibid., p. 20.

27. Ibid. See also "State Activities," in 5 Med. L. Rptr., January 22, 1980, inside back cover, for rules in twenty-eight states. Also, "In re California Rules of Court," ibid., pp. 2639-41, is relevant.
28. "Florida Judge Evaluates Camera Coverage of Trial," pp. 26-29.
29. Ibid.
30. "The Camera Comes to Court," *Freedom of Information Center Report*, no. 396, October 1978, p. 3.
31. Ibid.
32. Lyle Denniston, "Cameras in the Courtroom 1982," *Quill*, March 1982, p. 22.
33. "Maryland Bans Cameras from Crime Trials," *Editor & Publisher*, March 28, 1981, p. 37.

CHAPTER 7: BEYOND FAIR TRIAL, HOPE

1. American Bar Association, *The Rights of Fair Trial and Free Press: American Bar Association Standards* (Chicago: ABA, 1981). Also, "Panel Holds Hearings on Proposed Closure Rule," in "News Notes," 8 Med. L. Rptr., February 23, 1982, inside cover.
2. George Gallup, Jr., "Public Opinion and Freedom of the Press," January 17, 1980, a report to the First Amendment Congress, Philadelphia.
3. Address by William J. Brennan, Jr., *Dedication of Samuel I. Newhouse Law Center, Rutgers University—Newark, New Jersey, October 17, 1979*.
4. Ibid., p. 9.
5. Ibid., p. 10.
6. Schenck v. United States, 249 U.S. 47, 52 (1919).
7. New York Times Co. v. Sullivan, 376 U.S. 254 (1964). President Nixon's statement is in a press release, Office of White House Press Secretary, March 8, 1974, p. 4. The White House, Press Conference of Bryce N. Harlow, counsellor to the President, The Briefing Room, 11:47 a.m. EDT, March 8, 1974. Transcript copy.
8. "Reagan Calls TV Reporting Slanted," *Minneapolis Tribune*, March 16, 1982, p. 3A.
9. Gitlow v. New York, 268 U.S. 652, 666 (1927).
10. Whitney v. California, 274 U.S. 357, 372-75 (1927).
11. Miami Herald Publishing Co. v. Tornillo, 418 U.S. 241, 258 (1974).
12. Branzburg v. Hayes, 408 U.S. 665, 712 (1972).
13. Ibid., p. 727.
14. Ibid., pp. 739-40, 743.
15. David S. Broder, "The Media—Monitors of Virtue?" *Chicago Bar Record* 55:19 (1975). (Special Centennial issue.)

16. F. N. Thorpe, *The Federal and State Constitutions* (Washington, D.C.: Government Printing Office, 1909), vol. 7, p. 4380 (index).

17. State ex rel. Superior Ct. v. Sperry, 79 Wash. 2d 69, 483 P. 2d 608 (Supreme Ct. Wash. 1971).

18. Federated Publications v. Kurtz, 615 P. 2d 440 (Supreme Ct. Wash. 1980).

19. Ibid., pp. 449-52.

20. Federated Publications v. Swedberg, 633 P. 2d 74 (Supreme Ct. Wash. 1981).

21. Nebraska Press Assn. v. Stuart, 427 U.S. 539, 542 (1976).

22. Seattle Times v. Ishikawa, 640 P. 2d 716 (Supreme Ct. Wash. 1982).

23. Chicago Council of Lawyers v. Bauer, 522 F. 2d 242, 247-251 (7th Cir. 1975).

24. Hirschkop v. Snead, 594 F. 2d 356 (4th Cir. 1979).

Suggestions for Further Reading

The sources relied upon in the preparation of this book are acknowledged in the text and notes. The court cases since 1966, beginning with Sheppard v. Maxwell, constitute the main substance of the study. The value of cases and materials published prior to that time is limited by the changes mandated by the Sheppard case and other major constitutional interpretations by the Court, and by the active season of rulemaking by the state and federal courts.

Journalists and law enforcement officers who wish to put local events into nationwide perspective during their regular work should use a national loose-leaf service reporting and analyzing criminal law developments. Social science and criminal law, in the scholarly mix termed criminology, are treated in esoteric but solidly informative magazines such as the *American Sociological Review, American Journal of Sociology, Social Problems, Law and Society, Criminology*, and *Journal of Criminal Law and Criminology*.

THE COURT SYSTEM

Ruggero J. Aldisert, " 'The Nature of the Judicial Process' Revisited,'' *University of Cincinnati L.R.* 49:1 (1980).

Warren E. Burger, "Interdependence of Judicial and Journalistic Independence,'' *Georgetown L.J. 63:1195 (1975);* also in *New York State Bar Journal* 47:453 October 1975).

Lyle Denniston, *The Reporter and the Law*. New York: Hastings House, 1980. Jointly sponsored by the American Bar Association and American Newspaper Publishers Association.

Lotan Harold DeWolf, *Crime and Justice in America: A Paradox of Conscience*. New York: Harper & Row, 1975.

Abraham S. Goldstein, *Crime, Law and Society: Readings*. New York: Free Press, 1971.

Yale Kamisar, *Criminal Justice in Our Time*. Charlottesville: University Press of Virginia, 1965.

Hans Linde, "Advice to the Press," *Willamette L.R.* 13:211 (1977).

Barry Mishkin, *Criminal Justice and the News Media*. Cincinnati: Pamphlet Publications, 1979.

Peter F. Nardulli, *The Courtroom Elite: An Organizational Perspective on Criminal Justice*. Cambridge, Mass.: Ballinger, 1978.

National Conference on the Causes of Popular Dissatisfaction with the Administration of Justice, *Papers and Addresses*. St. Paul, Minn. 1976. Sponsored by U.S. Judicial Conference, American Bar Association, and Conference of Chief Justices.

Barbara Raffel Price and Phyllis Jo Baunach, *Criminal Justice Research*. Beverly Hills: Sage, 1979. For the American Society of Criminology, Philadelphia.

The Public Image of Courts: Highlights of a National Survey of the General Public, Judges, Lawyers and Community Leaders. Williamsburg, Va.: National Center for State Courts, 1978.

Paul C. Reardon, "State Court Reform: A Symposium. Introduction to State Court Reform." *American University L.R.* 31:207 (1982).

Bruce Dennis Sales, ed., *The Criminal Justice System*. New York: Plenum Press, 1977.

Colin Wakefield, "Trial and Pretrial Publicity in English Justice," *Nebraska L.R. 56:227 (1977)*.

CRIMINAL LAW POLICY AND ADMINISTRATION

American Bar Association Standards for Criminal Justice, vol. II. Boston: Little, Brown, 1980. See Chapter 8, "Fair Trial and Free Press," and "Commentary," pp. 7-14, 52-57, 60-61.

American Bar Association, Standing Committee on Association Communications, *The Rights of Fair Trial and Free Press: The American Bar Association Standards*. Chicago: American Bar Association, 1981.

David L. Bazelon, "Foreword—The Morality of Criminal Law: Rights of the Accused." *The Journal of Criminal Law and Criminology* 72:1143 (1981).

Vince Blasi, "Press Subpoenas: An Empirical and Legal Analysis," a study report for the Reporter's Committee on Freedom of the Press (1972).

Chilton R. Bush, ed. *Free Press and Fair Trial—Some Dimensions of the Problem*. Athens: University of Georgia Press, 1970.

William J. Campbell, "Delays in Criminal Cases," F.R.D. 55:229 (1972).

Hyman Gross, *A Theory of Criminal Justice*. New York: Oxford University Press, 1979.

Joseph M. Hassett, "A Jury's Pretrial Knowledge in Historical Perspective: The Distinction Between Pretrial Information and Prejudicial Publicity," in *Law and Contemporary Problems* 43:155 (1980).

William H. Levit, Dorothy W. Nelson, Vaughn C. Ball, Richard Chernick, "Expediting Voir Dire: An Empirical Study," *Southern Cal. L.R.* 44:916 (1971).

Courtney J. Mullin and Jeffrey Frederick, "The Uses of Social Science in Trials with Political and Racial Overtones: The Trial of Joan Little," *Law and Contemporary Problems* 41:205 (1977).

Note, "Prejudicial Publicity in Trials of Public Officials," *Yale L.J.* 85:123 (1975).

Note, "Protective Orders Against the Press and the Inherent Powers of the Courts," *Yale L.J.* 87:342 (1977).

Merle Pollock and Fred Cohen, "Problems of Pretrial Publicity," *Criminal Law Bulletin* 11:335 (1975).

Douglas Rendleman, "Free Press-Fair Trial Review of Silence Orders," *North Carolina L.R.* 52:127 (1973).

Andrew M. Schatz, "Gagging the Press in Criminal Trials," *Harvard Civil Rights-Civil Liberties L.R.* 10:608 (1975).

Charles E. Silberman, *Criminal Violence, Criminal Justice*. New York: Random House, 1978.

John E. Stanga, Jr., "Judicial Protection of the Criminal Defendant against Adverse Press Coverage," *William & Mary L.R.* 13:1 (1971).

Eric E. Younger, "The Sheppard Mandate Today: A Trial Judge's Perspective," *Nebraska L.R.* 56:1 (1977).

THE PROSECUTORIAL FUNCTION

Marvin E. Frankel and Gury P. Naftalis, *The Grand Jury: An Institution on Trial*. New York: Hill and Wang, 1977.

Richard S. Frase, "The Decision to File Federal Criminal Charges: A Quantitative Study of Prosecutorial Discretion," *University of Chicago L.R.* 47:246 (1979-80).

John F. Klein, *Let's Make a Deal: Negotiating Justice*. Lexington, Mass.: Lexington Books, 1976.

John H. Langbein, "Torture and Plea Bargaining," *University of Chicago L.R.* 46:3 (1978-79).

NEWSPAPERS, RADIO, TELEVISION

Floyd Abrams, Murray L. Gurfein, Charles Rembar, and Louis Nizer, *Not Fit to Print: The Individual vs. the Media.* New York: New York County Lawyers Assn. Foundation, 1977.

American Society of Newspaper Editors, *Bulletin.* P.O. Box 17004, Washington, D.C. 20041.

Charles E. Ayres, "Chandler v. Florida: Television, Criminal Trials and Due Process," *Supreme Court Review,* p. 157, 1981.

David L. Bazelon, "On the 40th Anniversary of Federal Communications Commission," *Congressional Record—Senate,* November 26, 1974, p. 37493.

Jeremy Cohen, "Cameras in the Courtroom and Due Process: A Proposal for a Qualitative Difference Test," *Washington L.R.* 57:277 (1982).

Robert E. Drechsel, *News Making in the Trial Courts.* New York: Longman, 1983.

James Goodale, Herald Price Fahringer, speakers; Edward Thompson, moderator; George Barasch, chairman, "Television in the Courtroom: Limited Benefits, Vital Risks?" *Communication & Law,* 3:35 (1981).

A. M. Rosenthal, "The Free Press Under Attack: Reflections of a Newspaper Editor," *Bar Leader* (ABA), March-April 1982, p. 25.

David Shaw, *Journalism Today: A Changing Press for a Changing America.* New York: Harper & Row, 1977.

William J. Small, *Political Power and the Press.* New York: W. W. Norton, 1972.

PROFESSIONALISM

Harry Ashmore, "A Case for Professionalism," *Bulletin,* American Society of Newspaper Editors, November-December 1970, p. 1.

William H. Erickson, "First Amendment Limitations on the Confidentiality of Lawyer Disciplinary and Disability Proceedings," *Kentucky L.J.* 67:823 (1978-79).

Robert C. Finley, "Free Press-Fair Trial: A Commonsense Accommodation," *New York State Bar Journal* 41:9 (1969).

Geoffrey C. Hazard, Jr., *Ethics in the Practice of Law.* New Haven: Yale University Press, 1978.

A. Howard and S. Newman, *Fair Trial and Free Expression: A Background Report*. Subcommittee on Constitutional Rights of the Senate Committee on the Judiciary, 94th Cong., 2d Session, 71-73. Committee Print 1976.

Landmark Communications, Inc., v. Virginia, 435 U.S. 829 (1978).

John B. Oakes, "Price of Freedom of Press: Responsibility," *New York State Bar Journal* 50:466 (1978).

James C. Thompson, Jr., *Some Probings by a Media Keeper*. Bloomington: Indiana University, Poynter Center, January 1978.

THE FIRST AMENDMENT

W. W. Van Alstine, "Hazards to Press of Claiming a Preferred Position," *Hastings L.J.* 28:761 (1977).

C. E. Baker, "Process of Change and the Liberty Theory of the First Amendment," *Southern Cal. L.R.* 55:293 (1981).

Margaret A. Blanchard, "The Institutional Press and Its First Amendment Privileges," *Supreme Court Review*, 1978. Chicago: University of Chicago Press, 1979.

Kent Greenwalt, "Speech and Crime," *American Bar Found. Research Jrnl* (1980), p. 645. The Samuel Pool Weaver Constitutional Law Essay.

Tamara Jacobs, "The Chilling Effect in Press Cases: Judicial Thumb on the Scales," *Harvard Civil Rights-Civil Liberties L.R.* 15:685 (1980).

David L. Lange, "The Role of the Access Doctrine in the Regulation of the Mass Media: A Critical Review and Assessment," *North Carolina L.R.* 52:1 (1973).

Anthony Lewis, "A Public Right to Know About Public Institutions: The First Amendment as Sword," *Supreme Court Review*, 1980, p. 1.

Susan P. McCarthy, "The First Amendment Newsman's Privilege: From Branzburg to Farber," *Seton Hall L.R.* 10:333 (1979-80).

David M. O'Brien, "Reassessing the First Amendment and the Public's Right to Know in Constitutional Adjudication," *Villanova L.R.* 26:1 (1980).

Don R. Pember, *Privacy and the Press: The Law, the Mass Media and the First Amendment*. Seattle: University of Washington Press, 1972.

David M. Rabban, "The First Amendment in Its Forgotten Years," *Yale L.J.* 90:514 (1981).

William A. Read, *The First Amendment Meets the Second Revolution*. Cambridge: Harvard University Press, 1979.

T. Scott, "Jurisdiction Over the Press: A Survey and Analysis," *Federal Communication L.J.* 32:19 (1980).

Potter Stewart, " 'Or of the Press,' " *Hastings L.J.* 26:631 (1975).

THE JOURNALIST'S PRIVILEGE

J. A. Barist, "First Amendment and Regulation of Prejudicial Publicity—An Analysis," *Fordham L.R.* 36:425 (1968).

Vince Blasi, "The Newsman's Privilege: An Empirical Study," *Michigan L.R.* 70:229 (1971).

Elizabeth Anne England, "Newsperson's Privilege in California: The Controversy and Resolution," *Hastings L.J.* 29:375 (1978).

James A. Guest and Alan L. Stanzler, "The Constitutional Argument for Newsmen Concealing Their Sources," *Northwestern L.R.* 64:18 (1969).

John B. Kuhns, "Reporters and Their Sources: The Constitutional Right to a Confidential Relationship," *Yale L.J.* 80:365 (1970).

Aaron Latham, "How the *Washington Post* Gave Nixon Hell," *New York Magazine,* May 14, 1973, p. 49.

Note, "Shield Laws: The Legislative Response to Journalistic Privilege," *Cleveland St. L.R.* 26:453 (1977).

Robert M. O'Neill, "Shield Laws: Partial Solution to a Pervasive Problem," *New York Law Forum* 20:515 (1975).

K. D. Sowle, "Defamation and the First Amendment: The Case for a Constitutional Privilege of Fair Report," *New York University L.R.* 54:469 (1979).

M. I. Spak, "Predictable Harm: Should the Media Be Liable?" *Ohio State L.J.* 42:671 (1981).

Maurice Van Gerpen, *Privileged Communication and the Press.* Westport, Conn.: Greenwood Press, 1979.

Kevin R. Vienna, "Comment: Discovery and the First Amendment," *William & Mary L.R.* 21:331 (1979).

Cases Cited

Index

About the Author

J. Edward Gerald has served as Professor at the Universities of Missouri and Minnesota, as Visiting Teacher at the University of Texas, Indiana University, and the University of Utah, and as Visiting Scholar at the Brookings Institution. He also is a journalist with practical understanding of the tasks of reporting and editing and was one of the founders of the pioneering Minnesota News Council. His books include *The Press and the Constitution*, *The British Press under Government Economic Controls*, and *Social Responsibility of the Press*.